SUPPLY MANAGEMENT TOOLBOX

HOW TO MANAGE YOUR SUPPLIERS

PETER L. GRIECO, JR.

PT Publications, Inc.

2273 Palm Beach Lakes Boulevard, Suite C
West Palm Beach, FL 33409-3401

Author Of The Best Selling Companion Book Supplier Certification II

Library of Congress Cataloging in Publication Data

Grieco, Peter L., Jr., 1942-
      Supply Management Tool box: How to Manage Your
Suppliers / Peter L. Grieco, Jr.
             p. cm.
       ISBN 0-945456-11-5 : $34.95
       1. Materials management.   I. Title.
TS161.G753   1994
658.7--dc20   94-1144
                                       CIP

Copyright © 1995 by PT Publications, Inc.

Printed in the United States of America.

All rights reserved. This book or any parts thereof
may not be reproduced in any form without
the permission of the publisher.

TABLE OF CONTENTS

ACKNOWLEDGMENTS

I would like to thank all of our clients for their good ideas, common sense and courage to be part of the Continuous Improvement Process. This book is dedicated to their effort to meet one of America's most serious challenges. Special thanks also go out to Mel Pilachowksi, Wayne Douchkoff, Tom Petroski, Bill Agee, Maureen Quinn, Louise Stewart, Mark Grieco and Chris Worel, my colleagues at Pro-Tech who have challenged me and contributed their input to this book. I thank them all for the time they took to review each chapter and make suggestions.

A special mention is reserved for Pro-Tech's capable and hardworking office staff of Leslie Boyce, Samra Wilson and Sarah Worel who always perform with excellence. Much appreciation is due to Steven Marks, my editor and friend, for all the years of his support. I wish also to thank Kevin Grieco for his design of our book cover. John Choate, vice president of manufacturing at Econologic Technologies, Inc., also deserves credit for his assistance in compiling a glossary of purchasing terms.

We at Pro-Tech would also like to acknowledge in advance all the people who use this book and its tools to bring their organizations into the twenty-first century. These people command our respect for their tireless efforts to make their companies and facilities into World Class institutions.

DEDICATION

For Mary who provides me with the happiness of life.

For all the purchasing professionals who are changing
the way we do business from an order-placing mentality
to the supply management of partnerships.

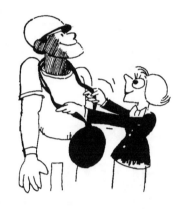

Purpose
and Use of
this Book

About the Author

Peter L. Grieco, Jr. is President and Chief Executive Officer of Professionals for Technology Associates, Inc., an international consulting and education firm. He was active in the development of Apple Computer's Macintosh Automated Focus Factory in Fremont, California. His industry experience encompasses both repetitive and discrete manufacturing processes. He has more than twenty-five years of experience as a practitioner and educator in the manufacturing environment. He has held numerous operation and financial positions, as well as having responsibility for numerous sales management and marketing departments. Mr. Grieco is the co-author of the latest JIT/TQC textbooks: "Made in America: The Total Business Concept," "Just-In-Time Purchasing," "Supplier Certification II," "Behind Bars: Bar Coding Principles and Applications," "The World of Negotiations: Never Being a Loser," "People Empowerment: Achieving Success from Involvement," and "World Class: Measuring Its Achievement." He attended Central Connecticut State University and Wharton School of Finance (Moody's School of Commerce). He is a frequent lecturer for professional societies, seminars, conferences, and university programs on Operations Management and Just-In-Time/Total Quality Control related topics.

HELP DESK HOTLINE

1-800-272-4335

In order to answer the questions of our readers, we have established a Help Desk Hotline at our corporate headquarters in West Palm Beach, Florida. We invite you to call us with your queries about how to use the forms and tools in this book.

We also invite you to use our HELP DESK HOTLINE to find out more about other books we publish as well as a videotape series entitled **Supplier Certification: The Path to Excellence**. In addition to books, software and videotapes, we offer over 80 courses which can be scheduled for intensive, in-house seminars. Call us for details.

FORMS SOFTWARE

For those who wish to utilize and print the forms in this book, PT Publications has developed a software package available for both Macintosh and IBM-PC computers.

Call or write to us for information at (407) 687-0455, Fax (407) 697-2303, PT Publications, 2273 Palm Beach Lakes Blvd., #C, West Palm Beach, FL 33409-3401.

INTRODUCTION

A good tool box has the right tool for any situation that arises. That type of tool box is what we had in mind when we started brainstorming about this book. Our VideoEducation Series, *Supplier Certification: The Path to Excellence*, and our book, *Supplier Certification II: A Handbook for Achieving Excellence Through Continuous Improvement*, were both being well received, but we weren't going to be content with not improving on what we were offering. We saw the need for another tool to put in the box and to use in conjunction with not only our Supplier Certification book and videotapes, but with our many other fine books on World Class Management such as *Just-In-Time Purchasing: In Pursuit of Excellence* and *The World of Negotiations: Never Being a Loser*. These other books cover vital areas such as Set-up Reduction, World Class Assessment, Employee Empowerment and Involvement, Just-In-Time and Total Quality Management.

For our new book, we wanted to look specifically at the area of Supply Management and how it relates to the topics just mentioned. We wanted to provide readers with more than explanations. We wanted to provide them the forms, checklists, surveys, audits and charts necessary to implement their own process for monitoring and controlling the supply base.

Although our original idea was to write this book for the companies who were setting out to implement a supply management program, we quickly saw that the book would be valuable to those who had already started a program. For whatever reason, perhaps the program wasn't going as well as it should. We had the tools, gained from our experience and from our clients' experiences, to help put the program back to work. These tools are in this book.

Furthermore, we saw that this book was not only for those putting a Supply Management program into effect. This book was also for those companies that were about to be rated or put through a Supplier Certification program. Our book would let them know what to expect and even help them to conduct self-audits, so that they could begin the improvement process themselves in order to obtain customer satisfaction.

USING THIS BOOK

It is strongly advised that your library contain *Supplier Certification II, Just-In-Time Purchasing: In Pursuit of Excellence* and *The World of Negotiations* to use with this book. They can provide you with the depth that a tool book cannot. The four books combined will provide you with both depth and range over the concept and process of implementation.

For those of you who require internal training, we suggest our VideoEducation Series. It will give you a first-hand look at how some companies have put these tools to work as well as what can be done and what has been accomplished.

If there are any questions or if we can be of further assistance, please don't hesitate to call our Help Desk hotline at 1-800-272-4335. It has been the suggestions and stories of hundreds of people like you that has made our work continuously improve as well.

Permission to use the forms in this book can be obtained by writing to us. Or, you can purchase our software package which allows you to print the forms from your computer. Please write or call for more information.

Chapter One

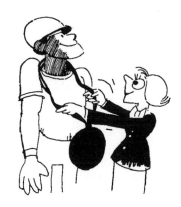

The Concept of Supply Management

and Supply Management Strategy

How to Use the Tools in this Chapter

The purpose of this chapter is to help you prepare a manual demonstrating your organization's concept of Supply Management. This manual will often be a supplier's first contact with the philosophy and practice of Supply Management. Therefore, you must present the material in a way which will reduce fear and anxiety, which are often the initial reactions to change. For a more thorough treatment of how to manage the process of change, we refer you to our book, **PEOPLE EMPOWERMENT:** *Achieving Success from Involvement*, (PT Publications, West Palm Beach, FL). You will find Chapter 3 particularly helpful in understanding how change should be introduced.

One of the most effective ways to reduce fear and anxiety is to present an accurate protrayal of the program being introduced. You will see that the sample text in this chapter does five things:

1) **Invites the supplier to listen or read.**

2) **Defines the concept of Supply Management.**

3) **Delineates the steps a supplier will take as a participant in the program.**

4) **States the expectations that both partners will meet in the program.**

5) **Establishes a timetable and process.**

We certainly recommend that you adapt our sample text to your particular needs. You may also decide to hire graphic designers to add illustrations, photos and charts. Just don't forget to get across the important points and to make the manual professional, rather than flashy and confusing.

AN INVITATION. . .

TO OUR MOST VALUED SUPPLIERS

Supply Management begins with one simple premise: We are all suppliers and we are all customers. To us, this means we started to look at our company's products and services from the perspective of the customer. What does a customer want and need? They want suppliers who claim quality ownership; who believe in the zero-defect concept; who consistently meet their requirements for quality, quantity, cost, and delivery.

No supplier can achieve this World Class level of performance without engaging in some type of program which eliminates the causes of wasted time, money and labor. A successful Supply Management program relies upon the just-in-time delivery of zero-defect material, parts, subassemblies and finished products throughout the supply network. This puts a premium on making it right the first time. Thus, the emphasis is on defect prevention, rather than routine inspection. Consequently, the burden of proof will not rest upon Inspectors, but on the makers or suppliers of a part. Quality cannot be inspected into a part; it must be there already.

In other words, we are trying to achieve quality at the source. But how do we get that quality? By entering into a partnership with a supplier which is based on trust and cooperation. No supplier can do it alone.

Suppliers will become a part of our organization for the life of the part and the life of the company. This is the key to reducing the supply base.

SUPPLIER PARTNERSHIPS

In the World Class arena where agile companies compete, it is far more profitable and reliable to develop long-term relationships with suppliers in which they are partners, not victims. This necessitates a level of trust and cooperation not usually found in today's business world. But we are asking your company to join us in a long-term partnership.

Supply Management is not easy. It requires time and effort. When we have achieved a 95 percent quality level, we then strive for 98 percent. When we reach that level, we go for 99 percent. Once there, we go for 99.8 percent. There is no stopping in Supply Management, no resting on our laurels. It is a commitment to the elimination of all waste in your company.

And why strive for anything less? We aren't saying that you will get there in one quarter or one year. We are saying that if you don't set the above conditions as a goal and strive for continuous improvement, then you won't even have the luxury of maintaining your present position. You will begin to slide backwards. Many American and foreign companies already subscribe to the definition above and are enjoying the lower costs and increased profits which ensue. And if your competition is not already embarking on a Supply Management program, you can be sure that they will be very shortly. It is too costly not to begin implementation of such a program.

WHAT IS A SUPPLY BASE PROGRAM?

Our supply base program is designed to source suppliers who are willing to join us in our quest for excellence and to reap the rewards of being a favored partner. To find these special suppliers requires an exhaustive sourcing effort which looks at their operations to determine which suppliers have the internal controls in place to ensure 100% on-time delivery of products and services, 100% conformance to quality requirements, 100% accuracy in product counts and be the lowest cost producer. Suppliers who have attained this level of excellence or who show that they can achieve it through our program will be known as Certified Suppliers and will thus receive a larger share of our business.

Any supplier who agrees to enter our supply base program will be evaluated using a set of strict supplier criteria developed by empowered teams at your company in conjunction with teams at our company. The purpose is to ensure consistency and objectivity in evaluating each element of your operations that impact on the shipment of products or provision of services to us.

We would like to empasize from the very beginning of our journey together that we will consider all information gained during the survey process as STRICTLY CONFIDENTIAL. We strongly believe that trust is a two-way street and the basis of all partnerships.

As for the supply base program itself, we have outlined the following steps to give you a better idea of what you can expect:

STEP 1. Complete a list of selection criteria. This sets the stage for the rest of the process.

STEP 2. Complete a presurvey questionnaire which covers ownership, financial condition, key operating personnel and the focus of the supplier's operations.

STEP 3. Conduct a site assessment with the Supply Management team. The written assessment, which is provided to the supplier after the results are tabulated and analyzed, would identify areas of strength and areas in need of improvement.

STEP 4. The next step is the supplier's responsibility. We would expect them to draw up a corrective action plan addressing those areas identified in our assessment as in need of improvement. Their plan must show how they will measure performance and monitor progress toward goals.

STEP 5. When the supplier has achieved the objectives set forth in their corrective action plan, they will submit their results to us. Based upon our review, we will decide whether or not to ask the supplier to begin the final certification process at this time.

STEP 6. Certification means meeting the criteria mentioned earlier — 100% quality, accuracy and on-time delivery. Through various sampling techniques, we will monitor performance to ensure that the supplier consistently meets the certification criteria. Suppliers must meet at least a 95% statistical confidence level that they can continue to perform at the certification level.

STEP 7. When suppliers have shown that they can consistently maintain high levels of performance and that they are willing to continuously improve, they are designated as a Certified Supplier. As a partner, the supplier will be part of our product/service design teams and will be granted long-term contracts with our company. We are looking for suppliers who are willing to strategically align with us.

STEP 8. After certification, we will conduct unannounced or agreed-upon site visits to verify your compliance to the certification criteria. If there are any deviations, we will work with the supplier to devise and implement corrective action. At the end of six months, the supplier's corrective actions will be evaluated. If the supplier has failed to comply with the criteria, their status as a certified supplier will be revoked.

STEP 9. We will install a supplier rating system in order to track the Continuous Improvement Program.

STEP 10. Our objective is to reduce our supply base and to give the majority and even 100% of our business to our certified suppliers. To that end, we will work with our partners to achieve an environment of continuous improvement.

Below is a capsule view of what we expect our suppliers to do over the next three years:

OBJECTIVE	After One Year	After Two Years	Three Years and Beyond
Quality — 100% conformance to specifications.	99.0%	99.5%	Six Sigma
On-time delivery — +/- 0 days to acknowledged delivery date.	99.0%	99.9%	Six Sigma
Quantity accuracy — +/- 0% deviation from order quantity.	99.0%	99.9%	Six Sigma

An Invitation To Supply Management

Chapter Two

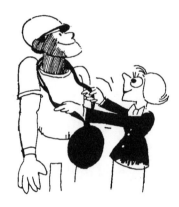

Developing a Supply Management Strategy

Chapter Two Contents

How to Use the Tools in this Chapter

The intent of this chapter is to provide each of you with a foundation for devising a Supplier Strategy. We have found that many companies today jump right into sourcing suppliers, services or materials without a strategic plan. To rectify that situation, we are providing you with some simple tools which require your company to develop a proactive process. This is far superior to reacting to events as they happen.

The Material Positioning tools were developed based upon the recognition that two of the most important factors determining supply strategy are influence on company results and procurement risks. We feel that it is extremely important to understand your market and the level of procurement risk.

Use the first tool, Influence on Company Results, as a way to determine on a scale of 0-5 what degree of influence the selected material/commodity has on your competitiveness. For each of the categories, describe the factors which affect it and rate their degree of influence. These factors and their weights may be different for different end-products. This tool helps you identify the pressures we sometimes don't see and consequently don't address.

The second tool, Procurement Risk, is used to chart on a scale of 0-5 the varying levels of procurement risk. An assessment of the four competitive forces of bargaining power, substitution, rivalry and entry barriers determines the procurement risk you face. The strength/weakness of these forces may be different for each material/commodity.

After you have scored the Influence on Company Results and Procurement Risk tools, position the material/commodity on the Material Positioning Matrix. The quadrant it occupies will determine the most appropriate strategies for this material/commodity. The third tool is an action planning worksheet for the selected strategies.

The following test for the soundness of your company's strategy can and should be used by top executives to monitor performance. The Test of a Good Supply Strategy is a means for you to determine how well you have conceived your strategy. Answer all of the questions with a "yes" or "no" and then rate yourself on the scale which follows.

The last tool, Implementing a Supply Strategy is a series of questions and charts for you to fill out which will help you to put your strategy into action and to keep it on track.

Strategic Material Positioning Methodology

- ## Tool #1

  ### 1. Determine influences on company results

  - Determine market success elements
  - Weight elements relative to market success
  - Calculate index of influence on company result

- ## Tool #2

  ### 2. Calculate procurement risk

  - Determine relative strength of competitive forces
    - Bargaining power
    - Rivalry
    - Substitution
    - Entry barriers

  ### 3. Position material on matrix

- ## Tool #3

  ### 4. Select appropriate strategy

Strategic Material Positioning and Strategy Selection

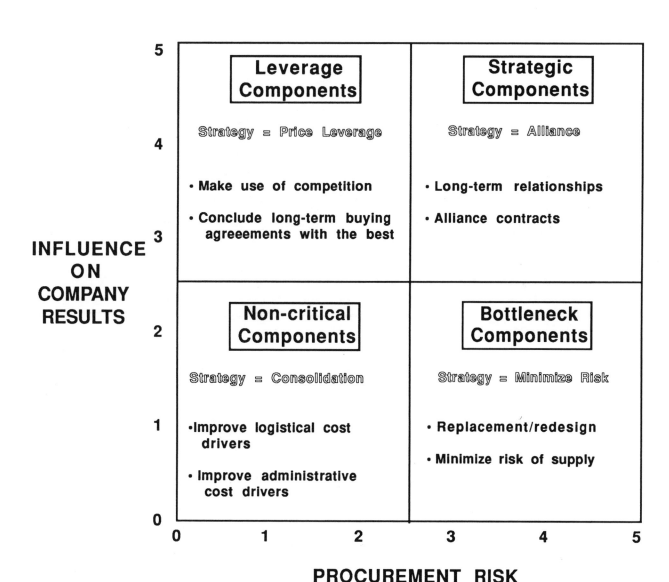

INFLUENCE ON COMPANY RESULTS

5

4

3

2

1

0

Leverage Components

Strategy = Price Leverage

- Make use of competition
- Conclude long-term buying agreeements with the best

Strategic Components

Strategy = Alliance

- Long-term relationships
- Alliance contracts

Non-critical Components

Strategy = Consolidation

- Improve logistical cost drivers
- Improve administrative cost drivers

Bottleneck Components

Strategy = Minimize Risk

- Replacement/redesign
- Minimize risk of supply

0   1   2   3   4   5

PROCUREMENT RISK

Tool #1:
Strategic Material/Commodity Positioning
Determining Influence on Company Results

(sidebar) Influence on Company Results

Let's review what factors are influencing your company the most in order to increase your competitiveness. Each commodity has a different level and weighted factor, and will influence company results.

How to use:
1) Determine relative weight of four factors as determined by your market.
2) Determine influence of their material/commodity on each of the four factors.
3) Calculate the weighted influences, their sum and then chart the figure obtained on the Material Position Matrix on Page 2-10.

MATERIAL/COMMODITY _____

	A Market Success Relative Weight	B Influence of Material (Scale 0-5)	C Weighted Influence (A x B)
COST World Pricing Domestic Pricing Cost of Inventory Activity Based Costing Total Cost Management Etc.	_____	_____	_____
QUALITY Product Quality Service Quality Reliability Etc.	_____	_____	_____
TIME Long-term Agreements Flexibility Short Lead Times Freight Terms Etc.	_____	_____	_____
TECHNOLOGY Commodity Leader Market Position Equipment Processes Innovations Vision (Future) Etc.	_____	_____	_____
Total	1.0 _____	**Sum of C's** _____ **= Influence Index** _____	

Procurement Risk
Competitive Forces

Now let's review the second factor that determines material positioning.

I. BARGAINING POWER

A. BUYER POWER
1. Volume purchases
2. Significant material content
3. Standard product/undifferentiated product
4. Low switching costs
5. Low profit
6. Potential for backward integration
7. Fully knowledgable

B. SELLER POWER
1. Monopoly/Oligopoly
2. Important product to customer
3. High switching cost
4. Potential for forward integration
5. Complex/differentiated product

II. SUBSTITUTION

A. Cost of switching
B. Willingness to switch
C. Level of differentation

III. RIVALRY

A. Industry growth
B. Number of competitors
C. Capital intensity

IV. ENTRY BARRIERS

A. Capital requirements
B. Technology/patents
C. Government policies
D. Level of differentation
E. Availability of raw materials
F. Availability of distribution network

Procurement Risk
Spider Diagram

The closer to the center of the spider diagram, the lower the procurement risk.

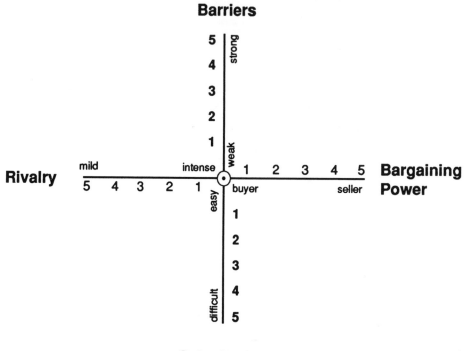

Example

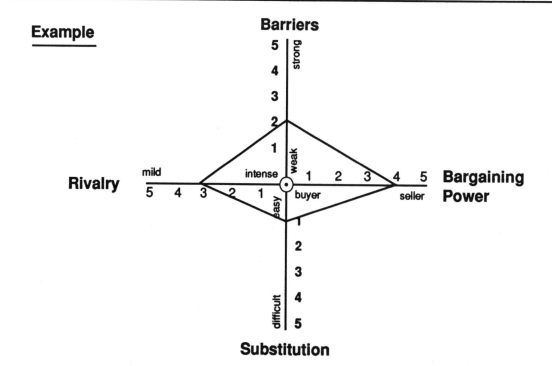

Strategic Material/Commodity Positioning
TOOL #2: PROCUREMENT RISK

How to Use:
1. Determine on a scale of 0 to 5 the relative strength of the four competitive forces listed below. Use the list of competitive forces on Page 2-7 to help you calculate the relative strength.
2. Add the relative weights of the procurement risks and divide by 4. Chart the figure obtained on the Material Positioning Matrix on Page 2-10.

MATERIAL/COMMODITY _____

Procurement Risk (Scale 0-5)

BARGAINING POWER
_____
_____
_____
_____

buyer .... seller
0   1   2   3   4   5

_____

SUBSTITUTION
_____
_____
_____
_____

easy .... difficult
0   1   2   3   4   5

_____

RIVALRY
_____
_____
_____
_____

intense .... mild
0   1   2   3   4   5

_____

BARRIERS
_____
_____
_____
_____

weak .... strong
0   1   2   3   4   5

_____

SUM/4 = _____

RISK INDEX

Material Positioning Matrix

Material Positioning Matrix

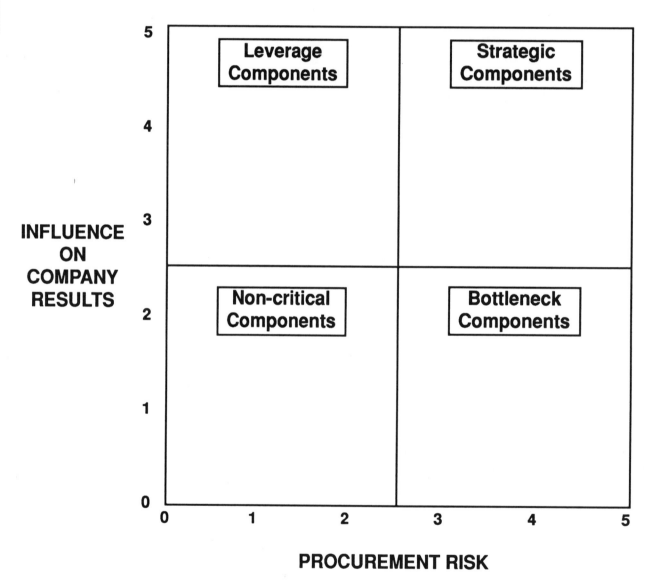

Chapter Three

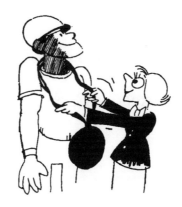

Benchmarking in Supply Management

Chapter Three Contents

How to Use the Tools
in this Chapter

Benchmarking Results, the first tool in this chapter allows you to calculate where your company stands in relation to industry leaders and World Class Levels. You can use this process to benchmark your present status as well as where you have been over several years. In addition, you can use benchmarking as a means of establishing targets you hope to achieve in coming years.

Identifying World Class Companies is used to view how companies you would like to benchmark compare with your company. This tool allows you to see how different companies rank against each other in various categories as well as in overall performance.

The third tool, Benchmarking Performance Characteristics, is often used in conjunction with the second tool since it provides a graphic snapshot of one particular company across all of the performance characteristics. We suggest that you make a chart for every company you are studying or evaluating. By doing this over a period of time, you can quickly see any variations or improvements in performance which may indicate a company to benchmark or use as a supplier.

The next tool, Benchmarking Team Member Checklist, is used to aid you in selecting members of the Benchmarking Team. We have found that the list we have provided works very well. You may want to adapt the list to your company's requirements.

How to Create a Benchmarking Objective is a set of guidelines you will need to follow as you establish objectives in your Continuous Improvement Process.

Bridging the Performance Gap is an excellent tool for determining how your company's performance varies from World Class performance levels for a number of different measurements. The last three columns can be used to set goals for your company to achieve in the coming years as you narrow the gap.

Benchmarking Results

BENCHMARKING RESULTS

Objective:

Shipments with Zero Defects

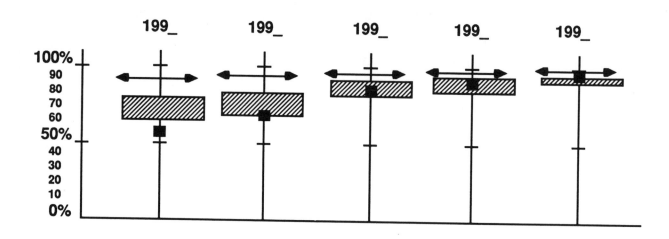

Measurement:

% of Shipments with No Defects

 **World Class Level**

Industry Leaders' Range

■ **Your Company's Level**

BENCHMARKING RESULTS

Objective:

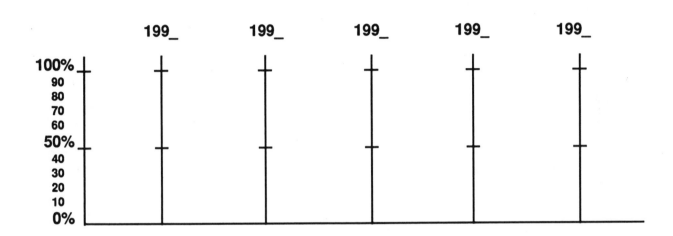

| | 199_ | 199_ | 199_ | 199_ | 199_ |

100%
90
80
70
60
50%
40
30
20
10
0%

Measurement:

 **World Class Level**

Industry Leaders' Range

■ **Your Company's Level**

Identifying World Class Companies

IDENTIFYING WORLD CLASS COMPANIES

For each characteristic, put the company's rank in the appropriate column (1 for best in class, 2 for average and 3 for below average). Add the rankings for each company and put in Total. Divide Total by the number of characteristics that you have established to derive an overall score. The score closest to 1.0 is the best.

Characteristics	Companies					
	XX	AA	BB	CC	DD	EE
1 Supply Mgmt. integral part of strategic plan	2	1	3	1	2	3
2 Education and training	1	3	2	2	2	2
3 Team building	3	1	2	3	2	3
4 Early supplier involvement	2	1	3	1	3	1
5 Concurrent engineering	2	3	1	3	3	3
6 CIP program	2	1	3	2	2	2
7 Activity Based Costing	1	2	3	3	3	3
8 Agile manufacturing	3	2	1	2	2	2
9 Six Sigma performance	3	2	3	2	2	1
10 Customer satisfaction	1	1	3	1	3	3
Total	20	17	24	20	24	23
Overall Score	2.0	1.7	2.4	2.0	2.4	2.3

IDENTIFYING WORLD CLASS COMPANIES

For each characteristic, put the company's rank in the appropriate column (1 for best in class, 2 for average and 3 for below average). Add the rankings for each company and put in Total. Divide Total by the number of characteristics that you have established to derive an overall score. The score closest to 1.0 is the best.

Characteristics	Companies					
	XX	AA	BB	CC	DD	EE
1						
2						
3						
4						
5						
6						
7						
8						
9						
10						
Total						
Overall Score						

Identifying World Class Companies

BENCHMARKING PERFORMANCE CHARACTERISTICS

Take the information in one company column from the IDENTIFYING WORLD CLASS COMPANIES chart and use the graph below to show their performance characteristics profile.

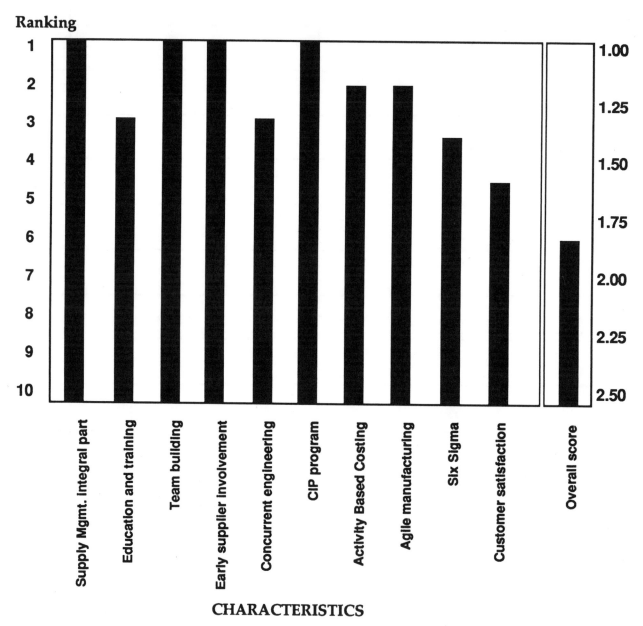

BENCHMARKING PERFORMANCE CHARACTERISTICS

Take the information in one company column from the IDENTIFYING WORLD CLASS COMPANIES chart and use the graph below to show their performance characteristics profile.

Benchmarking Performance

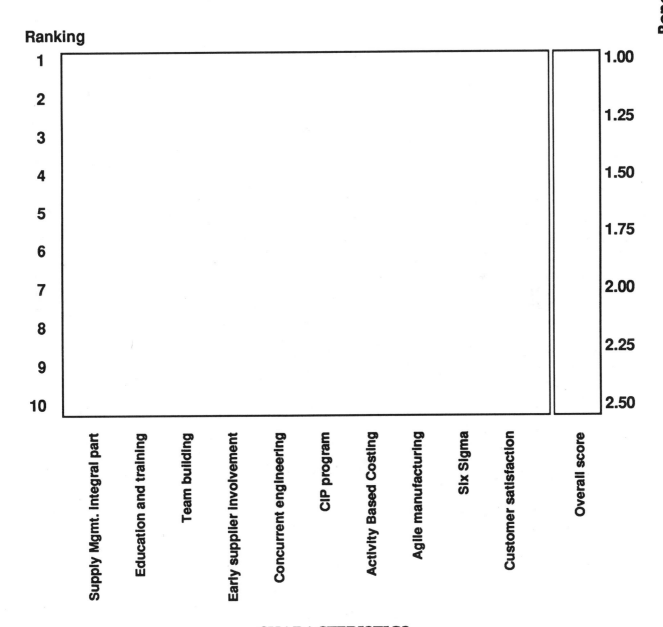

Ranking

1	1.00
2	1.25
3	
4	1.50
5	1.75
6	
7	2.00
8	2.25
9	
10	2.50

Characteristics (x-axis): Supply Mgmt. Integral part, Education and training, Team building, Early supplier involvement, Concurrent engineering, CIP program, Activity Based Costing, Agile manufacturing, Six Sigma, Customer satisfaction, Overall score

CHARACTERISTICS

BENCHMARKING
TEAM MEMBER CHECKLIST

	POSSIBLE POINTS	SCORE
Skills in area to be benchmarked	20	____
Understands processes and measurements	10	____
Trained in benchmarking	15	____
Understands team dynamics	10	____
Able to "clone" idea in other areas	10	____
Known and respected in organization	8	____
Trained in problem solving	20	____
Able to perform cost analyses	7	____
TOTAL	100	____

HOW TO CREATE
A BENCHMARKING OBJECTIVE

Benchmarking Objective

1. Identify key areas in your supply base
    which can be improved through
    benchmarking and rank them in order.

    _____
    _____
    _____
    _____
    _____

2. Choose the major area and state the
    objective you would like to achieve.

    _____
    _____
    _____
    _____
    _____

3. Define one specific action you can take
    to meet your objective.

    _____
    _____
    _____
    _____
    _____

4. Identify and define the cost drivers
    for the specific action defined in #3.

    _____
    _____
    _____
    _____
    _____

5. What measurements are required
    for the cost drivers in #4.

    _____
    _____
    _____
    _____
    _____

3-12

Performance Gap

BRIDGING THE PERFORMANCE GAP

Performance Measurements	Your Company's Performance	World Class Company's Performance	Performance Gap	1st Year Goal	2nd Year Goal	3rd Year Goal
On-time delivery	95%	99%	4%	98%	99.5%	99.999%
Defects per lot	2%	.001%	1.999%	1%	.01%	.001%
Accurate counts	97%	100%	3%	98.5%	99.8%	100%
Number of suppliers	345	70	275	280	170	85
Number of suppliers certified	10	60	50	20	40	60
Six Sigma performance	3.6	5.8	2.2	3.9	4.5	5.5
Value analysis (Cost reduction)	Unknown	5%/yr	100%/yr	5%/yr	5%/yr	5%/yr
Receipts to inventory (WIP)	10%	50%	50%	30%	40%	50%
Purchase order changes	25/mo	2/mo	23/mo	15/mo	8/mo	2/mo
Number of defects	9%	0%	9%	5%	2%	.001%

© 1995 PT Publications, Inc.

BRIDGING THE PERFORMANCE GAP

Performance Measurements	Your Company's Performance	World Class Company's Performance	Performance Gap	1st Year Goal	2nd Year Goal	3rd Year Goal
On-time delivery						
Defects per lot						
Accurate counts						
Number of suppliers						
Number of suppliers certified						
Six Sigma performance						
Value analysis (Cost reduction)						
Receipts to inventory (WIP)						
Purchase order changes						
Number of defects						

Performance Gap

Chapter Four

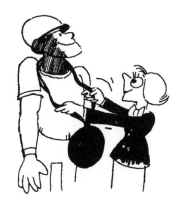

Developing Criteria for Supplier Selection

Chapter Four Contents

How to Use the Tools in this Chapter

One of the most important issues in developing supplier selection criteria is to involve as much of the company as possible in order to assure the overall success of the program. The selection criteria memo is sent by the Supplier Certification team to representatives of different functions in the company to elicit their support and gain their input. With this in mind, let's look at how to use the memo and the criteria checklist on pages three and four.

The actual criteria chosen to select suppliers will vary according to the size and nature of the business. Each company will have to tailor and develop its own checklist. However, there are criteria which are common to every industry. The process of development is extremely important. It is an exercise in creating an integrated approach within an organization. Our *Supplier Certification* VideoEducation Series illustrates how companies develop their own supplier selection criteria using the guidelines laid down in Chapter Two of our book, **Supplier Certification II:** *A Handbook for Achieving Excellence Through Continuous Improvement.*

Once you have drawn up a list of criteria, the next step is to refine the categories so there is no duplication. You can use the criteria definitions on pages 19 through 24 to help you with this task. We suggest that you read our latest book, **Activity Based Costing:** *The Key to World Class Performance* for more costing information.

With a clearly defined list of criteria, you can proceed to the next step using the Product and Service Criteria on pages six through 14 as your tool. You need to group the criteria into categories which address major areas of concern to your company. Some of the areas we have addressed in our sample tool are Product Development, Quality Management, Total Cost and so on. Your list of categories will come from the definitions you have written and the input you have gathered from other functions within your company. They identify what is important to your organization.

The level of importance for each category will be instrumental in establishing point values for each factor. Once again, you can use our sample survey as a tool to establish point values for each of your factors. We suggest assigning a point value to each criterion so that the categories add up to a total of 100 points. Many companies utilize a 1000-point system as well.

The checklist of supplier criteria in the last step is used when you compare each supplier survey. In order to make it easier to compare the results of different surveys, use the forms shown on 15 through 18. They give a capsulized review of each company's performance and allow you to see, at a glance, each company's weaknesses and strengths. We have provided you with a blank sample of the form and one that is filled in so that you can see how it is used.

Involvement Memo

TO: Plant Staff, Managers and Supervisors

FM: Supplier Certification Team

RE: SELECTION CRITERIA FOR NEW SUPPLIERS

....

The Supplier Certification Steering Group is seeking your input to develop criteria which can be applied when selecting new suppliers. We would like you to represent your function in reviewing the attached draft of selection criteria and by adding any other elements which you think are important to the process.

If you disagree with any criteria we've listed, please cross it off and provide your explanation of its non-applicability. When completed, please check the three elements you deem most important when selecting a new supplier.

Please return the form to the attention of

_____ by _____.

Selecting criteria is the first step in our journey toward implementing a successful Supplier Certification program.

(List your first pass criteria below.)

_____   _____

_____   _____

_____   _____

_____   _____

_____   _____

_____   _____

_____   _____

_____   _____

1 = Must Have 2 = Nice to Have 3 = Not Applicable	**Selection Criteria Checklist**	Applicable?		**Explanation of non-applicability**
		Yes	**No**	
	Quality Systems			
	Quality Management			
	Quality History			
	Six Sigma Program			
	ISO 9000			
	Manufacturing Process Control			
	Manufacturing Process Capability			
	Manufacturing to Specifications			
	Calibration History			
	Tool Tracking			
	Housekeeping			
	Preventive Maintenance			
	Compliance of Materials			
	Material Control Systems			
	Management Commitment			
	Education and Training Programs			
	Technical Support			
	Cost Controls			
	Competitive Pricing			
	Financial Stability			
	Business and Industry Knowledge			
	Facilities Management			
	Equipment Management			
	Order Entry Process Control			
	Distribution Process Control			
	Customer Service			
	On-time Delivery			
	Compliance to Govt. Regulations			
	Environmental Programs			
	Positive Labor Relations			
	Document Controls			
	Logistic/Geographic Compatibility			
	Product Warranty and Reliability			
	Research and Development			
	Subcontractor Policy			
	Ethics			
	Percent of Business			

Involvement Memo

SELECTION CRITERIA
for Products & Services

MAJOR CATEGORIES

	CATEGORY	POINTS
1.	Product	25
2.	Total Cost	10
3.	Quality Management	15
4.	Administration	5
5.	Product Development	10
6.	Supply Management	10
7.	Process Management	20
8.	Logistics	5
	TOTAL	100

© 1995 PT Publications, Inc.

Form SMTB-13

PRODUCT

	Value	Score
1. Product Conformance to Customer Requirements • Existence of technical capability • Manufacturing method, time and lot size • Raw material conformance • Performance benchmark • Landed cost/price • Life cycle expectations • Future improvements/goals • Spare part service and availability/policy • Reliability (MTBF) — Mean Time Between Failures • References — customers	50	
2. Assembly Requirements • Methodology • Handling • Compatibility to our process • Flexibility	10	
3. Packing • Transportation • Stocking • Cost, nonvalue-added • Bar coding capability • Can be recycled	5	
4. Environmental Requirements • Temperature • Moisture • Mechanical stress • Impurities • Local laws/regulations adherence	10	
5. Standard Requirements • EC, UL, CSA • Company requirements	5	
6. Design • Design for producibility • Concurrence methods	10	
7. Warranty • Coverage period • Length of contract	5	
8. Customer Service • Maintenance requirements • Spare parts availability • Service manual included	5	

Selection Criteria

TOTAL COST

	Value	Score

1. **Development Cost of a New Product** — Value: 10
   * Starting cost of a new production line, prototype costs, etc.

2. **Total Cost of Standard Production** — Value: 20

   A. Direct cost
   * Material cost (major components/other components/raw materials)
   * Direct labor cost

   B. Total overhead cost
   * Overhead costs must be determined as % of direct cost (manufacturing overhead costs, testing costs, other overhead costs)
   * R&D and engineering overhead costs
   * Data on supplier's total overhead %s
   * If no supplier data or information on overhead costs, then estimate as follows:

     * Human resource costs
     * Indirect labor cost added to overhead
     * Salary costs—administration
     * Space costs per square foot
     * Space of offices and manufacturing area
     * Investment costs
     * Other overheads (for special instances)

3. **Packaging Cost** — Value: 5

4. **Estimated Reasonable Profit Level** — Value: 3

5. **Transportation and Freight Costs** — Value: 5
   * Transportation costs must be determined as % of the total costs plus the profit (averages 2.7% of Cost of Goods Sold)

6. **Duty Cost** — Value: 2
   * Duty cost must be determined as % of the total cost plus the profit

7. **Cost of Special Payment Terms (Not Invoice Discounts)** — Value: 8
   * Calculated costs of different terms of payment

8. **Soft/Weak Country Currency Options** — Value: 5

9. **Discount for Early Payment** — Value: 2

10. **Cost of Inventory** — Value: 20

11. **Cost of Quality** — Value: 20
    * Failure
    * Appraisal
    * Prevention

QUALITY MANAGEMENT

	Value	Score

Selection Criteria

1. **Management review**
   - **Functions represented in reviews**
   - **Scope (audit reports, quality costs, number of customer complaints, feedback from personnel)**
   - **Corrective actions (policy and procedure)**

   Value: 20

2. **Strategic quality planning**
   - **Base for planning**
   - **Customer satisfaction study**
   - **National or international quality award**
   - **Quality plan for the company and quality goals for departments**
   - **QFD — Quality Functional Development**

   Value: 25

3. **Commitment to quality**
   - **Commitment by management**
   - **Commitment by organization**
   - **Mission/Vision statement**

   Value: 10

4. **Organization of the quality system**
   - **Clearly defined policy to guide the organization**
   - **Method for systematic performance of quality measurements**
   - **Certification: self-certified, QA system certified by third party**

   Value: 20

5. **Continuous improvement**
   - **Internal audits performance**
   - **Product quality level follow-up (number of warranty cases/costs)**
   - **Customer returns**
   - **Measure of improvements, quality metrics:**
     - **Total cycle time**
     - **First pass yield**
     - **Customer satisfaction**
     - **Quality costs**
   - **Problem-solving techniques employed**

   Value: 20

6. **National Quality Awards**
   - **Malcolm Baldrige**
   - **ISO 9000**
   - **European Quality Award**

   Value: 5

Selection Criteria

ADMINISTRATION

	Value	Score
1. Organization • Clearly defined organization chart • Partnership with suppliers/customers	5	
2. Personnel Policy • Hiring policy • Training and education policy	15	
3. Ownership • Question if subsidiary of main competitor • Public corporation • Private corporation	20	
4. Financial • Return on assets/investments • Annual report • Credit rating • Dun & Bradstreet report	10	
5. Business Strategy • Clear tasks, targets, goals • Technological targets • Market position • Benchmarking	10	
6. Systems of Handling Customer Feedback and Returns	25	
7. Information Systems	10	
8. Integration	5	

Selection Criteria

PRODUCT DEVELOPMENT

	Value	Score
1. **R&D Resources** • Budget and allocation	20	
2. **R&D Organization** • Project management methods • Staffing • New product capability	10	
3. **R&D Facilities** • Laboratory instruments • Information systems, etc. • Space	10	
4. **Patents and Innovations** • Number of patents • Patent policy • Ownership method	5	
5. **Investments in R&D** • % of revenue spent on R&D • R&D costs/revenues	5	
6. **Technology Management** • Technology roadmaps • Product roadmaps • Process roadmaps	5	
7. **Documentation System** • Procedures to manage design changes	20	
8. **Quality Management System** • Concurrent engineering • Taguchi • DFM/DFP • FEMA	10	
9. **Design Reviews** • Clearly defined design reviews • Design on time and schedule	10	
10. **Engineering Cycle Time Management**	5	

Selection Criteria

SUPPLY MANAGEMENT

	Value	Score

1. **Supplier Policy** — Value: **25**
   - Partnership practice (supplier agreements)
   - Quality policy statement
   - First pass yield requirements

2. **Supplier Survey** — Value: **10**
   - Assessments procedure (metrics, feedback, follow-up)
   - Assessments subjects
   - Accept/reject criteria
   - Selection criteria utilized

3. **Supplier Audits** — Value: **5**
   - Method
   - Frequency
   - Staffing
   - Cooperation

4. **Supplier Certification Process** — Value: **5**
   - Quality certification
   - Certified supplier
   - Requirements of program

5. **Purchase Procedure** — Value: **30**
   - Material risk management (single, sole, multiple supplier base)
   - Purchase policy and procedures
   - Blanket orders/system contracts, supplier quality agreements
   - Supplier metrics and measurements

6. **Logistic requirements** — Value: **10**
   - Geographic
   - Deliveries
   - Standard packaging

7. **Cooperation** — Value: **15**
   - How many partners currently exist
   - Customer/supplier relationship
   - Partnership objectives

PROCESS MANAGEMENT
Manufacturing

	Value	Score
1. **Process Capability** • Does specific equipment and capacity exist • Investment rate and age of machinery • Standardization of equipment and tooling	20	
2. **Process Control** • Existence of process mapping • Systematic identification of products • Statistical Process Control • Total cycle time employed • Spread and target worksheet	25	
3. **Process Status** • Continuous improvement plan • Demonstrated process control	10	
4. **Process Personnel Training and Responsibilities** • Minimum requirements • User and service manuals for key machinery and processes • Handling guidelines exist for manufacturing, packaging and transportation	10	
5. **Process Maintenance** • Corrective action methods employed • Preventive maintenance system • Zero breakdown process	10	
6. **Process Flexibility/Measurement** • Flexibility in changes of product design and production schedule, quantity, etc.	15	
7. **Cycle Time Management** • Set-up reduction • Administration Cycle Time Reduction • Manufacturing Cycle Time Reductions	10	

Selection Criteria

Selection Criteria

LOGISTICS

	Value	Score

1. **Packing, Package, Standardization** — *Value: 15*
   - How supplier packages and marks product
   - Standardization methods
   - Package engineering availability

2. **Deliveries** — *Value: 25*
   - Total cycle time
   - Frequency
   - Transportation methods: air, truck, sea, etc.
   - Terms of delivery — FOB points
   - On-time delivery
   - Insurance

3. **Paper Documents** — *Value: 10*
   - Documentation
   - Media: mail, EDI, fax, etc.

4. **Flexibility of Standardized Packaging Methods** — *Value: 15*
   - Is it possible to change the standard methods to meet customer requirements

5. **Quality of Delivered Products** — *Value: 35*
   - Certification
   - Sampling tests — AQL, zero defects
   - 100% test required

Criteria Worksheet (Existing Supply Base)

	Pts.	Supplier 1	Supplier 2	Supplier 3	Supplier 4	Supplier 5
1. General Information (from Presurvey)						
Company Name		Local Mfg.	Pacific Rim	European		
Company Location		USA	Japan	Germany		
2. Current Performance (from Databases)						
On-time Delivery (%)		70%	45%	80.5%		
Quality (%)		88.5%	99.5%	98.5%		
Actual Delivery Time (weeks)		17	20	18		
Flexibility		3	3	5		
Rating		3.70	3.14	3.50		
3. Product (from Specifications, Quotations)	25					
Product Range Coverage		65%	50%	100%		
Product Suitability		2	1	2		
Suitability for Process		4	4	2		
Environmental Safety		1	1	1		
Warranty Period (months)		24 months	24 months	24 months		
Expected Availability Period (weeks)		52	36	N/A		
4. Total Cost	10					
Price Level Rating		2	3	5		
Terms of Payment		45 days	60 days	30 days		
Terms of Delivery		Dist	Origin	Dist		
Cost Breakdown Available		N/A	N/A	Yes		
Cost Structure Analyzed		N/A	N/A	Yes		
Total Cost Index		2	3	4		
Custom Duty		1	1	1		
Currency Rate		Yes	Yes	N/A		

Selection Criteria

Selection Criteria

	Pts.	Supplier 1	Supplier 2	Supplier 3	Supplier 4	Supplier 5
5. Quality Management System	15					
System Reviewed (dd-mm-yy)		3-2-XX	4-7-XX	4-7-XX		
System Score		75	48	84		
6. Administration	5					
System Reviewed (dd-mm-yy)		3-4-XX	4-8-XX	4-8-XX		
System Score		70	78	92		
7. Product Development	10					
System Reviewed (dd-mm-yy)		3-7-XX	4-10-XX	4-10-XX		
System Score		76	56	97		
8. Supply Management	10					
System Reviewed (dd-mm-yy)		3-10-XX	4-13-XX	4-13-XX		
System Score		60	71	81		
9. Process Management	20					
System Reviewed (dd-mm-yy)		3-12-XX	5-15-XX	5-15-XX		
System Score		75	84	85		
10. Logistics	5					
Packaging		1	1	1		
Handling		2	1	1		
Freight/Duty		2	2	1		
Ranking						

Criteria Worksheet (Existing Supply Base)

Selection Criteria	Pts.	Supplier 1	Supplier 2	Supplier 3	Supplier 4	Supplier 5
1. General Information (from Presurvey)						
Company Name						
Company Location						
2. Current Performance (from Databases)						
On-time Delivery (%)						
Quality (%)						
Actual Delivery Time (weeks)						
Flexibility						
Rating						
3. Product (from Specifications, Quotations)	25					
Product Range Coverage						
Product Suitability OK						
Suitability for Process						
Environmental Safety						
Warranty Period (months)						
Expected Availability Period (years)						
4. Total Cost	10					
Price Level Rating						
Terms of Payment						
Terms of Delivery						
Cost Breakdown Available						
Cost Structure Analyzed						
Total Cost Index						
Custom Duty						
Currency Rate						
Cost of Quality						

© 1995 PT Publications, Inc.

Selection Criteria

	Pts.	Supplier 1	Supplier 2	Supplier 3	Supplier 4	Supplier 5
5. Quality Management System	15					
System Reviewed (dd-mm-yy)						
System Score						
6. Administration	5					
System Reviewed (dd-mm-yy)						
System Score						
7. Product Development	10					
System Reviewed (dd-mm-yy)						
System Score						
8. Supply Management	10					
System Reviewed (dd-mm-yy)						
System Score						
9. Process Management	20					
System Reviewed (dd-mm-yy)						
System Score						
10. Logistics	5					
Packaging						
Handling						
Freight/Duty						
Ranking						

SUPPLIER SELECTION CRITERIA DEFINITIONS

1. **QUALITY SYSTEMS...** Supplier employs formal quality systems that ensure continuous process control throughout both direct and support functions. The systems are formally documented for all processes that contribute to the receipt, production, handling, storage, and distribution of products produced for or distributed to customers. These quality systems are based upon statistical methodologies that comply with ANSI, ASTM, UL, CSA, ASQC, ISO 9000 or other applicable international standards.

   A supplier's quality system clearly states who has responsibility for control and release of nonconforming materials, and the conditions under which they can be released for further processing. The documentation required includes identification, segregation, and evaluation, thus designating any processed materials that have been identified at any stage as not meeting the customer's specifications must be scrapped or reworked under guidelines approved by the customer. This identifies the source of error in either operating or support functions, as well as by the Supplier's suppliers, and the corrective actions required to ensure prevention of same in the future.

   A supplier's quality system must support the position that "no measurements are to be taken with an instrument of unknown accuracy." The system defines the frequency of calibration, along with the selection, control, and maintenance of test equipment. The system includes a requirement for internal audits to verify whether quality activities comply with the customer's requirements and to determine the effectiveness of the quality system. Results of these audits are documented and reviewed by Supplier's management for any required corrective action.

2. **QUALITY MANAGEMENT...** Suppliers's organizational structure supports and promotes a focus on quality and customer service as evidenced by a formal written quality policy, measurable quality objectives and performance metrics, and an organizational structure with clearly defined lines of authority and responsibility for quality. Promoting operator control versus inspection/ appraisal techniques ensures continuous process control, and provides operators with the associated quality and technical training to support these activities. Procedures for inspection and test at receiving, in-process, and final stations are in place and understood by operating personnel. All required inspections are clearly defined, along with the responsible party and frequency. Test procedures covering the following are monitored by Supplier:

   - How and when a sample is to be taken.
   - Equipment to be used for the test.
   - Results obtained versus acceptance criteria.

Criteria Definitions

Criteria Definitions

- Method of recording results.
- To whom results are to be reported.
- What action to take if results are outside acceptable limits.
- How the material is released for further processing.

3. **MANUFACTURING PROCESS CONTROL...** Supplier has implemented in-process manufacturing process control procedures that confirm critical quality characteristics maintained through statistical methodologies. Data to support Supplier's manufacturing control is gathered and analyzed, with corrective actions documented to ensure noncompliances are resolved. Supplier's controls focus on preventive versus appraisal methodologies. Procedures are in place that document that production and installation processes are performed under controlled conditions, including use of approved equipment, inspection techniques, and associated gage calibration techniques. Supplier supports these controls through the documented instruction and training of its work force.

4. **MANUFACTURING PROCESS CAPABILITIES...** Supplier can demonstrate that its internal processes are statistically capable of meeting or exceeding the specifications and requirements of the customer's products and services. In-process capabilities are documented by Supplier for all critical stations and are available for review by the customer.

5. **COMPLIANCE OF MATERIALS...** Supplier procures raw materials, finished goods and subcontracted services that meet or exceed the specifications of the customer's products and services. Compliance is confirmed through documented supplier assessments, audits, and performance monitoring techniques. Corrective action procedures covering noncompliances are documented, along with the results. Purchasing procedures are in place documenting how purchase orders are produced, controlled, and authorized.

6. **MATERIAL CONTROL PROCESSES...** Supplier's procedures and practices cover how each product is stored, handled, and packaged. Storage must take into account shelf-life, contamination, and electrostatic control. Supplier's procedures define package materials to be used, labeling requirements, bar code requirements, and environmental protection requirements. Order processing and release procedures are clearly defined in Supplier's procedures, along with inventory planning criteria to prevent inventory obsolescence and surpluses.

7. **MANAGEMENT COMMITMENT...** Supplier's management commitment is evident through the deployment of the customers' requirements in the management's vision statement and company operating procedures. These procedures document how the company is to operate to meet customer requirements and include the following:

- How control is established throughout direct and indirect functions.

- How customer orders are to be processed and controlled.
- How product or service defects are to be addressed.
- How employees are to be trained.
- How the product and processes are to be tested.
- How information is to be processed and controlled.
- Who is responsible for quality.
- Management's role in ensuring quality requirements are met.
- Management's periodic auditing of the quality system to ensure the continued suitability and effectiveness of the system.
- What is expected from each functional area.
- Detailed instructions on how the policies and procedures are to be implemented.
- Technical data, control parameters, and specifications.

Management has defined the level of expertise required for each job, and the people doing the job have been evaluated against the requirements. Training records are available which demonstrate employee capabilities and skill levels.

8.   **TECHNICAL SUPPORT...** Supplier provides technical support to enhance the customer's current and projected product lines, repair and installation services, and anticipated future growth and innovation. This technical support includes technically qualified (in the specific industry) sales engineers/representatives to assist in problem resolution and product planning, an R&D support staff to support the customer in new product development, technical instruction manuals and installation guides for products provided to the customer, and customer training (where applicable). Supplier provides said services at no cost or at a nominal cost to the customer.

9.   **COST CONTROLS...** Supplier is actively involved in cost containment programs that demonstrate positive results during the prior year in maintaining or reducing product or service costs to Supplier's customers. Supplier is committed to sharing the results of any cost reduction and containment programs with the customer and to work with them to further develop and/or expand cost reduction programs for the future benefit of both parties.

10. **FINANCIAL STABILITY...** Supplier can demonstrate that it is financially sound and is effectively using its assets to generate cash flows from internal operations that are sufficient to sustain continuing business operations. Supplier agrees that should any financial condition change, that it will advise the customer immediately.

11. **BUSINESS AND INDUSTRY KNOWLEDGE...** Supplier and Supplier's employees and representatives are knowledgeable of the specific industry and related industry segments as demonstrated by Supplier's products, services, and customer base. Supplier is active in the industry through involvement in trade groups, technical associations, and industry publications. Supplier consistently provides the customer with insight into market and industry trends

Criteria Definitions

and shifts, as well as new product or service developments. Supplier has demonstrated commitment to long-term growth within the customer's industry segments and has committed its resources to same.

12. **FACILITIES MANAGEMENT…** Supplier's facilities and equipment are maintained to ensure continuous, uninterrupted delivery of products and services through the utilization of preventive and predictive maintenance. Supplier must demonstrate that maintenance schedules are effectively and routinely followed (through MTBF or similar measurements), and that results are used to implement corrective action to ensure that process controls are guaranteed. Supplier's facilities management processes contain provisions for safety-related monitoring programs, such as OSHA, to ensure a safe workplace for its employees.

13. **ORDER ENTRY PROCESS CONTROL…** Supplier's order entry processes are monitored by management to ensure the accurate and timely processing of customer orders. Monitoring includes performance metrics that focus on:

- Customer satisfaction.
- On-time deliveries.
- Product quality.
- Customer complaint resolution.
- Pricing accuracy.
- Invoicing accuracy.
- Order entry cycle time.
- Order entry accuracy.

These metrics are used by Supplier's management, operations, and marketing personnel to implement continuous improvement processes to better serve Supplier's customers.

14. **DISTRIBUTION PROCESS CONTROL…** Supplier's distribution processes are tightly controlled to ensure that its customers receive the exact products they have ordered, in the exact quantities, and delivered on time. Packaging and handling techniques employed by Supplier ensure that products are delivered in good condition, free of in-transit or handling damage. Supplier furnishes the shipping documentation (packing slips, invoices, freight bills, etc.) as specified by the customer. Supplier is also capable of supporting bar coding requirements.

15. **CUSTOMER SERVICE…** Supplier can demonstrate that its customer service function is clearly defined and supported by management, as evidenced by direct communication channels to senior management and the use of performance metrics to monitor customer service levels. Supplier's customer service function provides prompt response (measured in hours) for information or assistance (technical or general) through direct lines of communication (telephone, mail, and fax) and EDI.

4-23

Criteria Definitions

Supplier's customer service function provides flexible delivery schedules and quantities without an adverse impact on pricing.

16. **COMPLIANCE TO REGULATIONS...** Supplier is capable of demonstrating it is in compliance with any and all applicable governmental (federal, state, and local) regulatory requirements associated with:

- Equal Employment Opportunity Commission.
- Occupational Safety and Health Administration.
- Hazardous Waste Disposal and Handling.
- Environmental Protection Agency.

Supplier has documented procedures, policies, and practices in place to ensure environmentally responsible and community supportive operations. Supplier can further document that all products are in strict compliance with applicable regulations, and that any product containing materials or chemicals covered under the regulations are labeled appropriately pursuant to applicable requirements.

17. **LABOR RELATIONS...** Supplier promotes a stable and productive working relationship with its employees through employee involvement and employee work team methodologies. Supplier provides training and educational opportunities for its employees to broaden their skills and enhance their decision-making abilities. Safety programs are employed by Supplier to ensure that a safe working environment exists for the work force. Supplier is an equal opportunity employer.

Supplier's documentation verifies that its labor relations are sound and productive, and thus, pose no threat to delivery schedules or quality levels for products or services provided to the customer.

18. **DOCUMENT CONTROL PROCESSES...** Supplier maintains a formal document control process which ensures conformance to specifications, bills-of-material, engineering change notices, drawing revision levels, and supporting documentation are current and available to appropriate operating personnel. This control process is contained in written procedures which are included as part of Supplier's employee training program. Supplier routinely confirms the validity of its documentation and employs the required verification upon receipt of an order for products or services.

19. **LOGISTICS...** Supplier's facility is geographically located near main transportation arteries (rail, truck, air, barge/seaport) to ensure Supplier is capable of supplying products and services to the customer on a timely and economical basis.

Criteria Definitions

20.   **PRODUCT WARRANTY AND RELIABILITY...** Supplier can demonstrate that product reliability has been confirmed through FMEA, DOE, or other similar analyses in applications routinely experienced by its customers. Documented results of these analyses will be provided for review. Supplier provides industry-standard warranty periods on all products and services rendered to the customer. Supplier has a formal procedure for handling warranty claims and has documented evidence of adherence. Supplier's warranty claims processing procedures are available for review by the customer.

NOTE: Refer to pages 35 through 46 of *Supplier Certification II: A Handbook for Achieving Excellence through Continuous Improvement* (PT Publications, West Palm Beach, FL).

Chapter Five

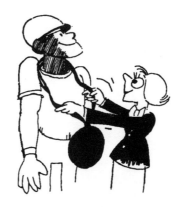

Supplier
Commodity
Management

Chapter Five Contents

How to Use the Tools in this Chapter

There are various techniques available for managing supplier commodities. Most companies, however, need to review their existing supplier base first to determine a reasonable number of suppliers that can be worked with in an efficient and productive manner.

One approach is to determine, by commodity codes and product types, how many suppliers are required by each category and in the aggregate. In this manner, you can determine how much of your existing supplier base to retain and how many new suppliers you need to find or certify.

Our first form, the Summary Commodity Listing, is for recording the aggregate number of suppliers for each commodity type. Each company will complete this analysis of their total supply base for all types of commodities — MRO, direct, indirect as well as distribution of service-related commodities. The intent is to see how much of each commodity you are buying from all of your suppliers.

The second group of forms depict Sourcing Worksheets which you can use to take a snapshot of your present supply base by commodity — direct material, indirect material, MRO, service industry and distributors. Sourcing Worksheets take the raw share percentages and begin the determination of which suppliers can presently meet requirements and how many will need to be added or phased out if they can't become certified.

The Bar Graphs which follow the worksheets are used to demonstrate how many suppliers you have at present versus how many you had in the last evaluation period. We recommend that graphs such as this be clearly displayed for all personnel to see. By adding new graphs over time, your people can see the progress they are making. In all of our books, we have repeatedly emphasized the need for visual reminders of progress.

The next tool you can use is a Pie Chart showing how dollars are expended in the procurement process. Divide the chart and put in the percentages which reflect spending levels at your company. Again, visual reminders like this provide your organization with a quick and accurate picture of how money and resources are being used.

The Progress Charts are designed to show the progress of your Supply Management program by commodity. Using this chart allows you to track the progress of suppliers. The intent is to identify which commodities are in the process and what stage they are at in the process. The charts allow you to track their progress over a year-long period. There would be a progress chart such as this for each supplier going through the process.

The purpose of the Supply Management Road Map is to show the progress of the implementation of the entire supply base project. We have given you a blank form and a form which has been filled in as an example.

The Calendar of Events is a tool for keeping track of the different tasks performed by team members. The Team Member Format is also a team tool. It shows what functions are represented on various teams responsible for each commodity. You can utilize this chart to show both the name of the person to manage the commodity and the functions required to complete the team.

Lastly, the Supplier Certification Candidate Chart shows where each supplier is in the process of certification. Like all of the forms mentioned, it provides management with visibility into the process. Put the name of the supplier being certified and the name of the team leader in the first column. As the supplier completes a step, put the date of completion in the appropriate cell.

How to Use the Tools

SUMMARY COMMODITY LISTING

Commodity Listing

PURCHASED MATERIAL
PER COMMODITY TYPE VALUE/VOLUME

CODE	COMMODITY TYPE	# OF SUPPLIER	PART #	USAGE 12 Months $$	VOLUME 12 Months Pcs.	SHARE %	ACTIVE
05000	Semiconductors						
10000	Passive Components						
15000	Electromagnetic Components						
20000	Assemblies						
25000	Distributors						
30000	Cabins, Racks and Accessories						
35000	Capital Equipment						
40000	Buildings						
45000	Software Products						
50000	Energy						
55000	Office Supplies						
60000	Telephone						
65000	Sheet Metal						
70000	Injection Molding						
75000	Fur						
80000	Printing Material						
85000	Advertising Supplies						
90000	Grain						
95000	Packaging						
Totals							

SOURCING WORKSHEET — Direct Material

Commodity	Code		Present No. of Suppliers	Required No. of Suppliers	Suppliers Meeting Req't	Required New Suppliers	Yearly Dollar Volume Purchased	Number of Part Numbers	Twelve Months Usage
Totals									

Sourcing Worksheet

SOURCING WORKSHEET — Indirect Material

Sourcing Worksheet

Commodity	Code		Present No. of Suppliers	Required No. of Suppliers	Suppliers Meeting Req't	Required New Suppliers	Yearly Dollar Volume Purchased	Number of Part Numbers	Twelve Months Usage
Totals									

© 1995 PT Publications, Inc.

SOURCING WORKSHEET - MRO

Commodity	Code		Present No. of Suppliers	Required No. of Suppliers	Suppliers Meeting Req't	Required New Suppliers	Yearly Dollar Volume Purchased	Number of Part Numbers	Twelve Months Usage
Totals									

Sourcing Worksheet

Supplier Commodity Management   **Form SMTB-16**

SOURCING WORKSHEET - Service Industry

Sourcing Worksheet

Commodity	Code		Present No. of Suppliers	Required No. of Suppliers	Suppliers Meeting Req't	Required New Suppliers	Yearly Dollar Volume Purchased	Number of Part Numbers	Twelve Months Usage
Totals									

SOURCING WORKSHEET - Distributors

Commodity	Code		Present No. of Suppliers	Required No. of Suppliers	Suppliers Meeting Req't	Required New Suppliers	Yearly Dollar Volume Purchased	Number of Part Numbers	Twelve Months Usage
Totals									

Sourcing Worksheet

Bar Graph

NUMBER OF SUPPLIERS
(sample)

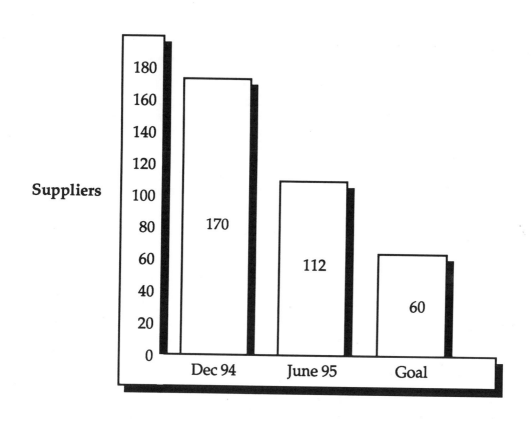

Suppliers

170	112	60
Dec 94	June 95	Goal

Notes:

_____

_____

_____

_____

_____

_____

_____

Bar Graph

NUMBER OF SUPPLIERS
direct material

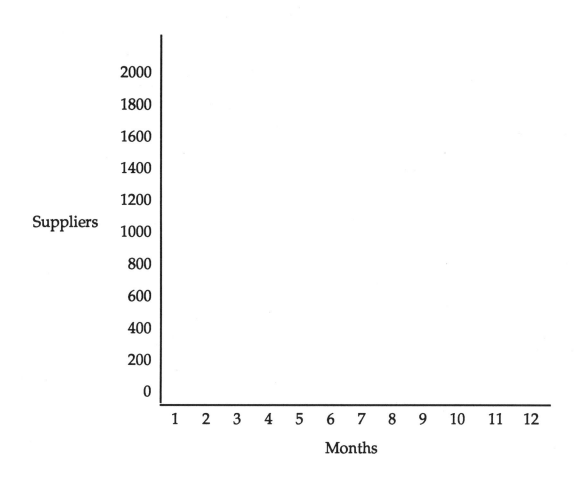

Notes:

_____

_____

_____

_____

_____

_____

_____

NUMBER OF SUPPLIERS
indirect material

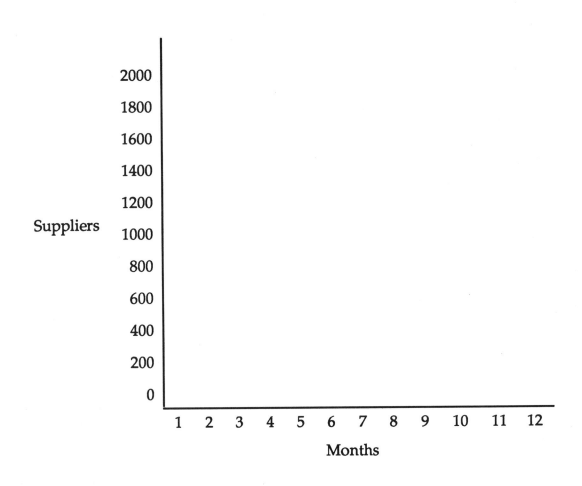

Notes:

_____

_____

_____

_____

_____

_____

_____

NUMBER OF SUPPLIERS
MRO

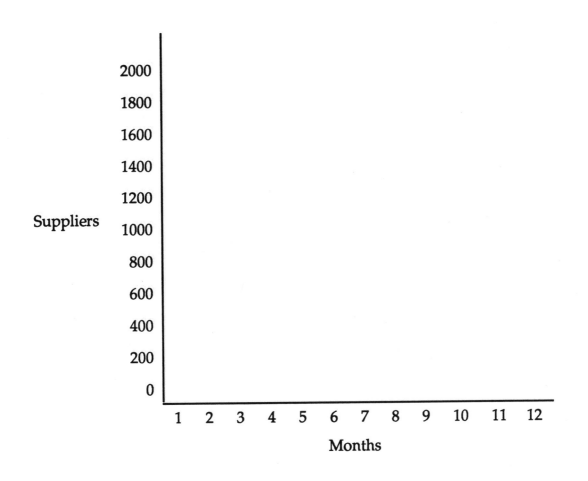

Notes:

_____

_____

_____

_____

_____

_____

_____

Bar Graph

NUMBER OF SUPPLIERS
distributors

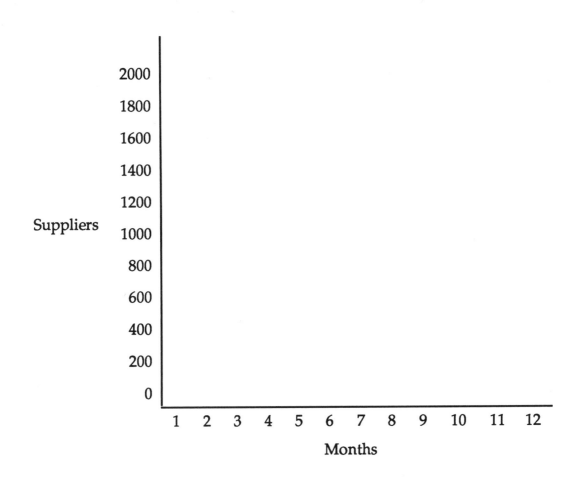

Notes:

_____

_____

_____

_____

_____

_____

_____

NUMBER OF SUPPLIERS
service industry

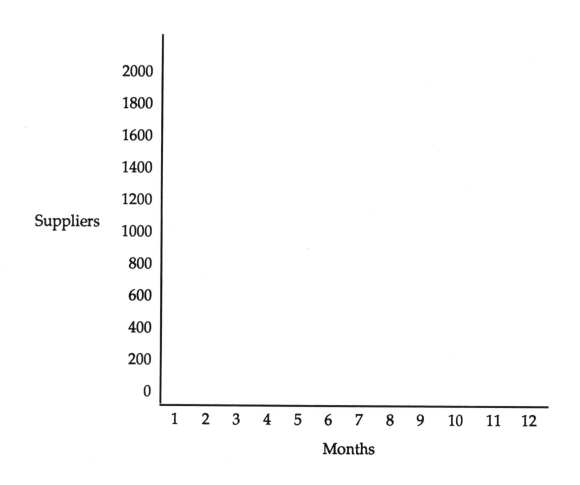

Notes:

_____

_____

_____

_____

_____

_____

_____

_____

Bar Graph

NUMBER OF SUPPLIERS
total supplier base

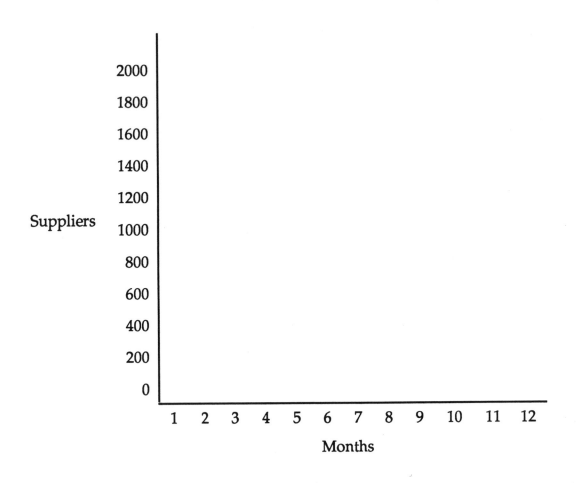

Suppliers

2000
1800
1600
1400
1200
1000
800
600
400
200
0

1   2   3   4   5   6   7   8   9   10   11   12

Months

Notes:

_____

_____

_____

_____

_____

_____

_____

PROCUREMENT
DISTRIBUTION OF DOLLARS
EXPENDED

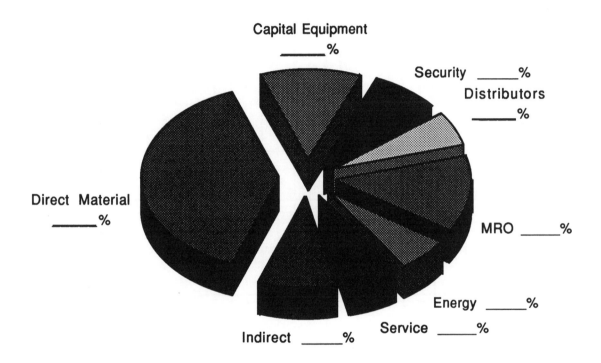

Capital Equipment _____%

Security _____%

Distributors _____%

Direct Material _____%

MRO _____%

Energy _____%

Service _____%

Indirect _____%

Progress Chart

PROGRESS CHART: Supply Base

Process-Step	Commodity	Jan	Feb	Mar	Apr	May	Jun	Jul	Aug	Sep	Oct	Nov	Dec	Remarks
Supplier Selection Criteria														
Presurvey														
Supplier Survey														
Final Selection														
Partnership Statement														
Certification Process: Phase 1 2 3														
Rating and Valuation														
Certification Phase 4														
Maintenance and Audit: Phase 5														

© 1995 PT Publications, Inc.

SUPPLY MANAGEMENT IMPLEMENTATION ROAD MAP

Supply Manager _____

Commodity _____

Supply Road Map

Cycle Time

Weeks

# of Part #s

# of Suppliers

1 2 3 4 5 6 7 8 9 10 11 12 13 14 15 16 17 18 19 20 21 22 23 24 25 26 27 28 29 30 31 32 36 40 44 48 52 2

- Data Collection
- Supplier Selection Criterias
- Analysis
- Sourcing Plan
- Required # of Suppliers
- Supplier Presurvey
- Supplier Survey
- Partnership Statement
- Certification Process
- Rating and Valuation (CIP)
- Audit

© 1995 PT Publications, Inc.

SUPPLY MANAGEMENT IMPLEMENTATION ROAD MAP

Supply Road Map

Commodity _____

Supply Manager _____

Cycle Time

Weeks

# of Part #s

# of Suppliers

Week columns: 1 2 3 4 5 6 7 8 9 10 11 12 13 14 15 16 17 18 19 20 21 22 23 24 25 26 27 28 29 30 31 32 36 40 44 48 52

Row labels:
- Data Collection
- Supplier Selection Criteria
- Analysis
- Sourcing Plan
- Required # of Suppliers
- Supplier Presurvey
- Supplier Survey
- Partnership Statement
- Certification Process
- Rating and Valuation (CIP)
- Audit

CALENDAR OF EVENTS (for the Year)

(Identify day of week and time period)

Task	Responsibility	Objective	Meeting Times	Jan	Feb	Mar	Apr	May	Jun	Jul	Aug	Sep	Oct	Nov	Dec
Team 1 2 3 4 5 Meetings	Person(s)	Sourcing Cost Reduction													
Consultant Visits	Person(s)	Project Assistance													
Steering Comm. Meetings	Person(s)	Project Review													
Project Reports Due	Person(s)	Status													
Meas. Due	Person(s)	Performance													
Supplier Visits	Person(s)	Supplier Reduction													

Calendar of Events

© 1995 PT Publications, Inc.

Team Format

COMMODITY TEAMS	FUNCTIONS REQUIRED					PROJECT INVOLVEMENT		
	Pur-chasing	Engi-neering	Manufac-turing	Quality	Others	1	2	3
Sheet metal								
Winding wires								
Insulating material								
Injection molding								
Welding construction								
Sheets								
Fastening parts								
Bearings								
Castings								
Electronics								
Fans								
Instrumentation								
Copper								
Plastic								

Supplier Certification Candidate Chart

Candidate Chart

Phase V																
Team Assignments																
Team Review																
Phase IV																
Phase III																
Phase II																
Phase I																
Team Review																
Track Corr. Action																
Corrective Action Plan																
Suppl. Plan Review																
Min. Requirements																
Plans Established																
Review Survey																
Team Meeting																
Survey																
Cand. Intro.																
Commit Letter																
Team Preparation																
Supplier Symposium																
Notify Candidate																
Start History																
Committee Confirms																
Select Candidate																
Team Leader / Supplier Candidate																

Chapter Six

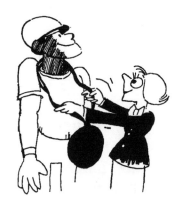

The Supplier Presurvey Form

Chapter Six Contents

How to Use the Tools in this Chapter

We recommend that a Presurvey Questionnaire be sent out before you conduct a supplier survey. This presurvey is for informational purposes only and not all the questions are applicable to all the companies that are asked to fill it out. Besides company ownership, financial information and type of business, the questionnaire attempts to ascertain how sophisticated the supplier's current quality practices are and whether the supplier is moving toward Statistical Process Control (SPC) and Total Quality Management (TQM).

Its purpose is also to find out if the supplier is already certified by another company. If it is, then the certification process will go much faster for a pre-certified supplier. In addition, this tool reduces the number of suppliers down to a more manageable level: just those with whom you should conduct a survey. You simply cannot survey all suppliers in every commodity. Use the tool in this chapter to identify the best.

This presurvey can be completed either during a visit to the supplier, by mail or by any other method that obtains the results you require.

PRESURVEY QUESTIONNAIRE

The purpose of this questionnaire is to get acquainted with various aspects of the supplier's company. We need the information to evaluate their organization. Suppliers will also need to be provided with complete assurance that this questionnaire is *strictly confidential*. The contents will only be used internally and exclusively for the evaluation of the supplier's readiness in our "ACHIEVING EXCELLENCE THROUGH CONTINUOUS IMPROVEMENT" program.

INSTRUCTIONS: All of the following questions should be answered by the supplier. Any questions that do not pertain to the supplier's business operations should be identified as not applicable (N/A). If the answer to a particular question is "none," please write that down. We regret that we will be unable to process incomplete questionnaires. Attach additional sheets when necessary to address specific questions.

Questionnaire

PRESURVEY

GENERAL INFORMATION:

Company Name _____ Company SIC _____

Mailing Address_____

_____

_____

Telephone Number (____) _____ Fax Number (____) _____

STATUS OF OWNERSHIP:

___ Proprietorship   ___ Division
___ Partnership   ___ Years in business
___ Corporation   ___ Public
___ Subsidiary   ___ Private
___ Affiliate

Parent Company (if applicable) _____

Has your company done business with us in the past? ___ Yes ___ No
If yes, when? _____

BUSINESS STATUS:

___ Small   ___ Large
___ Minority Owned   ___ Medium
___ Woman Owned   ___ Handicapped (not for profit)
___ Foreign

TYPE OF BUSINESS:

___ Manufacturing   ___ Raw Material
___ Service   ___ Assembly
___ Distributor

FACILITIES:

Plant Size _____
Plant Condition _____ Equipment Condition _____
Number of production shifts _____
Total Number of Employees _____
        ___ Production   ___ Engineering
        ___ Service   ___ R&D
        ___ Administration   ___ Sales and Marketing

List all your facilities by location _____
_____
_____

CONTACTS:

	Contact Person	Telephone
Sales	_____	_____
Quality	_____	_____
Purchasing	_____	_____
Delivery	_____	_____
Production Control	_____	_____
General Manager	_____	_____

LISTING OF KEY PERSONNEL:

President & CEO _____
Vice President - Operations _____
Vice President - Finance _____
Vice President - Marketing _____
Vice President - Engineering _____
Production Manager _____
Quality Manager _____
Customer Services Manager _____

PAYMENT AND DELIVERY TERMS:

Normal payment terms _____
Normal FOB point _____

Questionnaire

FINANCIAL INFORMATION:

D&B rating _____

Taxpayer identification number _____

Financial statements provided for year(s) _____ (attached) _____

Annual sales revenues for last three years:

    (YEAR)   (SALES REVENUES)

    _____   _____

    _____   _____

    _____   _____

Do you currently track cost of quality? ___ Yes ___ No

Are your records available for audit? ___ Yes ___ No

What are your annual shipments (average 2 years)? _____

What percentage of your annual shipments are procured
    by our company? ___%

What is your total past due committed shipments (in dollars)? _____

Credit references we can contact:

  (COMPANY)   (ADDRESS)   (TELEPHONE)

_____

_____

_____

_____

_____

PRODUCTS AND VOLUMES:

Products produced _____

_____

_____

Services performed _____

_____

_____

Volumes produced (Lot Size)

    ___ Low   ___ Medium   ___ High

ENGINEERING CAPABILITIES:

Desirable engineering services your company offers _____

_____

_____

_____

ADDITIONAL COMMENTS:

_____

_____

_____

_____

QUALITY MANAGEMENT: Yes   No

Are you a certified supplier for any other customer?   ___   ___
     If yes, who? _____

Are you ISO 9000 registered?   ___   ___
     If yes, under what category?
     ___ (9001)   ___ (9003)
     ___ (9002)   ___ (9004)

Have you committed the organization to TQM?   ___   ___
What type of quality system do you employ? _____
Do you routinely provide certifications
     with your shipments of products?   ___   ___
Do you have a written Quality Manual?   ___   ___
Do you use a formal supplier certification process
     in your procurement activities?   ___   ___
Do you routinely track customer service levels for:
     ___ On-time delivery?
     ___ Quality?
     ___ Count accuracy?
What type of material control system do you have? _____

PROCESS CONTROL:

Record the elements that apply to the process control system used in your company:

	Yes	No
Statistical Process Control	___	___
Process Routing	___	___
Routing ID by Customer Number	___	___
Tooling Controlled	___	___
Special Handling	___	___
In-Process Revision System	___	___
Time Standards Used	___	___

Questionnaire

LIST OF EQUIPMENT USED IN PRODUCTS SOLD OR SERVICES PROVIDED TO OUR COMPANY:

_____

_____

_____

_____

_____

ATTACHMENTS:

Please attach any documents you feel will assist us in evaluating your organization.

THE INFORMATION CONTAINED HEREIN IS COMPLETE AND ACCURATE TO THE BEST OF MY KNOWLEDGE AND BELIEF.

_____   _____

Signature of Authorized Representative   **Title**

_____

Print Name

_____   _____

Company Name   **Date**

PLEASE RETURN TO THE ATTENTION OF:

DOCUMENTS REQUIRED WITH PRESURVEY:

- [ ] **Annual Survey**
- [ ] **Quality Policy and Manual**
- [ ] **Company Brochures and Literature**
- [ ] **Facility Listing — Equipment and Process**
- [ ] **Annual Reports**
- [ ] **Financial Statements**

FOR INTERNAL USE ONLY: DATE:

Comments

Reviewed by _____

Chapter Seven

Supplier
Survey&Audit
Form

Chapter Seven Contents

How to Use the Tools in this Chapter

In Chapter Four, we provided several major areas of criteria which you can use when surveying suppliers. These criteria need to be put into a survey format which will allow you to collect information critical to supply management. This chapter provides you with one example of a supplier survey. Many companies use more than one survey. We have provided you with samples of those surveys in Chapters Eight, Nine, Ten and Eleven. You will find that for every supplier you survey, a different type of survey form may be utilized.

Each survey consists of a Survey Scoring Summary and several sections covering an individual area such as Total Quality Management, Housekeeping or Process Control. The last page is a Summary Sheet which shows how the supplier scored on each question in each of the sections of the survey.

All five of the surveys are preceded by a tool called an Evaluation Criteria Point Value. We evaluate suppliers by assigning a point value to each of the criterion in our supplier survey and audit form. The purpose of this procedure is to objectively quantify a supplier's capabilities in order to fairly and accurately document the current level of operations. We feel that the use of the point values listed in our tool on Page 7-4 assures suppliers of consistent, unbiased evaluations.

A team from your company would conduct the survey in this chapter by visiting the plant and interviewing appropriate people. The questions in each section would be asked and the responses noted. Any additional comments can be added at the end of each section. Scores can be added at the time of the survey or later when the team has time to sit down and evaluate the information they have gathered. Scores are then added up and placed in the summaries.

The forms on Pages 7-21 through 7-25 should also be used in conjunction with the surveys in Chapters Eight through Eleven. Fill in the type of supplier at the top of the page.

The Qualification Survey Summary on Page 7-21 is a summation of the activities taken during the survey and what actions the supplier needs to take in order to begin the Certification Process. This form is sent to the supplier.

The tool on Page 7-22 (Supplier Qualification Candidate) is used to indicate to the Supply Management Steering Committee that a supplier is ready to participate in the Certification Process. This form is forwarded to the committee which then sends a copy of the completed survey to the supplier and a recommendation. As for the recommendation, there are three categories — NOT RECOMMENDED, RECOMMENDED and CONDITIONALLY RECOMMENDED. We have supplied you with an example of each at the end of this chapter.

Survey Form

SURVEY & AUDIT FORM

TYPE OF SUPPLIER: _____

Evaluation Criteria Point Value

Question Score		Approach	Deployment	Results
Points				
0	Poor	• No system evident • No management recognition evident	• None	• Anecdotal
2	Weak	• Beginnings of system/process • Limited resource commitment	• Some activities started • Deployment in some areas	• Some evidence of output • Limited results
4	Fair	• Prevention-based system defined • Less than total mgmt support	• Deployed in some major areas and some support areas	• Inconsistent, but positive results
6	Approved	• Sound system in place with evidence of evaluation/improvement cycles • Some evidence of business integration • Proactive leadership emerging	• Deployed in most major areas and some support areas • Mostly consistent and accepted	• Positive trends in most areas • Evidence that results caused by approach
8	Qualified	• Well-designed system/process with evidence of Continuous Improvement Program • Good to excellent integration • Total mgmt support	• Consistent across all major areas and most support areas • Consistent and pervasively accepted	• Positive trends and demonstrated results • All requirements met
10	Excellent	• Systematic prevention that anticipates customer needs • Total management leadership and commitment • Publicly acknowledged and industry recognized	• Consistent across all major areas and support areas • All operations	• Excellent, sustained results • Exceeds requirements • World Class

GENERAL SURVEY & AUDIT FORM

Date _____

Survey Form

Supplier Company	
Address	
Survey Contact Person	**Name**
	Phone
	Fax
Survey/Audit Team	**Supply Leader**

Survey Scoring Summary

Selection Category	Total Points Available	Points Awarded	Weight Factor	Score
1 Total Quality Management	100	_____	.10	_____
2 Total Cost	100	_____	.08	_____
3 Material Control	100	_____	.10	_____
4 Process Control	100	_____	.10	_____
5 Safety and Housekeeping	100	_____	.05	_____
6 Documentation and Record Control	100	_____	.05	_____
7 Organization and Administration	100	_____	.05	_____
8 Customer Service and Satisfaction	100	_____	.08	_____
9 Information Management	100	_____	.06	_____
10 Supply Management	100	_____	.08	_____
11 Design and Product Development	100	_____	.07	_____
12 Capacity	100	_____	.05	_____
13 Delivery and Shipping	100	_____	.08	_____
14 GMP, Labor Relations, and Regulatory Compliance	100	_____	.05	_____
Total	1400		1.00	

TOTAL SCORE _____

Survey Form

CATEGORY 1: Total Quality Management

	YES	NO	POINTS
1. Does the supplier use a formal quality system?	___	___	___
2. Is there a written corporate quality policy?	___	___	___
3. Does the supplier have a QA manual? ___ Supplied ___ Latest Revision	___	___	___
4. Are all levels of the plant trained in Total Quality Management?	___	___	___
5. Is precision measuring equipment calibrated and records well maintained?	___	___	___
6. Are records of inspection and process control accurate and current?	___	___	___
7. Is there a segregated QC lab or inspection area?	___	___	___
8. Is quality data used as a basis for corrective action?	___	___	___
9. Does the operator have the authority to stop the production line if there is a quality problem?	___	___	___
10. Is supplier's quality system based upon statistical methodologies?	___	___	___
11. Does supplier's quality system have a written procedure for corrective action when a defect occurs?	___	___	___
12. Does the supplier have a system of internal surveys and audits to ensure the proper functioning of its quality system?	___	___	___
13. Does the supplier's organizational structure support the customer's quality requirements?	___	___	___
14. Does the supplier support operator control versus product inspection?	___	___	___
15. Are meetings of quality teams held regularly?	___	___	___
16. Is achieving World Class status part of the supplier's quality improvement plans?	___	___	___
17. Is the supplier's quality system certified by another customer? Who? _____	___	___	___
18. Does the supplier share quality data and histories with the customer?	___	___	___
19. Are all quality data and results of performance measurements on file and current?	___	___	___
20. Are defective material reports supplied to customer?	___	___	___

TOTAL POINTS (Record in "Points Awarded" column of Survey Scoring Summary):

Comments: _____
_____
_____
_____
_____

Survey Form

CATEGORY 2: Total Cost

	YES	NO	POINTS

1. Does the supplier have a cost accounting system which supports the pursuit of World Class status?
2. Is supplier willing to share cost data with the customer, allowing the examination of historical, actual and projected cost data?
3. Does the supplier track operating budgets and forecasts?
4. Is the supplier willing to enter into long-term contracts and extend cost reductions to all partners?
5. Does the supplier have an Activity Based Costing or total cost system?
6. Is the supplier willing to commit to product life cycle costing?
7. Does the supplier track performance against profitability goals?
8. Does the supplier track performance against contract terms?
9. Are the supplier's prices competitive?
10. Does percentage of goods and services sold to our company exceed 30% of total goods and services sold to all customers?
11. Can the supplier demonstrate that there are teams actively working on cost reduction and waste elimination?
12. Does the supplier track the cost of quality?
13. Does the supplier have effective control of overtime?
14. Does the supplier have effective control of inventory?
15. Does the supplier have effective control of labor costs?
16. Can the supplier show that it is financially stable using generally accepted accounting principles as audited by an independent accounting firm?
17. Is the supplier able to demonstrate a trend of continuous sales and profitability growth over the past five years?
18. Has the supplier changed ownership or management frequently over the past five years?
19. Does the supplier have an adequate cash flow?
20. Does the supplier have a history of frequent price increases?

TOTAL POINTS (Record in "Points Awarded" column of Survey Scoring Summary):

Comments: _____
_____
_____
_____
_____

Survey Form

CATEGORY 3: Material Control

		YES	NO	POINTS
1.	Are storage areas adequately controlled and supervised?	___	___	___
2.	Is material segregated and identified by part number/customer/other?	___	___	___
3.	Is material with a limited shelf life clearly and accurately identified and controlled?	___	___	___
4.	Does the supplier have adequate procedures to detect and document transit damage, counts and correct deliveries?	___	___	___
5.	Are the procedures to assure proper storage conditions and to guard against damage from handling effectively employed?	___	___	___
6.	Are the procedures for identifying and tracing raw materials adequate?	___	___	___
7.	Does the supplier protect material from the environment?	___	___	___
8.	Does the supplier have an effective system of identifying and controlling in-process materials?	___	___	___
9.	Does the supplier have a fast and effective procedure for tracing and responding to customer inquiries?	___	___	___
10.	Is there a written procedure for receiving materials?	___	___	___
11.	Does the supplier have written procedures for the release of material to other departments, particularly manufacturing?	___	___	___
12.	Does the supplier have plans for the automation of material storage and retrieval? For example, Bar Coding.	___	___	___
13.	Does the supplier have an effective inventory control program that seeks to maximize inventory turns?	___	___	___
14.	Does the supplier use physical inventories or cycle counts to ensure inventory accuracy? What is the current level of accuracy? ___%	___	___	___
15.	Is there a formal routing method in place to ensure that materials are in the right place at the right time?	___	___	___
16.	Is there a plan for reducing or eliminating surplus and obsolete inventories?	___	___	___
17.	Does the supplier use or have EDI capability?	___	___	___
18.	Does the supplier maintain data on its process capabilities?	___	___	___
19.	Has the supplier put in place performance measurements for quality, on-time delivery and count accuracy?	___	___	___
20.	Does the supplier communicate the results of performance measurements to its customers?	___	___	___

TOTAL POINTS (Record in "Points Awarded" column of Survey Scoring Summary): _____

Comments: _____
_____
_____
_____
_____

CATEGORY 4: Process Control

		YES	NO	POINTS

Survey Form

1. Does the supplier use Statistical Process Control?
2. Is there a plan for preventive maintenance on equipment?
3. Is there evidence of a set-up reduction program?
4. Are drawing and specification changes well documented and controlled?
5. Does the supplier monitor work-in-process in order to maintain schedule adherence?
6. Does the supplier take effective corrective action in order to put production back on schedule if there is a slippage?
7. Does the supplier have an adequate procedure for managing capacity availability?
8. Is the Master Production Schedule centrally managed?
9. Is there an ongoing program of education and training in process control for all levels of the organization?
10. Is there a written procedure for process control that defines the methods of reporting and their frequency and timing?
11. Is there a written procedure for process audits that defines the methods of reporting and their frequency and timing?
12. Does the supplier have a written procedure that defines the methods for recording corrective actions and root causes?
13. Are process controls set up at all critical points in the process?
14. Is process control data prepared and distributed on a timely schedule to give advance warning of developing problems?
15. Does the data show when the process is in control and when it is improving?
16. Does the process control system trigger corrective action when the process is not in control limits?
17. Are process changes controlled, authorized and documented?
18. Is there evidence of a set-up reduction program to allow for quick change?
19. Does the supplier use statistically designed experiments to solve quality problems and optimize process conditions for continuous quality improvement?
20. Does the supplier use a "pull" vs. "push" technique to drive production?

TOTAL POINTS (Record in "Points Awarded" column of Survey Scoring Summary):

Comments: _____

CATEGORY 5: Safety and Housekeeping

Survey Form

		YES	NO	POINTS
1.	Are all areas of the plant kept clean and free of nonessential items?	___	___	___
2.	How safe are manufacturing work areas? (Proper ventilation, good lighting, safe noise levels, safety glasses, etc.)	___	___	___
3.	Does the plant monitor compliance to regulatory agencies? (OSHA, EPA, etc.)	___	___	___
4.	Does the supplier have a preventive maintenance program in place for both the equipment and the facilities?	___	___	___
5.	Are there regular safety inspections?	___	___	___
6.	Is there an education and training program in place for employees to learn good safety and housekeeping practices?	___	___	___
7.	Are the facilities and equipment in good working order?	___	___	___
8.	Does all transportation comply with established vehicle safety standards?	___	___	___
9.	Is there a written safety program?	___	___	___
10.	Are housekeeping audits conducted on a regular schedule?	___	___	___
11.	Does the supplier have a written procedure for reporting deviations from preventive maintenance standards?	___	___	___
12.	Do safety and housekeeping procedures comply with industry standards?	___	___	___
13.	Does the supplier have a formal safety review program?	___	___	___
14.	Does the supplier take timely corrective action when an accident occurs?	___	___	___
15.	Are safety and housekeeping incidents thoroughly documented?	___	___	___
16.	Are there written safety instructions for special or dangerous procedures?	___	___	___
17.	Are there written housekeeping instructions for special or dangerous procedures?	___	___	___
18.	Does the supplier have a policy in which all employees are responsible for preventive maintenance?	___	___	___
19.	Are preventive maintenance records available for customer perusal?	___	___	___
20.	Does management support safety and housekeeping efforts?	___	___	___

TOTAL POINTS (Record in "Points Awarded" column of Survey Scoring Summary): _____

Comments: _____

_____

_____

_____

_____

Survey Form

CATEGORY 6: Documentation and Record Control

		YES	NO	POINTS
1.	Is documentation accurate and current?	___	___	___
2.	Does the supplier have a positive recall system to find up-to-date procedures, specifications and drawings?	___	___	___
3.	Are records kept of inspections and process control?	___	___	___
4.	Is there a procedure in place for the distribution of documents?	___	___	___
5.	Are obsolete specifications, procedures, requirements and drawings purged from the system?	___	___	___
6.	Are proposed changes communicated to all departments needing the information?	___	___	___
7.	Are proposed changes communicated to the customer?	___	___	___
8.	Are test procedures readily available for review?	___	___	___
9.	Does the supplier have a list of documents to be controlled?	___	___	___
10.	Has the supplier defined a retention time for records?	___	___	___
11.	Is there a back-up system in place?	___	___	___
12.	Are records stored in a safe and secure location?	___	___	___
13.	Have procedures been put in place to protect against computer tampering or sabotage?	___	___	___
14.	Have procedures been put in place to protect against computer viruses?	___	___	___
15.	Are all associated employees trained in the document and record control system?	___	___	___
16.	Is the system audited on a periodic basis?	___	___	___
17.	Are the results of these audits available for review by customers?	___	___	___
18.	Does the supplier have a system of controlled access?	___	___	___
19.	Is the supplier ISO 9000 registered?	___	___	___
20.	Does management support documentation and record control efforts?	___	___	___

TOTAL POINTS (Record in "Points Awarded" column of Survey Scoring Summary):

Comments: _____
_____
_____
_____

CATEGORY 7: Organization and Administration

Survey Form

		YES	NO	POINTS
1.	Is area performance communicated to management on a regular basis?	___	___	___
2.	Is management receptive to new ideas and changes in order to ensure continuous improvement?	___	___	___
3.	Does management support a partnership relationship with customers and suppliers?	___	___	___
4.	Is the supplier's organizational structure documented?	___	___	___
5.	Has management identified and implemented employee education and training programs for the acquisition of World Class skills?	___	___	___
6.	Does the supplier have an employee involvement program in place?	___	___	___
7.	Is the supplier moving toward being able to compete in an agile business environment?	___	___	___
8.	Has management identified a business plan describing commitments of capital and resources?	___	___	___
9.	Is the supplier's organizational structure well defined?	___	___	___
10.	Does the supplier have a program for reducing cycle time?	___	___	___
11.	Does the supplier regularly communicate performance results to employees?	___	___	___
12.	Does the supplier use the results of internal audits to initiate corrective actions?	___	___	___
13.	Does supplier notify customers of potential nonconformances or late deliveries in advance of the scheduled due date?	___	___	___
14.	Does the supplier regularly visit suppliers and customers to solicit input?	___	___	___
15.	Are administrative and product/service quality systems given equal weight?	___	___	___
16.	Is supplier involved in professional or industry organizations?	___	___	___
17.	Does the supplier's mission statement reflect customer requirements?	___	___	___
18.	Has the supplier made it clear to all levels that quality is everybody's responsibility?	___	___	___
19.	Does the organization or administration of the supplier's company impede change?	___	___	___
20.	Does the supplier's management actively look to embrace appropriate new technologies?	___	___	___

TOTAL POINTS (Record in "Points Awarded" column of Survey Scoring Summary): _____

Comments: _____

_____

_____

_____

_____

CATEGORY 8: Customer Service and Satisfaction

		YES	NO	POINTS

1. Are employees courteous and knowledgeable?
2. Does the supplier respond to inquiries in less than 24 hours?
3. Does the supplier handle claims objectively and promptly?
4. Does the supplier provide technical and commercial assistance for both new and existing products?
5. Is the supplier willing to listen to recommendations for usage and improvement?
6. Is the supplier able to demonstrate a customer service function with a clearly defined organization?
7. Does the supplier measure the performance of customer service?
8. Does the supplier measure the customer satisfaction level?
9. Is the supplier's management actively involved in achieving customer satisfaction?
10. Is the supplier's level of customer service comparable to its competition's?
11. Does the supplier regularly communicate performance results to employees?
12. Does the supplier have teams in place to direct the achievement of continuous improvement in customer service?
13. Has the supplier established World Class goals?
14. Does the supplier regularly visit customers to solicit input?
15. Does the supplier have a documented procedure for handling customer complaints?
16. Are records kept of complaints and are they used to drive corrective action?
17. Can customer service personnel resolve complaints without seeking management approval?
18. Has the supplier made it clear to all levels that service is everybody's responsibility?
19. Does the supplier provide adequate field support?
20. Does the supplier strictly enforce ethical business practices?

TOTAL POINTS (Record in "Points Awarded" column of Survey Scoring Summary):

Comments: _____
_____
_____
_____
_____

Survey Form

CATEGORY 9: Information Management

Survey Form

	YES	NO	POINTS

1. Does the supplier have clearly defined information management policies and procedures?
2. Is the phasing in of new information management technologies done in a proscribed, formal manner?
3. Does the supplier solicit input from customers when planning new information management procedures?
4. Are there procedures in place for translating customer requirements into design requirements?
5. Has management identified and implemented employee education and training programs for the acquisition of World Class skills?
6. Are all information management requirements documented and maintained in an accurate and timely fashion?
7. Does the supplier have a system for tracking the development of its information management system?
8. Has management identified information management requirements in its business plan?
9. Is the information management function's organizational structure well defined?
10. Does the supplier employ all relevant industry standards?
11. Does the supplier measure performance and report results to employees?
12. Does the supplier use measurement results to initiate corrective actions?
13. Does supplier notify customers of potential nonconformances?
14. Is there a documented procedure for releasing updates to the information management system?
15. Is there a documented procedure for releasing changes to the information management system?
16. Is the testing of the information management system done independently?
17. Does the supplier create testing conditions similar to actual working conditions?
18. Is the supplier's information management system compatible with our system?
19. Does the supplier have EDI capability?
20. Does the supplier's management actively look to embrace appropriate new technologies?

TOTAL POINTS (Record in "Points Awarded" column of Survey Scoring Summary):

Comments: _____

CATEGORY 10: Supply Management

	YES	NO	POINTS

Survey Form

1. Does the supplier base its method for selecting its own suppliers on process control, quality and delivery ratings? ___ ___ ___
2. Is there a documented procedure for tracking nonconformances? ___ ___ ___
3. Does management support a partnership relationship with its suppliers? ___ ___ ___
4. Are the sub-tier suppliers' facilities geographically close to major transportation arteries? ___ ___ ___
5. Have sub-tier suppliers implemented employee education and training programs for the acquisition of World Class skills? ___ ___ ___
6. Do sub-tier suppliers have employee involvement programs in place? ___ ___ ___
7. Are sub-tier suppliers moving toward being able to compete in an agile business environment? ___ ___ ___
8. Do sub-tier suppliers use a system to track on-time delivery to the supplier? ___ ___ ___
9. Is the supplier's responsibility for logistics well defined? ___ ___ ___
10. Do the sub-tier suppliers have a program for reducing cycle time? ___ ___ ___
11. Does the sub-tier supplier regularly communicate performance results to its customers? ___ ___ ___
12. Does the sub-tier supplier use the results of internal audits to initiate corrective actions? ___ ___ ___
13. Does the sub-tier supplier notify customers of potential nonconformances or late deliveries in advance of the scheduled due date? ___ ___ ___
14. Does the supplier regularly visit sub-tier suppliers to solicit input? ___ ___ ___
15. Does the supplier review freight costs on a regular basis? ___ ___ ___
16. Is the sub-tier supplier involved in professional or industry organizations? ___ ___ ___
17. Does the sub-tier supplier's mission statement reflect customer requirements? ___ ___ ___
18. Has the sub-tier supplier made it clear to all levels that quality is everybody's responsibility? ___ ___ ___
19. Does the organization or administration of the sub-tier supplier's company impede change? ___ ___ ___
20. Does the sub-tier supplier's management actively look to embrace appropriate new technologies? ___ ___ ___

TOTAL POINTS (Record in "Points Awarded" column of Survey Scoring Summary):

Comments: _____
_____
_____
_____
_____

Survey Form

CATEGORY 11: Design and Product Development

		YES	NO	POINTS

1. Is the supplier's system of managing and storing customer supplied design documentation effective? ___ ___ ___
2. Is the supplier's change control process for customer initiated revisions reliable? ___ ___ ___
3. Is customer documentation distributed internally to all departments that require the information? ___ ___ ___
4. Does the supplier have an effective system of notifying customers of design problems? ___ ___ ___
5. Has the supplier implemented employee education and training programs for the acquisition of World Class skills? ___ ___ ___
6. Does the supplier have employee involvement programs in place? ___ ___ ___
7. Is the supplier moving toward being able to compete in an agile business environment? ___ ___ ___
8. Does the supplier document the solutions to design problems and use them for continuous improvement? ___ ___ ___
9. Is the supplier's disaster recovery capability adequate? ___ ___ ___
10. Is the supplier working on new product development for future needs? ___ ___ ___
11. Is there a system in place for monitoring the effectiveness and timeliness of design activities? ___ ___ ___
12. Are computer design tools used in the design of new products, technologies or services? ___ ___ ___
13. Are statistical tools used in the development of new products, technologies or services? ___ ___ ___
14. Is there a policy for patents and are any pending? ___ ___ ___
15. Does the supplier have a long-term technology plan? ___ ___ ___
16. Are a sufficient number of employees involved in professional or industry organizations? ___ ___ ___
17. Is the process for designing and developing new products, technologies or services fully documented to ensure reproducibility? ___ ___ ___
18. Does the supplier establish specific quality objectives in the design of new products, technologies or services? ___ ___ ___
19. Does the supplier review the design process on a periodic basis? ___ ___ ___
20. Does the supplier use Concurrent Engineering? ___ ___ ___

TOTAL POINTS (Record in "Points Awarded" column of Survey Scoring Summary):

Comments: _____
_____
_____
_____
_____

© 1995 PT Publications, Inc.

CATEGORY 12: Capacity

		YES	NO	POINTS

1. Does the supplier have documented process plans? ___ ___ ___
2. Does the supplier have the appropriate diversification of equipment to produce our planned products? ___ ___ ___
3. Are the employees qualified to perform their job functions? ___ ___ ___
4. Does the supplier have a set-up/queue reduction program in place? ___ ___ ___
5. Has the supplier implemented employee education and training programs for the acquisition of World Class skills? ___ ___ ___
6. Does supplier have employee involvement programs in place? ___ ___ ___
7. Is the supplier moving toward being able to compete in an agile business environment? ___ ___ ___
8. Does the supplier have a capacity planning/tracking system in place? ___ ___ ___
9. Does the supplier use the capacity planning/tracking system to determine availability of capacity to accept purchase order delivery dates? ___ ___ ___
10. Does the supplier conduct regular reviews of process capability? ___ ___ ___
11. Are the results of these reviews forwarded to Design Engineering to be used in product development? ___ ___ ___
12. Does the supplier use problem solving tools to identify and resolve capacity problems? ___ ___ ___
13. Is there a program in place to reduce process variability? ___ ___ ___
14. Are statistical techniques used to measure process capability against product specifications? ___ ___ ___
15. Are written procedures provided to operators to prevent the process from moving out of control? ___ ___ ___
16. Does the supplier solicit input from customers? ___ ___ ___
17. Does the supplier obtain process capability studies from sub-tier suppliers? ___ ___ ___
18. Is there a documented calibration system with periodic audits? ___ ___ ___
19. Are final acceptance procedures documented, controlled and followed? ___ ___ ___
20. Are lots kept intact and traceable throughout the process? ___ ___ ___

TOTAL POINTS (Record in "Points Awarded" column of Survey Scoring Summary):

Comments: _____
_____
_____
_____

Survey Form

CATEGORY 13: Delivery and Shipping

		YES	NO	POINTS
1.	Is there same day pull of orders?	___	___	___
2.	Is there shipment of open orders within one working day?	___	___	___
3.	Are orders 100% accurate?	___	___	___
4.	Are deliveries 100% on-time?	___	___	___
5.	Has the supplier implemented employee education and training programs for the acquisition of World Class skills?	___	___	___
6.	Does the supplier monitor on-time delivery performance?	___	___	___
7.	Does the supplier maintain packaging specifications in an effective manner?	___	___	___
8.	Are there written procedures for packaging products?	___	___	___
9.	Are customer traffic and routing instructions visible in the shipping area?	___	___	___
10.	Are there written procedures for including proper enclosures with each shipment?	___	___	___
11.	Are there written procedures for shipping hazardous materials?	___	___	___
12.	Does the supplier have bar coding capability?	___	___	___
13.	Does the supplier notify customers of potential nonconformances or late deliveries in advance of the scheduled due date?	___	___	___
14.	Does the supplier have agreements with freight carriers that ensure on-time delivery?	___	___	___
15.	Are proper customer codes and labels attached to each shipment?	___	___	___
16.	Are approved lots kept intact in the shipping and packaging processes?	___	___	___
17.	Is nonconforming material properly identified and segregated?	___	___	___
18.	Does the supplier have ship-direct capabilities?	___	___	___
19.	Does the supplier have a shelf-life program for products?	___	___	___
20.	Does the supplier have written agreeements with transport companies for the return of defective goods?	___	___	___

TOTAL POINTS (Record in "Points Awarded" column of Survey Scoring Summary):

Comments: _____
_____
_____
_____
_____

CATEGORY 14: GMP, Labor Relations, and Regulatory Compliance

Survey Form

		YES	NO	POINTS
1.	Does the supplier understand and use Good Manufacturing Practices?	____	____	____
2.	Is the supplier in compliance with right-to-know laws?	____	____	____
3.	Does management support a partnership relationship with its suppliers?	____	____	____
4.	Has the supplier been cited by any agency for violations?	____	____	____
5.	Does the supplier have a published code of ethics?	____	____	____
6.	Does the supplier have a published policy on conflicts of interest?	____	____	____
7.	Is there evidence of open lines of communication between management and employees?	____	____	____
8.	Is there an established mandatory training program in the handling of dangerous goods?	____	____	____
9.	Are there published emergency response procedures and guidelines?	____	____	____
10.	Is the supplier in compliance with regulatory agencies?	____	____	____
11.	Is compliance monitored and controlled?	____	____	____
12.	Does the supplier promote the use of employee involvement and empowerment programs?	____	____	____
13.	Are cross-functional teams used for problem solving?	____	____	____
14.	Does the supplier provide education and training for all employees at every level?	____	____	____
15.	Is the supplier an equal opportunity employer?	____	____	____
16.	Has the supplier experienced any work stoppages in the last three years?	____	____	____
17.	Have labor disputes been settled without resorting to outside mediation?	____	____	____
18.	Has the supplier made it clear to all levels that they have the responsibility and authority to achieve continuous improvement?	____	____	____
19.	Does the organization or administration of the supplier impede change?	____	____	____
20.	Does the supplier have an equal or better than industry average for employee turnover rate, absenteeism, productivity, and advancement?	____	____	____

TOTAL POINTS (Record in "Points Awarded" column of Survey Scoring Summary):

Comments: _____
_____
_____
_____
_____

SUMMARY SHEET

Survey Form

QUESTION	SECTION													
	1	2	3	4	5	6	7	8	9	10	11	12	13	14
1														
2														
3														
4														
5														
6														
7														
8														
9														
10														
11														
12														
13														
14														
15														
16														
17														
18														
19														
20														
Total Pts.														

Type of Supplier: _____

QUALIFICATION SURVEY SUMMARY

Post Survey

Company Name		Surveyed By	
Address		Accompanied By	
City, State, Zip		Initial Survey	Resurvey
Phone		Survey Date	
Supplier Code		Contact	
Supplier Score		Minimum Required Score: 65	

RECOMMENDATIONS

_____
_____
_____
_____
_____
_____
_____
_____

ACTION PLAN IS DUE BY: _____

SUPPLIER ACKNOWLEDGMENT:

_____	_____
Signature	*Date*

Post Survey

SUPPLIER QUALIFICATION CANDIDATE

DATE:
    TO: Supplier Certification Steering Committee
FROM: Initiator (see below)
SUBJECT: Supplier Participation in Qualification Process

Please consider the supplier named below for participation in the Supplier Certification Qualification Process:

Supplier Name	Supplier Code
Street Address	Phone Number
City, State, Zip	Contact/Title

- This supplier has ___ open Purchase Order, ___ part numbers.

- Yearly volume $ _____

- They presently have a ___% Delivery Rating and a ___% Quality Rating.

- The primary commodities this supplier provides are
  _____
  _____

- They should be awarded long-term contract for ___ part numbers.

- Schedule site survey _____.

Initiator's Name	Initiator's Title

RECOMMENDED

Date

Supplier Name
Street Address
City/State/Zip

Dear _____:

On behalf of the Supplier Certification team, we would like to congratulate your company for successfully achieving the status of **QUALIFIED SUPPLIER**.

Achieving a score of ____ places your company in the upper 10% of our Supply Base. Although your score qualifies you, we also require a written statement and timetable which details your continuous improvement efforts.

Your commitment to the Continuous Improvement Process has resulted in our confidence that your company will supply us with the highest quality products and service complying with every aspect of the specifications. Our Supplier Certification Team will be contacting you to start Phase I in the implementation of the certification program.

Thank you for your efforts in meeting this milestone and for your continued participation in the process.

Sincerely,

(signature)

Post Survey

NOT RECOMMENDED

Date

Supplier Name
Street Address
City/State/Zip

Dear _____ :

We have completed our survey evaluation of your company and its operations on (date) with (names of company representatives) and (supplier representative) in attendance.

This letter is to inform you that your company has **not been recommended** to enter into the Supplier Certification Process due to the findings recorded during the evaluation survey.

Please notify us when you have completed a review of the deficiencies named in this report, executed an improvement plan and achieved a minimum required score of 65.

Should you have further questions, please contact me at (phone).

Thank you,

(signature)

CONDITIONALLY RECOMMENDED

Date

Supplier Name
Street Address
City/State/Zip

Dear _____:

On behalf of the Supplier Certification team, we would like to award your company a temporary status for enrollment in our Supplier Certification Program. Having achieved a score of _____, you are entitled to participate further in our certification process provided that you complete (1) an action plan and (2) corrective actions for the DEFICIENCIES highlighted in our report.

Your status will be changed to QUALIFIED when our team receives written evidence of the corrective actions noted above. At that time, we will audit your facility to determine that the minimum requirements have been met.

Should you have further questions, please contact me at (phone).

Thank you,

(signature)

Chapter Eight

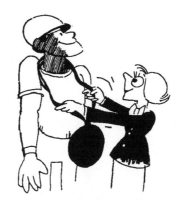

Direct Material Survey & Audit Form

Chapter Eight Contents

How to Use the Tools in this Chapter

In Chapter Four, we identified several major areas of criteria which you can use when surveying suppliers. These criteria need to be put into a survey format which will allow you to collect information critical to supply management. This chapter provides you with a supplier survey which focuses on Direct Material suppliers.

The Direct Material survey in this chapter consists of a Survey Scoring Summary and sections covering individual areas such as Quality, Human Resources, Measurement, Customer Satisfaction, Supply Management, Product Development and Logistics. The last page is a Summary Sheet which shows how the supplier scored on each question in each of the sections of the survey.

Suppliers are evaluated by assigning a point value to each of the criterion in our supplier survey and audit form. Use the tool called an Evaluation Criteria Point Value on Page 8-4 in order to fairly and accurately document the current level of operations.

A team from your company would conduct the Direct Material survey in this chapter by visiting the plant and interviewing appropriate people. The questions in each section would be asked and the responses noted. Any additional comments can be added at the end of each section. Scores can be added at the time of the survey or later when the team has time to sit down and evaluate the information they have gathered. Scores are then added up and placed in the summaries.

Refer to the Qualification Survey Summary on Page 7-21 for a tool to use in summarizing the activities taken during the survey and what actions the supplier needs to take in order to begin the Certification Process. This form is then sent to the supplier.

The tool on Page 7-22 (Supplier Qualification Candidate) is used to indicate to the Supply Management Steering Committee that a supplier is ready to participate in the Certification Process. This form is forwarded to the committee which then sends a copy of the completed survey to the supplier and a recommendation. As for the recommendation, there are three categories — NOT RECOMMENDED, RECOMMENDED and CONDITIONALLY RECOMMENDED. We have supplied you with an example of each of these letters on Pages 7-23 through 7-25.

SURVEY & AUDIT FORM

TYPE OF SUPPLIER: _____

Evaluation Criteria Point Value

Question Score (Points)		Approach	Deployment	Results
0	Poor	• No system evident • No management recognition evident	• None	• Anecdotal
2	Weak	• Beginnings of system/process • Limited resource commitment	• Some activities started • Deployment in some areas	• Some evidence of output • Limited results
4	Fair	• Prevention-based system defined • Less than total mgmt support	• Deployed in some major areas and some support areas	• Inconsistent, but positive results
6	Approved	• Sound system in place with evidence of evaluation/improvement cycles • Some evidence of business integration • Proactive leadership emerging	• Deployed in most major areas and some support areas • Mostly consistent and accepted	• Positive trends in most areas • Evidence that results caused by approach
8	Qualified	• Well-designed system/process with evidence of Continuous Improvement Program • Good to excellent integration • Total mgmt support	• Consistent across all major areas and most support areas • Consistent and pervasively accepted	• Positive trends and demonstrated results • All requirements met
10	Excellent	• Systematic prevention that anticipates customer needs • Total management leadership and commitment • Publicly acknowledged and industry recognized	• Consistent across all major areas and support areas • All operations	• Excellent, sustained results • Exceeds requirements • World Class

DIRECT MATERIAL
SURVEY AND AUDIT FORM

Date _____

Supplier Company	
Address	
Survey Contact Person	Name
	Phone
	Fax
Survey/Audit Team	Supply Leader	

Survey Scoring Summary

Selection Category	Total Points Available	Points Awarded	Weight Factor	Score
1 Quality Leadership	100	_____	.07	_____
2 Quality Data	100	_____	.06	_____
3 Quality Strategic Planning	100	_____	.05	_____
4 Human Resources	100	_____	.10	_____
5 Process Quality	100	_____	.17	_____
6 Measurement and Operational Results	100	_____	.04	_____
7 Customer Focus and Satisfaction	100	_____	.15	_____
8 Supply Management	100	_____	.08	_____
9 Time-Based Management	100	_____	.13	_____
10 Problem Solving	100	_____	.04	_____
11 Product Development	100	_____	.06	_____
12 Logistics	100	_____	.05	_____
Total	1200		1.00	

TOTAL SCORE   _____

CATEGORY 1: Quality Leadership

Survey Form

		YES	NO	POINTS
1.	Has the supplier's management organized regular management reviews?	___	___	___
2.	Do management reviews cover customer satisfaction, quality costs, audit reports, etc.?	___	___	___
3.	Are the principal functions (such as Marketing, R&D, Personnel, Quality, etc.) represented during review meetings?	___	___	___
4.	How are corrective actions implemented and monitored by members of the management review?	___	___	___
5.	Does management actively subscribe to the partnership principles of supply base management?	___	___	___
6.	Is quality leadership receptive to new ideas and techniques for continuous quality improvement?	___	___	___
7.	Has management identified special controls, processes, tools, and skills which are vital to maintaining the highest levels of quality?	___	___	___
8.	Has management released a Quality Policy or Statement?	___	___	___
9.	Is this Policy communicated to all levels of the organization?	___	___	___
10.	Is the Policy updated on a regular schedule?	___	___	___
11.	Does supplier's quality system have a documented Quality Assurance system?	___	___	___
12.	Is this QA system audited on a regular schedule?	___	___	___
13.	Is there a corrective action procedure in place for all departments?	___	___	___
14.	Are corrective actions based on quality data and audit reports?	___	___	___
15.	Are responsibilities clearly defined, understood, and documented?	___	___	___
16.	Is the QA system certified by a third party?	___	___	___

TOTAL POINTS: _____

POINTS AWARDED (Total Points X .625): _____
(Record in "Points Awarded" column of Survey Scoring Summary)

Comments: _____
_____
_____
_____
_____

CATEGORY 2: Quality Data

	YES	NO	POINTS
1. Does the supplier obtain quality related data and information from customers?	___	___	___
2. Is the supplier using a follow-up system for internal quality metrics to measure its performance?	___	___	___
3. Does the supplier use an effecive cost-of-quality system that leads to corrective actions?	___	___	___
4. Are these corrective actions based on quality metrics?	___	___	___
5. Is there a system to handle and protect documents?	___	___	___
6. Is there a back-up system for computer systems and documents?	___	___	___

TOTAL POINTS:

POINTS AWARDED (Total Points X 1.67):
(Record in "Points Awarded" column of Survey Scoring Summary)

Comments: _____
_____
_____

CATEGORY 3: Quality Strategic Planning

	YES	NO	POINTS
1. Does the supplier have a long-term Quality Improvement plan?	___	___	___
2. Is the implementation status of this plan regularly reviewed by management?	___	___	___
3. Are full customer satisfaction and achieving World Class status among the goals?	___	___	___
4. Are company-wide goals broken down further into departmental goals?	___	___	___
5. Are administrative quality systems also a part of the total Quality Improvement plan?	___	___	___
6. Are quality objectives established for the design of new products?	___	___	___
7. Does the supplier show evidence of continuous quality improvement in the introduction of new products?	___	___	___

TOTAL POINTS:

POINTS AWARDED (Total Points X 1.43):
(Record in "Points Awarded" column of Survey Scoring Summary)

Comments: _____
_____
_____

CATEGORY 4: Human Resources

		YES	NO	POINTS

Survey Form

1. Has the supplier defined and documented its organizational structure?

2. Does the supplier make all of its employees aware of its goals for quality, costs and customer satisfaction?

3. Are both employees and management informed on a regular basis of actual situation against goal? (e.g., on-time delivery, cycle time, inventory turns, quality costs, etc.)

4. Does the supplier's management support ongoing training and is there a documented organizational training plan?

5. Are a sufficient number of employees participating in professional societies and development programs?

6. Does the supplier encourage cross training and employee rotation as part of its plan for career progression?

7. Does the supplier have a clearly defined quality function that is responsible for internal audits of the quality system?

8. Is there an ongoing quality training program for all personnel?

9. Are all employees in the organization aware of the consequences of quality as it applies to their work?

10. Does the supplier conduct employee satisfaction surveys and are they used effectively?

11. Is there a timely and effective corrective action system for instances of injuries or absences?

TOTAL POINTS:

POINTS AWARDED (Total Points X .909):
(Record in "Points Awarded" column of Survey Scoring Summary)

Comments: _____
_____
_____
_____
_____

CATEGORY 5: Process Quality

	YES	NO	POINTS
1. Does supplier conduct regular reviews of the product process and establish goals to maintain improvement at the required rate?	___	___	___
2. Are quality tests built into the operations at logical points and is the resulting data maintained and promptly acted upon?	___	___	___
3. Are methods and techniques of statistical quality control effectively used in critical processes?	___	___	___
4. Are the procedures invoked for reacting to "out-of-control" process and product situations adequate and effective?	___	___	___
5. Is Statistical Process Control (SPC) at the operator level?	___	___	___
6. Does the supplier have a training program in SPC for management, middle management and operators?	___	___	___
7. Are the processes and products properly documented and controlled? Do they include customer requirements?	___	___	___
8. Are final acceptance procedures documented, controlled and followed? Are customer product audits conducted as required?	___	___	___
9. Does the supplier keep manufactured lots intact and traceable throughout the process?	___	___	___
10. Are there written safety instructions?	___	___	___
11. Does the supplier keep all areas of the plant clean and free of non-essential items?	___	___	___
12. Is the plant environment conducive to producing quality work?	___	___	___
13. Does the supplier have a process change control system? How are customers informed of changes?	___	___	___
14. Is the receipts, handling storage, packaging and release of all material specified and controlled to prevent damage or deterioration?	___	___	___
15. Does the supplier have an effecive system for managing and storing customer supplied documentation, such as drawings and specifications?	___	___	___
16. Is there an effective system for notifying customers of documentation problems?	___	___	___
17. Are current documents free of unauthorized changes?	___	___	___
18. Does the supplier have a properly documented calibration system with effective audits?	___	___	___
19. Does the supplier have a properly documented preventive maintenance system for all equipment and systems?	___	___	___
20. Does the supplier determine maximum tool life?	___	___	___

TOTAL POINTS:

POINTS AWARDED (Total Points X 1.00):
(Record in "Points Awarded" column of Survey Scoring Summary)

Comments: _____
_____
_____
_____

CATEGORY 6: Measurement and Operational Results

Survey Form

		YES	NO	POINTS

1. Does supplier record, track and analyze customer complaints? ____ ____ ____
2. Does the supplier use internal quality metrics to measure key processes? ____ ____ ____
3. Are procedures in place for measuring the on-time performance and quality level of the supplier's suppliers? ____ ____ ____
4. Does the supplier have a plan in place for managing and reducing its own supply base? ____ ____ ____
5. Does the supplier use an Activity Based Costing system? ____ ____ ____
6. Are costs split into different categories and is the supplier willing to share this information with the customer? ____ ____ ____
7. Does the accounting system include both preliminary calculations and actual data which has been split into different cost categories? ____ ____ ____

TOTAL POINTS:

POINTS AWARDED (Total Points X 1.43):
(Record in "Points Awarded" column of Survey Scoring Summary)

Comments: _____
_____
_____
_____
_____

CATEGORY 7: Customer Focus and Satisfaction

	YES	NO	POINTS

1. Does the supplier measure the customer's satisfaction level with its complete performance? ⸺ ⸺ ⸺
2. Are independent surveys used to establish benchmarks in relation to competitors? ⸺ ⸺ ⸺
3. Has the supplier established specific goals for achieving Total Customer Satisfaction, both internally and externally? ⸺ ⸺ ⸺
4. Is the goal of Total Customer Satisfaction clearly understood by all the supplier's employees? ⸺ ⸺ ⸺
5. Is management actively involved in regularly verifying that customer satisfaction plans are implemented? ⸺ ⸺ ⸺
6. Does the supplier have a procedure in place for handling all customer relations? ⸺ ⸺ ⸺
7. Is there a method for planning future requirements and expectations of customers? ⸺ ⸺ ⸺

TOTAL POINTS:

POINTS AWARDED (Total Points X 1.43):
(Record in "Points Awarded" column of Survey Scoring Summary)

Comments: _____
_____
_____
_____
_____
_____

Survey Form

CATEGORY 8: Supply Management

		YES	NO	POINTS
1.	Does the supplier have a Supplier Certification program for its own suppliers?	___	___	___
2.	Does the program seek to establish partnership agreements?	___	___	___
3.	Are the records of approved sources adequately maintained?	___	___	___
4.	Have quality metrics and improvement goals been established with the participation of suppliers?	___	___	___
5.	Does the supplier have a rating system and does it inform its suppliers of their performance?	___	___	___
6.	Does the supplier audit its own suppliers regularly and with qualified people?	___	___	___
7.	Is process capability data available for all suppliers?	___	___	___
8.	Are the requirements for supplied material clearly specified and documented?	___	___	___
9.	Does the supplier have a written procedure for receiving materials?	___	___	___
10.	Is there a procedure for recording incoming quantities and dates?	___	___	___
11.	Does the supplier properly protect incoming raw material from the environment?	___	___	___
12.	Does the supplier verify that incoming material fully conforms to the purchase order and specifications?	___	___	___
13.	Does the supplier have adequate procedures for identifying and tracing raw materials?	___	___	___
14.	Are raw material testing procedures documented properly?	___	___	___
15.	Does the supplier monitor raw material test results?	___	___	___
16.	Is there a corrective action system for nonconforming material?	___	___	___
17.	Is nonconforming raw material properly marked and segregated from approved material?	___	___	___

TOTAL POINTS:

POINTS AWARDED (Total Points X .588):
(Record in "Points Awarded" column of Survey Scoring Summary)

Comments: _____
_____
_____
_____
_____

CATEGORY 9: Time-Based Management

		YES	NO	POINTS

1. Does the supplier train its people in the principles of Time-Based Management?

2. Has the supplier mapped critical business processes in order to analyze cycle time?

3. Does the supplier have goals and plans for reducing cycle time for such processes as order handling, administration and handling of complaints?

4. Are key suppliers to the supplier involved in cycle reduction activities?

5. Has the supplier implemented a set-up reduction program to allow for quick change and reduced lot sizes?

TOTAL POINTS: _____

POINTS AWARDED (Total Points X 2.00): _____
(Record in "Points Awarded" column of Survey Scoring Summary)

Comments: _____
_____
_____

CATEGORY 10: Problem Solving

		YES	NO	POINTS

1. Does the supplier use problem solving techniques to identify, measure and resolve internal and external problems?

2. Do the problem solving efforts aim for permanent solutions?

3. Is there a policy/procedure using problem solving techniques to reduced variability in order to achieve the goal of 100% First Pass Yield?

4. Does the supplier use corrective actions that seek to remove root causes?

5. Does supplier use measurements to ensure that problems remain solved?

TOTAL POINTS: _____

POINTS AWARDED (Total Points X 2.00): _____
(Record in "Points Awarded" column of Survey Scoring Summary)

Comments: _____
_____
_____
_____

CATEGORY 11: Product Development

Survey Form

	YES	NO	POINTS

1. Does the supplier's management have a procedure for measuring the need for development resources?
2. Does the supplier have a system for monitoring design activities and evaluating them against targets?
3. Is the supplier making maximum use of computer design tools in the development of new products, technologies and services?
4. Does the supplier make maximum use of computer simulation in the design phase?
5. Are statistical tools used in the development of new products, technologies and services?
6. Does the supplier have a long-term technology map which ensures continuous improvement and the achievement of World Class?
7. Is the supplier moving toward being able to compete in an agile business environment in its development of new products?
8. Is the process for producing new products, technologies and services fully and properly documented?
9. Does the supplier include customer requirements in the planning of new products and services?
10. Does the supplier have a procedure in place for translating customer requirements into design requirements?
11. Do development policies and procedures exist for new products, technologies and services?
12. Does the supplier have a procedure to control critical functions for new products before production?
13. Does the supplier conduct design reviews on a scheduled basis?
14. Are products, technologies and services developed concurrently with the new processes needed to produce them?

TOTAL POINTS:

POINTS AWARDED (Total Points X .714):
(Record in "Points Awarded" column of Survey Scoring Summary)

Comments: _____

CATEGORY 12: Logistics

Survey Form

	YES	NO	POINTS

1. Does the supplier maintain a file for packaging specifications? __ __ __
2. Does the supplier have written procedures for packaging the product? __ __ __
3. Does the system allow for packages as defined by the customer? __ __ __
4. Do the packing materials conform to environmental regulations? __ __ __
5. Will the supplier accept the return of material, including packaging material? __ __ __
6. Does the supplier have written procedures for marking containers? __ __ __
7. Is there a written procedure for the use of proper identificatin labels? __ __ __
8. Does the supplier include reference codes and other data as requested by customer? __ __ __
9. Does the supplier have written procedures outlining the details of shipping a product? __ __ __
10. Does the supplier have bar coding capability? __ __ __
11. Are customer routing instructions visible on packages? Are traffic and routing guides maintained in the shipping department? __ __ __
12. Has the supplier ensured that the methods for shipping hazardous material are fully documented and understood? __ __ __
13. Is the responsibility for company logistics clearly defined? __ __ __
14. Does the supplier have procedures for handling non-received material? __ __ __
15. Will the supplier deliver directly to the customer's production line? __ __ __
16. Is the supplier capable of EDI (Electronic Data Interchange)? __ __ __
17. If the supplier is not using EDI, do they have definite plans for its introduction? __ __ __

TOTAL POINTS:

POINTS AWARDED (Total Points X .588):
(Record in "Points Awarded" column of Survey Scoring Summary)

Comments: _____

Direct Material Survey & Audit Form

Form SMTB-31

SUMMARY SHEET
DIRECT MATERIAL

Survey Form

QUESTION	SECTION											
	1	**2**	**3**	**4**	**5**	**6**	**7**	**8**	**9**	**10**	**11**	**12**
1												
2												
3												
4												
5												
6										▬	▬		
7		▬										
8			▬			▬	▬					
9												
10												
11												
12				▬								
13												
14												
15											▬	
16												
17	▬											
18								▬				▬
19												
20												
Total Pts.					▬							

Supply Management Tool Box
© 1995 PT Publications, Inc.

Chapter Nine

MRO
Survey&Audit
Form

Chapter Nine Contents

How to Use the Tools in this Chapter

In Chapter Four, we identified several major areas of criteria which you can use when surveying suppliers. These criteria need to be put into a survey format which will allow you to collect information critical to supply management. This chapter provides you with a supplier survey which focuses on MRO (Maintenance, Repair and Ordinary Supplies) suppliers.

The MRO survey in this chapter consists of a Survey Scoring Summary and sections covering individual areas such as Organization, Product/Service, Quality Management, Service Management, and Customer Satisfaction. The last page is a Summary Sheet which shows how the supplier scored on each question in each of the sections of the survey.

Suppliers are evaluated by assigning a point value to each of the criterion in our supplier survey and audit form. Use the tool called an Evaluation Criteria Point Value on Page 9-4 in order to fairly and accurately document the current level of operations.

A team from your company would conduct the MRO survey in this chapter by visiting the plant and interviewing appropriate people. The questions in each section would be asked and the responses noted. Any additional comments can be added at the end of each section. Scores can be added at the time of the survey or later when the team has time to sit down and evaluate the information they have gathered. Scores are then added up and placed in the summaries.

Refer to the Qualification Survey Summary on Page 7-21 for a tool to use in summarizing the activities taken during the survey and what actions the supplier needs to take in order to begin the Certification Process. This form is then sent to the supplier.

The tool on Page 7-22 (Supplier Qualification Candidate) is used to indicate to the Supply Management Steering Committee that a supplier is ready to participate in the Certification Process. This form is forwarded to the committee which then sends a copy of the completed survey to the supplier and a recommendation. As for the recommendation, there are three categories — NOT RECOMMENDED, RECOMMENDED and CONDITIONALLY RECOMMENDED. We have supplied you with an example of each of these letters on Pages 7-23 through 7-25.

MRO SURVEY & AUDIT FORM

Type of Supplier: _____

Evaluation Criteria Point Value

Question Score		Approach	Deployment	Results
Points				
0	Poor	• No system evident • No management recognition evident	• None	• Anecdotal
2	Weak	• Beginnings of system/process • Limited resource commitment	• Some activities started • Deployment in some areas	• Some evidence of output • Limited results
4	Fair	• Prevention-based system defined • Less than total mgmt support	• Deployed in some major areas and some support areas	• Inconsistent, but positive results
6	Approved	• Sound system in place with evidence of evaluation/improvement cycles • Some evidence of business integration • Proactive leadership emerging	• Deployed in most major areas and some support areas • Mostly consistent and accepted	• Positive trends in most areas • Evidence that results caused by approach
8	Qualified	• Well-designed system/process with evidence of Continuous Improvement Program • Good to excellent integration • Total mgmt support	• Consistent across all major areas and most support areas • Consistent and pervasively accepted	• Positive trends and demonstrated results • All requirements met
10	Excellent	• Systematic prevention that anticipates customer needs • Total management leadership and commitment • Publicly acknowledged and industry recognized	• Consistent across all major areas and support areas • All operations	• Excellent, sustained results • Exceeds requirements • World Class

Survey Form

MRO SUPPLIER
SURVEY AND AUDIT FORM

Date _____

Supplier Company	
Address	
Survey Contact Person	Name
	Phone
	Fax
Survey/Audit Team	Supply Leader	

Survey Scoring Summary

Selection Category	Total Points Available	Points Awarded	Weight Factor	Score
1 Organization	100	_____	.10	_____
2 Product/Service	100	_____	.25	_____
3 Quality Management	100	_____	.25	_____
4 Service Management	100	_____	.20	_____
5 Customer Satisfaction	100	_____	.20	_____
	500		1.00	
			TOTAL SCORE	_____

CATEGORY 1: Organization

Survey Form

		YES	NO	POINTS
1.	Does the supplier have a well defined and documented organizational structure?	___	___	___
2.	Does management support a partnership relationship with customers and suppliers?	___	___	___
3.	Is there an ongoing commitment to reducing cycle time in areas such as order handling, administration and handling of complaints?	___	___	___
4.	Is there a policy for hiring people with adequate education and skills?	___	___	___
5.	Has the supplier implemented employee education and training programs to meet customer requirements and quality targets?	___	___	___
6.	Does the supplier have a follow-up procedure for updating changes in governmental regulations?	___	___	___
7.	Has the supplier begun implementation of Electronic Data Interchange (EDI)?	___	___	___

TOTAL POINTS:

POINTS AWARDED (Total Points X 1.43):
(Record in "Points Awarded" column of Survey Scoring Summary)

Comments: _____
_____
_____
_____
_____

CATEGORY 2: Product/Service

Survey Form

	YES	NO	POINTS

1. Does the supplier have a policy for the development of new products/services? ____ ____ ____
2. Has the supplier properly documented the development process to ensure consistent reproducibility? ____ ____ ____
3. Does the supplier include customer requirements in the development of new products/services? ____ ____ ____
4. Are there specific quality objectives in place for the development of new products/services? ____ ____ ____
5. Does the supplier maintain adequate records about approved materials sources? ____ ____ ____
6. Is there a procedure for recording quality and dates of incoming material? ____ ____ ____
7. Do packing materials conform to environmental requirements? ____ ____ ____
8. Will the supplier accept the return of material, including packaging? ____ ____ ____
9. Does the supplier use the proper identification labels on each parcel of the shipment? ____ ____ ____
10. Do the markings include reference codes and other data that the customer requires? ____ ____ ____
11. Is there a detailed written procedure outlining the shipment of products? ____ ____ ____
12. Has the supplier documented the methods for shipping hazardous material and made them well understood? ____ ____ ____
13. Does the supplier have bar coding capability? ____ ____ ____

TOTAL POINTS:

POINTS AWARDED (Total Points X .769):
(Record in "Points Awarded" column of Survey Scoring Summary)

Comments: _____
_____
_____
_____
_____

CATEGORY 3: Quality Management

Survey Form

		YES	NO	POINTS
1.	Does the supplier hold regular management reviews?	___	___	___
2.	Are quality issues such as customer satisfaction, quality cost, and audit reviews handled at reviews?	___	___	___
3.	Does the supplier follow up on corrective actions during the review meetings?	___	___	___
4.	Is there a long-term quality improvement plan?	___	___	___
5.	Does the supplier follow the implementation of this plan during review meetings?	___	___	___
6.	Has management released a written quality policy/commitment?	___	___	___
7.	Is this quality policy/commitment communicated to the whole organization?	___	___	___
8.	Has management explained what the policy means to the work of each employee?	___	___	___
9.	Does the supplier regularly update the quality policy?	___	___	___
10.	Does the supplier have a clearly defined quality function for supporting quality directives?	___	___	___
11.	Does the supplier have a system of measuring quality performance?	___	___	___
12.	Does the supplier base its corrective actions on these quality metrics?	___	___	___

TOTAL POINTS:

POINTS AWARDED (Total Points X .833):
(Record in "Points Awarded" column of Survey Scoring Summary)

Comments: _____
_____
_____
_____
_____

CATEGORY 4: Service Management

		YES	NO	POINTS

1. Does the supplier maintain written safety instruction for its products and services?   ____ ____ ____
2. Do the written instructions take into account occupational health and safety regulations?   ____ ____ ____
3. Are the handling instructions and controls for hazardous materials correct and up to date?   ____ ____ ____
4. Is the corrective action system based on safety records?   ____ ____ ____
5. Does the supplier advocate a policy of cross-training and personnel rotation?   ____ ____ ____
6. Does the supplier have a system for immediate responses to urgent needs for repairs/services/products?   ____ ____ ____
7. Has the supplier named a contact person for each of its customers?   ____ ____ ____

Survey Form

TOTAL POINTS:

POINTS AWARDED (Total Points X 1.43):
(Record in "Points Awarded" column of Survey Scoring Summary)

Comments: _____
_____
_____
_____
_____

Survey Form

CATEGORY 5: Customer Satisfaction

	YES	NO	POINTS
1. Does the supplier have a system for effectively measuring customer satisfaction levels with the company's total performance?	___	___	___
2. Are independent surveys of competitors used to benchmark customer satisfaction results?	___	___	___
3. Does the supplier have both internal and external goals for achieving Total Customer Satisfaction?	___	___	___
4. Is the goal of 100% customer satisfaction understood by all levels of the organization?	___	___	___
5. Does the supplier make sure that plans for customer satisfaction are implemented?	___	___	___
6. Does the supplier have a system for handling customer relationships and complaints?	___	___	___
7. Does the supplier have a system for determining future requirements and expectations of customers?	___	___	___

TOTAL POINTS:

POINTS AWARDED (Total Points X 1.43):
(Record In "Points Awarded" column of Survey Scoring Summary)

Comments: _____
_____
_____
_____
_____

MRO SUMMARY SHEET

QUESTION	SECTION				
	1	2	3	4	5
1					
2					
3					
4					
5					
6					
7					
8					
9					
10					
11					
12					
13					
14					
15					
16					
17					
18					
19					
Total Pts.					

Chapter Ten

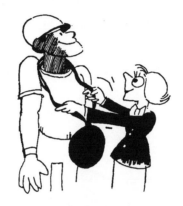

Distributor Survey & Audit Form

Chapter Ten Contents

How to Use the Tools in this Chapter

In Chapter Four, we identified several major areas of criteria which you can use when surveying suppliers. These criteria need to be put into a survey format which will allow you to collect information critical to supply management. This chapter provides you with a supplier survey which focuses on Distributors that buy from original manufacturers and store material, assemblies and parts to be sold to other businesses.

The Distributor survey in this chapter consists of a Survey Scoring Summary and sections covering individual areas such as Quality Management, Administration, Supply Management, Service Management, Logistics and Customer Satisfaction. The last page is a Summary Sheet which shows how the supplier scored on each question in each of the sections of the survey.

Suppliers are evaluated by assigning a point value to each of the criterion in our supplier survey and audit form. Use the tool called an Evaluation Criteria Point Value on Page 10-4 in order to fairly and accurately document the current level of operations.

A team from your company would conduct the Distributor survey in this chapter by visiting the plant and interviewing appropriate people. The questions in each section would be asked and the responses noted. Any additional comments can be added at the end of each section. Scores can be added at the time of the survey or later when the team has time to sit down and evaluate the information they have gathered. Scores are then added up and placed in the summaries.

Refer to the Qualification Survey Summary on Page 7-21 for a tool to use in summarizing the activities taken during the survey and what actions the supplier needs to take in order to begin the Certification Process. This form is then sent to the supplier.

The tool on Page 7-22 (Supplier Qualification Candidate) is used to indicate to the Supply Management Steering Committee that a supplier is ready to participate in the Certification Process. This form is forwarded to the committee which then sends a copy of the completed survey to the supplier and a recommendation. As for the recommendation, there are three categories — NOT RECOMMENDED, RECOMMENDED and CONDITIONALLY RECOMMENDED. We have supplied you with an example of each of these letters on Pages 7-23 through 7-25.

Survey Form

DISTRIBUTOR SURVEY & AUDIT FORM

Type of Distributor: _____

Evaluation Criteria Point Value

Question Score		Approach	Deployment	Results
Points				
0	Poor	• No system evident • No management recognition evident	• None	• Anecdotal
2	Weak	• Beginnings of system/process • Limited resource commitment	• Some activities started • Deployment in some areas	• Some evidence of output • Limited results
4	Fair	• Prevention-based system defined • Less than total mgmt support	• Deployed in some major areas and some support areas	• Inconsistent, but positive results
6	Approved	• Sound system in place with evidence of evaluation/improvement cycles • Some evidence of business integration • Proactive leadership emerging	• Deployed in most major areas and some support areas • Mostly consistent and accepted	• Positive trends in most areas • Evidence that results caused by approach
8	Qualified	• Well-designed system/process with evidence of Continuous Improvement Program • Good to excellent integration • Total mgmt support	• Consistent across all major areas and most support areas • Consistent and pervasively accepted	• Positive trends and demonstrated results • All requirements met
10	Excellent	• Systematic prevention that anticipates customer needs • Total management leadership and commitment • Publicly acknowledged and industry recognized	• Consistent across all major areas and support areas • All operations	• Excellent, sustained results • Exceeds requirements • World Class

DISTRIBUTOR SURVEY AND AUDIT FORM

Survey Form

Date _____

Supplier Company	
Address	
Survey Contact Person	**Name**
	Phone
	Fax
Survey/Audit Team	**Supply Leader**	

Survey Scoring Summary

Selection Category	Total Points Available	Points Awarded	Weight Factor	Score
1 Quality Management	100	_____	.15	_____
2 Administration	100	_____	.10	_____
3 Supply Management	100	_____	.25	_____
4 Storage Management	100	_____	.20	_____
5 Logistics	100	_____	.20	_____
6 Customer Satisfaction	100	_____	.10	_____
	600		1.00	
			TOTAL SCORE	_____

CATEGORY 1: Quality Management

Survey Form

		YES	NO	POINTS
1.	Does the distributor hold regular management reviews?	___	___	___
2.	Are quality issues such as customer satisfaction, on-time delivery, delivery quality and audit reports handled at reviews?	___	___	___
3.	Does the distributor follow up on corrective actions during the review meetings?	___	___	___
4.	Has management released a written quality policy/commitment?	___	___	___
5.	Is this quality policy/commitment communicated to the whole organization?	___	___	___
6.	Has management explained what the policy means to the work of each employee?	___	___	___
7.	Does the distributor regularly update the quality policy?	___	___	___
8.	Does the distributor have a documented quality assurance system?	___	___	___
9.	Does the distributor have a clearly defined quality function for supporting quality directives?	___	___	___
10.	Are responsibilities clear, known and documented?	___	___	___
11.	Does the distributor have an ongoing quality training program for all personnel?	___	___	___
12.	Is the QA system certified by a third party?	___	___	___
13.	Does the distributor have a system for basing corrective actions on customer feedback?	___	___	___
14.	Does the distributor have a system of measuring on-time performance, delivery quality, etc.?	___	___	___
15.	Does the distributor base its corrective actions on these quality metrics?	___	___	___

TOTAL POINTS:

POINTS AWARDED (Total Points X .667):
(Record in "Points Awarded" column of Survey Scoring Summary)

Comments: _____
_____
_____
_____
_____

CATEGORY 2: Administration

Survey Form

	YES	NO	POINTS
1. Does the distributor have a well defined and documented organizational structure?	___	___	___
2. Does management support a partnership relationship with customers and suppliers?	___	___	___
3. Is the distributor receptive to new ideas and changes for continuous quality improvement?	___	___	___
4. Is there an ongoing commitment to reducing cycle time in areas such as order handling, administration and handling of complaints?	___	___	___
5. Does the distributor use an internal interest rate in its cost accounting?	___	___	___
6. Does the distributor split total cost into different categories and is it willing to share this information with customers?	___	___	___
7. Has the distributor communicated its goals on quality, costs, and customer satisfaction to all employees?	___	___	___
8. Is area performance reported to both management and employees on a regular basis?	___	___	___
9. Does the distributor's management sufficiently support ongoing training and is it documented by an organizational training plan?	___	___	___
10. Does the distributor provide a quality education training program for all employees?	___	___	___
11. Does the distributor provide training in the principles of Time-Based Management?	___	___	___
12. Are administrative quality systems given equal importance as product/service quality systems?	___	___	___
13. Does the distributor's cost accounting system split cost data into different cost categories for preliminary calculations and actual data?	___	___	___
14. Is the cost of quality system effective and does it lead to corrective actions?	___	___	___
15. Does the distributor have a back-up system for computer systems, files and documents?	___	___	___

TOTAL POINTS:

POINTS AWARDED (Total Points X .667):
(Record in "Points Awarded" column of Survey Scoring Summary)

Comments: _____
_____
_____
_____
_____

Survey Form

CATEGORY 3: Supply Management

	YES	NO	POINTS

1. Is there a Supplier Selection and Certification program in place? ____ ____ ____
2. Has the distributor established partnership agreements? ____ ____ ____
3. Does the distributor keep adequate records of approved sources? ____ ____ ____
4. Has the distributor established quality metrics and improvement goals in conjunction with its suppliers?
5. Are suppliers rated and informed about their performance? ____ ____ ____
6. Does the distributor use qualified people to audit suppliers? ____ ____ ____
7. Is data available about the supplier's process capabilities? ____ ____ ____
8. Are supplier's materials clearly specified and documented? ____ ____ ____
9. Does the distributor have a system for informing customers about supplier specification changes?
10. Is there a written procedure for receiving materials? ____ ____ ____
11. Does the distributor have a procedure for recording incoming quantities and dates?
12. Does the distributor adequately protect incoming material from the environment?
13. Is there a procedure which is followed that fully confirms the purchase order and specifications of incoming material?
14. Are the procedures for identifying and tracing distributed materials adequate?
15. Is information about supplier testing procedures available? ____ ____ ____
16. Does the distributor monitor test results from the suppliers? ____ ____ ____
17. Is there a corrective action system for nonconforming material? ____ ____ ____
18. Is nonconforming material properly segregated from approved material?

TOTAL POINTS:

POINTS AWARDED (Total Points X .556):
(Record in "Points Awarded" column of Survey Scoring Summary)

Comments: _____
_____
_____
_____
_____

CATEGORY 4: Storage Management

	YES	NO	POINTS

1. Does the distributor keep lots intact and traceable through the entire material chain? ____ ____ ____

2. Is there a system for identifying which materials are approved or rejected? ____ ____ ____

3. Does the distributor properly identify and segregate nonconforming material from qualified material? ____ ____ ____

4. Is the receipt, handling, storage, packaging and release of all material specified and controlled to prevent damage, deterioration and obsolescence? ____ ____ ____

5. Are only authorized personnel able to store and retrieve material? ____ ____ ____

6. Does the distributor handle important documents properly and protect them adequately? ____ ____ ____

7. Is there a written procedure and distribution list for communicating changes to documents? ____ ____ ____

8. Does the distributor remove obsolete drawings and specifications from use? ____ ____ ____

9. Are current documents free of handwritten and unofficial changes? ____ ____ ____

10. Does the distributor have procedures and documents for proper storage and inventory control of hazardous materials? ____ ____ ____

11. Are timely and effective corrective actions taken that are based on records of work injuries and absences? ____ ____ ____

12. Is there a shelf like program for distributed products? ____ ____ ____

13. Is there a written safety manual? ____ ____ ____

14. Is the facility kept clean and free of all non-essential items? ____ ____ ____

15. Does the distributor have a written procedure for electrostatic discharge protection when electrical components are used? ____ ____ ____

16. Does the distributor have a procedure for informing customers of out-of-stock or discontinued products? ____ ____ ____

TOTAL POINTS:

POINTS AWARDED (Total Points X .625):
(Record in "Points Awarded" column of Survey Scoring Summary)

Comments: _____
_____
_____
_____
_____

Survey Form

10-10

CATEGORY 5: Logistics

		YES	NO	POINTS
1.	Does the distributor maintain packaging specifications?	____	____	____
2.	Are there written procedures for packaging the product?	____	____	____
3.	Do the procedures permit the definition of packaging by customers?	____	____	____
4.	Do the packaging materials conform to environmental regulations?	____	____	____
5.	Does the distributor accept the return of material, including packaging material?	____	____	____
6.	Does a written procedure exist for marking containers for shipping?	____	____	____
7.	Does the distributor use the proper identification lables for each container that is shipped?	____	____	____
8.	Do these markings include reference codes and other data supplied by the customer?	____	____	____
9.	Does the distributor have written procedures outlining the details of shipping a product?	____	____	____
10.	Does the distributor have bar coding capability?	____	____	____
11.	Are customer routing instructions visible on packages? Are traffic and routing guides maintained in the shipping department?	____	____	____
12.	Has the distributor ensured that the methods for shipping hazardous material are fully documented and understood?	____	____	____
13.	Is the responsibility for company logistics clearly defined?	____	____	____
14.	Does the distributor have procedures for handling non-received material?	____	____	____
15.	Will the distributor deliver directly to the customer's production line?	____	____	____
16.	Is the distributor capable of EDI (Electronic Data Interchange)?	____	____	____
17.	If the distributor is not using EDI, do they have definite plans for its introduction?	____	____	____

TOTAL POINTS:

POINTS AWARDED (Total Points X .588):
(Record in "Points Awarded" column of Survey Scoring Summary)

Comments: _____
_____
_____
_____
_____

Survey Form

CATEGORY 6: Customer Satisfaction

	YES	NO	POINTS

1. Does the distributor have a system for effectively measuring customer satisfaction levels with the company's total performance? ____ ____ ____

2. Are independent surveys of competitors used to benchmark customer satisfaction results? ____ ____ ____

3. Does the distributor have both internal and external goals for achieving Total Customer Satisfaction? ____ ____ ____

4. Is the goal of 100% customer satisfaction understood by all levels of the organization? ____ ____ ____

5. Does the distributor make sure that plans for customer satisfaction are implemented? ____ ____ ____

6. Does the distributor have a system for handling customer relationships and complaints? ____ ____ ____

7. Does the distributor have a system for determining future requirements and expectations of customers? ____ ____ ____

TOTAL POINTS:

POINTS AWARDED (Total Points X 1.43):
(Record in "Points Awarded" column of Survey Scoring Summary)

Comments: _____
_____
_____
_____
_____

Distribution Survey & Audit Form

Form SMTB-33

DISTRIBUTION SUMMARY SHEET

Survey Form

QUESTION	SECTION					
	1	2	3	4	5	6
1						
2						
3						
4						
5						
6						
7						
8						
9						
10						
11						
12						
13						
14						
15						
16						
17						
18						
19						
Total Pts.						

Chapter Eleven

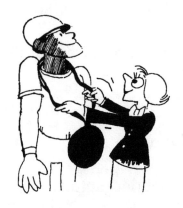

Software Survey & Audit Form

Chapter Eleven Contents

How to Use the Tools in this Chapter

In Chapter Four, we identified several major areas of criteria which you can use when surveying suppliers. These criteria need to be put into a survey format which will allow you to collect information critical to supply management. This chapter provides you with a supplier survey which focuses on Software suppliers.

The Software survey in this chapter consists of a Survey Scoring Summary and sections covering individual area such as Organization, Quality Management, Customer Requirements, Project Management, Software Development Process, System/Acceptance Testing and Logistics/Support Activities. The last page is a Summary Sheet which shows how the supplier scored on each question in each of the sections of the survey.

Suppliers are evaluated by assigning a point value to each of the criterion in our supplier survey and audit form. Use the tool called an Evaluation Criteria Point Value on Page 11-4 in order to fairly and accurately document the current level of operations.

A team from your company would conduct the Software survey in this chapter by visiting the plant and interviewing appropriate people. The questions in each section would be asked and the responses noted. Any additional comments can be added at the end of each section. Scores can be added at the time of the survey or later when the team has time to sit down and evaluate the information they have gathered. Scores are then added up and placed in the summaries.

Refer to the Qualification Survey Summary on Page 7-21 for a tool to use in summarizing the activities taken during the survey and what actions the supplier needs to take in order to begin the Certification Process. This form is then sent to the supplier.

The tool on Page 7-22 (Supplier Qualification Candidate) is used to indicate to the Supply Management Steering Committee that a supplier is ready to participate in the Certification Process. This form is forwarded to the committee which then sends a copy of the completed survey to the supplier and a recommendation. As for the recommendation, there are three categories — NOT RECOMMENDED, RECOMMENDED and CONDITIONALLY RECOMMENDED. We have supplied you with an example of each of these letters on Pages 7-23 through 7-25.

Survey Form

SOFTWARE SURVEY & AUDIT FORM

Type of Supplier: _____

Evaluation Criteria Point Value

Question Score		Approach	Deployment	Results
Points				
0	Poor	• No system evident • No management recognition evident	• None	• Anecdotal
2	Weak	• Beginnings of system/process • Limited resource commitment	• Some activities started • Deployment in some areas	• Some evidence of output • Limited results
4	Fair	• Prevention-based system defined • Less than total mgmt support	• Deployed in some major areas and some support areas	• Inconsistent, but positive results
6	Approved	• Sound system in place with evidence of evaluation/improvement cycles • Some evidence of business integration • Proactive leadership emerging	• Deployed in most major areas and some support areas • Mostly consistent and accepted	• Positive trends in most areas • Evidence that results caused by approach
8	Qualified	• Well-designed system/process with evidence of Continuous Improvement Program • Good to excellent integration • Total mgmt support	• Consistent across all major areas and most support areas • Consistent and pervasively accepted	• Positive trends and demonstrated results • All requirements met
10	Excellent	• Systematic prevention that anticipates customer needs • Total management leadership and commitment • Publicly acknowledged and industry recognized	• Consistent across all major areas and support areas • All operations	• Excellent, sustained results • Exceeds requirements • World Class

SOFTWARE
SURVEY AND AUDIT FORM

Date _____

Supplier Company	
Address	
Survey Contact Person	Name
	Phone
	Fax
Survey/Audit Team	Supply Leader	

Survey Scoring Summary

Selection Category	Total Points Available	Points Awarded	Weight Factor	Score
1 Organization	100	_____	.20	_____
2 Quality Management	100	_____	.10	_____
3 Customer Requirements	100	_____	.15	_____
4 Project Management	100	_____	.10	_____
5 Software Development Process	100	_____	.25	_____
6 System/Acceptance Testing	100	_____	.10	_____
7 Logistics/Support Activities	100	_____	.10	_____
	700		1.00	
			TOTAL SCORE	_____

CATEGORY 1: Organization

Survey Form

		YES	NO	POINTS

1. Has the supplier defined and documented its organizational structure?

2. Has the supplier made responsibilities clear, known and documented?

3. Does the supplier have a procedure for selecting responsible individuals as customer contacts?

4. Has the supplier clearly defined who is in charge of acquiring, maintaining, reviewing and distributing applicable regulations and published standards?

5. Does the supplier have a process for qualifying and validating personnel and tools?

6. Does the supplier have a program for systematically developing the professional skills of its employees through training?

7. Has the supplier named people who can substitute for each person who works in a critical position?

8. Does the supplier have a system for reviewing employee suggestions?

9. Does the supplier have an internal recognition system for all employees?

10. Does the supplier have internal standards for documentation, programming, program saving and testing?

11. Does this program have procedures for identifying, tracking, managing and reporting changes and revisions?

12. Does the supplier have a back-up and security system in place for procedures, instructions, computer systems, files and documents?

13. Does supplier have a security system for protecting customer software, present software work, files and documents?

14. Does the supplier have a business plan?

15. Does the supplier have an effective and efficient information delivery system in use?

16. Is supplier and/or project performance reported to both management and employees on a regular basis?

17. Does the supplier's management study future requirements in order to continue striving for Total Customer Satisfaction?

18. Does the supplier's performance in customer satisfaction show improvement over the long run?

19. Does the supplier have long-term experience in partnership agreements with customers?

TOTAL POINTS:

POINTS AWARDED (Total Points X .526):
(Record in "Points Awarded" column of Survey Scoring Summary)

Comments: _____
_____
_____
_____

CATEGORY 2: Quality Management

Survey Form

		YES	NO	POINTS
1.	Has management included all functions in management reviews?	___	___	___
2.	Are quality issues such as customer satisfaction, quality costs and audit reports handled during management reviews?	___	___	___
3.	Does the supplier have long-term plans and programs for quality improvement and corrective actions?	___	___	___
4.	Does management regularly follow up on the progress of the software quality improvement plan?	___	___	___
5.	Is the supplier working toward the achievement of total customer satisfaction and/or World Class status?	___	___	___
6.	Has the quality improvement plan been broken down into goals for each department?	___	___	___
7.	Has the supplier's top management released a written software quality policy, quality values or quality commitment?	___	___	___
8.	Has the supplier communicated and deployed the quality policy to the entire organization?	___	___	___
9.	Do all personnel understand how the quality policy relates to their work?	___	___	___
10.	Does the supplier have a documented software quality assurance system?	___	___	___
11.	Does the supplier have procedures, instructions and mechanisms for applying quality plans to software work?	___	___	___
12.	Does the supplier base corrective actions on audit reports?	___	___	___
13.	Is the quality assurance system certified by a third party?	___	___	___
14.	Does the supplier have a documented procedure for handling customer complaints?	___	___	___
15.	Is there a follow-up system for software quality metrics and corrective actions?	___	___	___

TOTAL POINTS:

POINTS AWARDED (Total Points X .667):
(Record in "Points Awarded" column of Survey Scoring Summary)

Comments: _____
_____
_____
_____
_____

11-8

CATEGORY 3: Customer Requirements

Survey Form

	YES	NO	POINTS
1. Has the supplier designated who is in charge of reviewing and accepting customer requirements and documents?	___	___	___
2. Does the supplier have a procedure for handling, accepting and updating customer requirements?	___	___	___
3. Does the supplier have a procedure for obtaining the minimum amount of information needed to fulfill project needs?	___	___	___
4. Has the supplier designated a person to help the customer in defining and redefining requirements?	___	___	___
5. Has the supplier defined a procedure for evaluating critical factors in software for reliability, safety, standards and performance?	___	___	___
6. Does the supplier have a system for ensuring that customer requirements are met during process reviews and the final acceptance test?	___	___	___
7. Does the supplier have a system for maintaining customer software after delivery?	___	___	___

TOTAL POINTS:

POINTS AWARDED (Total Points X 1.43):
(Record in "Points Awarded" column of Survey Scoring Summary)

Comments: _____
_____
_____
_____
_____
_____

CATEGORY 4: Project Management

		YES	NO	POINTS

1. Does the supplier have a software project planning procedure and is it followed? ___ ___ ___
2. Does the supplier regularly use software project planning tools? ___ ___ ___
3. Are software development projects planned formally and consistently? ___ ___ ___
4. Does the supplier have a system for controlling information during the project? ___ ___ ___
5. Are software project management metrics used to track project progress? ___ ___ ___
6. Does the staff use project control mechanisms and tools? ___ ___ ___
7. Does the supplier identify key risks to minimize their effects? ___ ___ ___
8. Does the supplier have a system for selecting subcontractors? ___ ___ ___
9. Does the system ensure that the software is ready in time and fulfills all customer requirements? ___ ___ ___

TOTAL POINTS:

POINTS AWARDED (Total Points X 1.11):
(Record in "Points Awarded" column of Survey Scoring Summary)

Comments: _____
_____
_____
_____
_____

Survey Form

Survey Form

CATEGORY 5: Software Development Process

		YES	NO	POINTS

1. Does the supplier have policies and procedures for new software development? Do they result in clearly defined project plans with appropriate measurables and approvals?   ___ ___ ___

2. Do software projects employ phasing and are the phases formally selected?   ___ ___ ___

3. Is the customer able to include its requirements in the planning of new software?   ___ ___ ___

4. Does the supplier have a system for translating customer requirements into design requirements?   ___ ___ ___

5. Does the supplier document software requirements and update them regularly?   ___ ___ ___

6. Is a tracing system used for software projects from requirements to design and code?   ___ ___ ___

7. Does the supplier have a system for ensuring coverage of the requirements?   ___ ___ ___

8. Are all outputs of the phased development approach defined and fulfilled?   ___ ___ ___

9. Does the supplier use approved design standards in software projects?   ___ ___ ___

10. Do the standards cover software requirements, design, coding, documentation and testing?   ___ ___ ___

11. Does the project team routinely maintain software design reviews?   ___ ___ ___

12. Does the approval procedure base entry and exit criteria on customer requirements?   ___ ___ ___

13. Is there a documented process for developing software configuration?   ___ ___ ___

14. Does the supplier have a procedure for managing software releases?   ___ ___ ___

15. Does the supplier have a procedure for managing software changes?   ___ ___ ___

16. Is there a system to notify project participants and customers of changes and to obtain approval?   ___ ___ ___

17. Does the supplier employ software verification activities?   ___ ___ ___

18. Does the supplier have a procedure for controlling sensitive hardware and software materials in all phases of development and during processing?   ___ ___ ___

TOTAL POINTS:

POINTS AWARDED (Total Points X .556):
(Record in "Points Awarded" column of Survey Scoring Summary)

Comments: _____
_____
_____
_____
_____

CATEGORY 6: System/Acceptance Testing

		YES	NO	POINTS
1.	Does the procedure to control system/acceptance testing guarantee sufficient levels of coverage and documentation?	___	___	___
2.	Is software testing activity independent?	___	___	___
3.	Do all projects ensure that the system/acceptance tests will cover the requirements?	___	___	___
4.	Are testers participating during the early phases of software projects?	___	___	___
5.	Does the project team create software test plans in parallel with early phase activities?	___	___	___
6.	Does the supplier perform testing under conditions similar to actual customer operating conditions?	___	___	___
7.	Are the customer's operational profiles used to define test runs?	___	___	___
8.	Does the supplier have a procedure for the formal acceptance of all phases of software development?	___	___	___
9.	Does the supplier measure the effectiveness of its software test process?	___	___	___
10.	Does the supplier have a formal safety review program for software products?	___	___	___

Survey Form

TOTAL POINTS:

POINTS AWARDED (Total Points X 1.00):
(Record in "Points Awarded" column of Survey Scoring Summary)

Comments: _____
_____
_____
_____
_____

Software Survey & Audit Form　　　　　　　　　**Form SMTB-34**

CATEGORY 7: Logistics/Support Activities

		YES	NO	POINTS
1.	Does the supplier have written procedures for packaging the product?	____	____	____
2.	Does this procedure allow for packages defined by the customer?	____	____	____
3.	Does the supplier use markings which include reference codes and other data required by the customer?	____	____	____
4.	Does the supplier have bar coding capability?	____	____	____
5.	Does the partnership agreement ensure delivery to the user?	____	____	____
6.	Does the supplier have a system for exchanging commercial and technical information with customers?	____	____	____

TOTAL POINTS:

POINTS AWARDED (Total Points X 1.67):
(Record in "Points Awarded" column of Survey Scoring Summary)

Comments: _____
_____
_____
_____
_____

SOFTWARE SUMMARY SHEET

Survey Form

QUESTION	SECTION						
	1	2	3	4	5	6	7
1							
2							
3							
4							
5							
6							▬
7			▬				
8							
9				▬			
10						▬	
11							
12							
13							
14							
15		▬					
16							
17							
18					▬		
19	▬						
Total Pts.							

Chapter Twelve

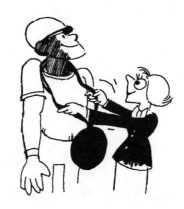

Supplier Symposium

Chapter Twelve Contents

How to Use the Tools in this Chapter

We have found that a supplier symposium in which the benefits of supply management are presented is a highly successful way to involve suppliers in a Supply Management program. The suppliers that you select will be based on the work that you did in the chapter on commodity management.

On the following pages are samples of material that should be prepared. First, there should be a letter of invitation and a follow-up letter confirming a positive response and announcing the agenda. A symposium should not only describe the Supply Management program to potential participants, but begin the process of signing up those who are interested in joining the effort. We have included a sample Supplier Enrollment Agreement to show you what this tool should contain. We have also included a sample agenda which shows the events of the supplier symposium in more detail.

The tool on Pages 9 to 17 is a very valuable one. It is a supplier's detailed introduction to Supply Management. We recommend that you use the generic booklet in this chapter or adapt it to your needs. Copies are distributed to particpants at the symposium or to any supplier interested in becoming part of supply base.

Symposium participants ideally should also participate in Cost Reduction workshops which look at the reduction of nonvalue-added activities. These suppliers will have passed the minimum level of the Supplier Survey and have expressed interest in signing a Partnership Agreement. The Enrollment Agreement can be signed prior to the survey or after the symposium.

Supplier Symposium

Form SMTB-35

Invitation Letter

INVITATION LETTER

Dear (Supplier's President):

(Your company's name) is developing a process of Supplier Certification to ensure the consistent quantity, quality and delivery of products and services from our suppliers that conform to our specifications.

We have adopted the process developed by Professionals for Technology Associates, Inc., which is being utilized by companies around the world.

The first step in this process will be conducting a Supplier Symposium on **(fill in the date)**, from 8:00 am to 4:30 pm at **(fill in place)**.

As a valued supplier to **(your company's name)**, we cordially invite you and your Quality Manager to join us for our kick-off to the Supplier Certification process.

Please RSVP to **(put in name and telephone number)**.

We look forward to meeting with you and sharing information about our Supplier Certification Program and to establish a long-term relationship which will be profitable to both of us.

Sincerely,

(Name of President)
President

ACKNOWLEDGMENT LETTER

Acknowledgment Letter

Dear **(Supplier's President)**:

We are pleased you accepted our invitation to attend our Supplier Symposium on **(fill in date)**.

Due to the enthusiastic response of our suppliers, we believe the day will be both beneficial and rewarding. Our meeting will be held at the Marriott Hotel in **(fill in place)**. A block of rooms has been reserved for those of you who are attending.

Our symposium agenda for the day will include:

Registration

Welcome
Introduction to (Your Company)
President

World Class Manufacturing
Vice President, Manufacturing

Total Quality Management
Vice President of Quality

Supplier Partnership
Director of Purchasing

(continued on next page)

Supplier Certification — Successful Programs
Peter L. Grieco, Jr., Chairman and CEO
Professionals for Technology Associates, Inc.

The Certification Program
Supplier Certification Team Members

Plant Tour

The program starts at 8:00 am and will conclude at 4:30 pm. Breakfast and lunch will be included. We will also be presenting you with a complimentary copy of Mr. Peter Grieco's book, **Supplier Certification II: Achieving Excellence Through Continuous Improvement**, at the symposium.

If you have any questions, please call **(put in name and telephone number)**.

Sincerely,

(Chairperson's Name)
Supplier Certification
Chairperson

SUPPLIER ENROLLMENT AGREEMENT

As a current or intended supplier of your company, we have reviewed the documentation contained herein which explains your Supplier Certification process and we agree to participate.

We understand that this process will involve site visits to our facility for the purpose of assessing our operating and administrative controls. We agree to work with your survey team in conducting the assessments.

We further agree to work with your company in the reduction of product and/or service costs for the mutual benefit of both parties. The goal is to move along a Continuous Improvement Path.

We believe that this agreement is a pledge between the supplier and the customer to create an atmosphere of cooperation. The intent is to bring improved productivity and higher profits to both companies.

_____   _____

Company Representative (Supplier)   Date

_____

Title

_____   _____

Company Representative (Customer)   Date

_____

Title

Enrollment Agreement

SUPPLIER SYMPOSIUM AGENDA

LOCATION:
DATE:

8:30 - 9:00	Arrival/Registration
9:00 - 9:30	Opening Remarks and Review of Objectives by President
9:30 - 10:30	Total Quality Management — Impact on Operations
10:30 - 10:45	Break
10:45 - 11:30	Supply Management Concepts and Applications — Partnering
11:30 - 12:00	Process Control of Manufacturing Operations

12:00 - 1:00	Lunch and Keynote Speaker
	    Why Supplier Certification?
	    Its Benefits and Savings

1:00 - 2:30	Design for Manufacturability — Concepts and Applications
2:30 - 3:30	Plant Tour
3:30 - 5:00	Supplier Cost Reduction Workshops
5:00 - 5:30	Conclusion and Assignments

SYMPOSIUM
booklet

© 1995 PT Publications, Inc.

THE GOALS OF SUPPLY MANAGEMENT

Eliminating waste and consistently achieving zero defects are the primary goals of Supply Management. These goals are synonymous with those of WC (World Class) and TQM (Total Quality Management) philosophies. Both Supply Management and WC/TQM address the elimination of waste and both have a win/win mentality. What's good for us is good for you. What we expect from you, you should expect from your own company.

Goal	Action
Total Quality Management	Ensures that the entire manufacturing cycle from design review through customer receipt meets quality standards established by the customer.
Quantity	Process and produce the lowest possible quantity by manufacturing on-time. The smaller the quantity, the easier it is to control.
Supplier Partnerships	Establish a relationship based on a win/win philosophy.
Logistics	Simplify the control and movement of material between functions and activities. Incorporate standard objectives.

WHAT IS SUPPLY MANAGEMENT?

Supply Management is one of the systems we use in our quest for World Class status. With over 50% of the sales dollars spent on purchased materials coming from outside suppliers, we recognize the impact that companies like yours have on our product. Because of that reliance, we saw the need for a process in which we would work with our suppliers to assure that they are supplying a total quality part, in the quantity we need, when we need it.

Supply Management is a process whereby our company and yours agree to **work as partners** to consistently provide a part that has 100% Quality, 100% On-time Delivery, and 100% Correct Quantities.

Those companies which join us in a successful Supply Management process can expect the following benefits:

> **Higher quality products which result in more satisfied customers, increased business, fewer returns and fewer warranty claims.**
>
> **Commitment of companies in the formation of long term relationships based on trust, cooperation and a balanced partnership.**
>
> **Quality parts leading to the elimination of scrap, returns, repairs, and rejects.**
>
> **Frequent deliveries which will aid you in implementing and maintaining programs in set-up reduction, inventory reduction as well as fewer obsolete parts and less damage to inventory.**
>
> **Smaller lot sizes which will allow you to be more agile and increase your flexibility to schedule changes in order to meet the customer's needs.**
>
> **Reduction in total cost so that you can make a more competitive product and increase sales.**
>
> **Greater job satisfaction which leads to fewer rejects, less rework and pride in the quality of work.**

We need suppliers who can help us achieve these benefits. We need suppliers who want to be part of a total team effort. The support and participation of suppliers, teams, and employees are vital to the success of the process.

SUPPLIER SELECTION CRITERIA

The actual criteria we choose to select suppliers will vary according to the size and nature of your business. However, there are criteria which are common to every industry. The checklist we have included in this booklet should be used as a guideline. They are the criteria that we think are important to the creation of a partnership in which we can all benefit.

Specifications	Market Involvement
Producibility	Capability
Financial Condition	Supplier's Mgmt. Commitment
Geographical Location	Capacity
Quality History	Facilities and Equipment
Customer Base	Labor Conditions
Education and Training	Cost Control
Process and Quality Control	Knowledgeable Sales Force
Competitive Pricing	On-time Delivery
Prior and Post Sales Support	Environmental Programs
Organization	Policies and Procedures
Preventive Maintenance	Housekeeping
Ethics	Percent of Business
Subcontractor Policy	Multiple Plants
Research and Development	Calibration History
Tool Tracking	Quantity
Smoking Policy	ISO 9000
Self Assessment	Six Sigma Program

A GUIDE TO
DOING BUSINESS WITH US

Symposium Booklet

Changing the one-way street of supplier relations to a two-way street means there will be new directions in the way we select suppliers. The one-way street of the fifties, sixties and early seventies was marked by a signpost which looked like this:

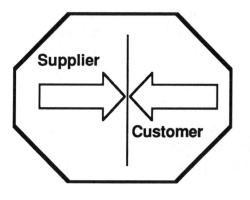

"Adversary" Supplier Relations

This was the era of adversarial relations in which customers made demands upon suppliers without extensive consultation in order to build an understanding between the two parties. By the late seventies, however, customers began to notice that this relationship had serious shortcomings. It was never entirely clear who was supposed to do what and when.

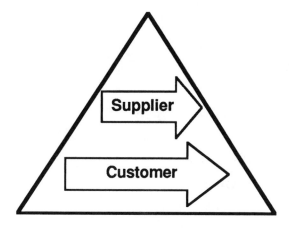

"Contract" Supplier Relations

The contract era of supplier relations lasted well into the eighties and, as the sign shows, did point both parties in the same direction. Contract administrators, or lawyers, were hired in procurement functions to review contracts so there would be no ambiguity about how customers would work with suppliers. What this era still left out was continual contact with the supplier to work on building a partnership. This is the work of the new era of supplier relations.

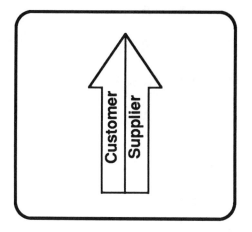

"Partnership" Supplier Relations

The partnership era shows both arrows side by side and pointing upwards as the supplier and manufacturer work together to improve quality, delivery, performance and cost. Thus, the first question we ask suppliers today is: Are you willing to become our partner in eliminating waste and embarking upon a continuous improvement process?

HOW TO BECOME CERTIFIED

We can achieve the primary objectives of Supply Management by entering into a partnership with a supplier which is based on trust and cooperation. Establishing that partnership entails gathering facts about a supplier, designing quality improvement processes, putting them into practice, and then auditing and maintaining the process based on results which are continuously gathered and jointly interpreted.

In this program, we can both think of ourselves as medical researchers who take a patient and not only find a cure, but find the means for the patient's continued well-being. The five phases of supplier certification are similar to the compilation of a medical history, the implementation of a nourishing diet and a schedule of exercise, and the institution of regular check-ups. Our goal is to develop a relationship in which a healthy supplier will act according to the regimen of TQM and World Class Objectives.

PHASE ONE: History, Status, Documentation

PHASE TWO: Supplier Program Review and Process Evaluation

PHASE THREE: Finalization

PHASE FOUR: Certification

PHASE FIVE: Ongoing Audit and Maintenance

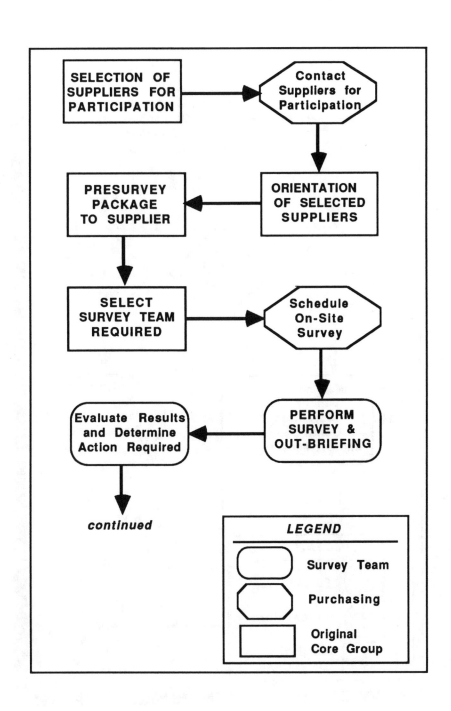

```
┌──────────────────┐        ╔════════════════╗
│  SELECTION  OF   │───────▶║    Contact      ║
│  SUPPLIERS  FOR  │        ║  Suppliers for  ║
│  PARTICIPATION   │        ║  Participation  ║
└──────────────────┘        ╚════════════════╝
                                     │
                                     ▼
┌──────────────────┐        ┌──────────────────┐
│   PRESURVEY      │◀───────│   ORIENTATION    │
│    PACKAGE       │        │   OF  SELECTED   │
│  TO SUPPLIER     │        │    SUPPLIERS     │
└──────────────────┘        └──────────────────┘
         │
         ▼
┌──────────────────┐        ╔════════════════╗
│     SELECT       │───────▶║   Schedule      ║
│  SURVEY  TEAM    │        ║   On-Site       ║
│   REQUIRED       │        ║   Survey        ║
└──────────────────┘        ╚════════════════╝
                                     │
                                     ▼
╭──────────────────╮        ╭──────────────────╮
│ Evaluate Results │◀───────│    PERFORM       │
│ and  Determine   │        │   SURVEY  &      │
│ Action  Required │        │  OUT-BRIEFING    │
╰──────────────────╯        ╰──────────────────╯
         │
         ▼
    *continued*
```

LEGEND

╭──────╮	Survey Team
╔══════╗	Purchasing
┌──────┐	Original Core Group

Symposium Booklet

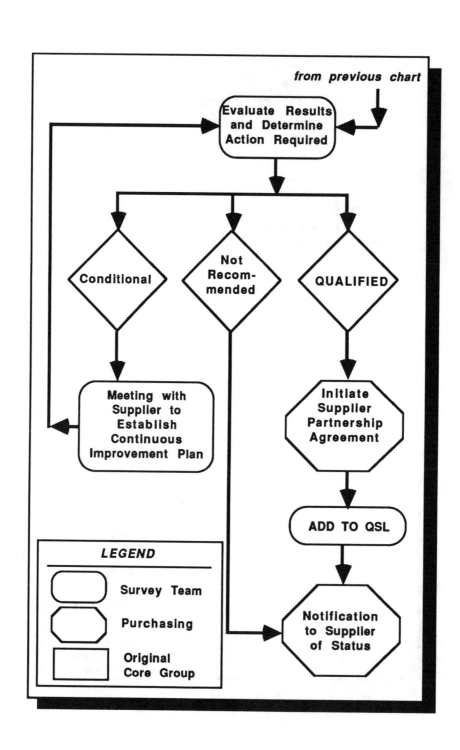

CONCLUSION

Benefits of Certification

We recognize that for a supplier to attain certified status, they must achieve and sustain a high level of outstanding effort, performance and reliability. We encourage suppliers to share their thoughts and concerns on any ideas regarding Supplier Benefits and Rewards. Suppliers must ultimately embrace the concepts of Supply Management to become efficient Certified Suppliers. We believe our supplier's ability to compete in their own markets will be enhanced through the improvements and benefits of Supply Management.

Other benefits include:

- **Strengthened relationships which seek mutual gains in quality, cycle time, service and cost reduction.**
- **Sharing in the growth and success of our company.**
- **Certified Suppliers will receive more of our business.**
- **Opportunity to participate in new products and business ventures.**
- **Certified Suppliers will have preference over other suppliers in early payment terms and elimination of invoices.**
- **Our company and our Certified Suppliers will share in the benefits of cost reduction efforts.**

PARTNERSHIP GOALS

100% Quality
100% Quantity
100% On-time

**We agree to continuously strive
to reduce cost and improve quality.**

Chapter Thirteen

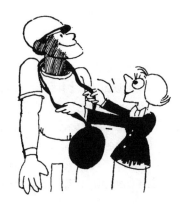

Supplier
Partnership
Agreement

Chapter Thirteen Contents

We would like to thank the Supply Management Team at ABB BIRR Switzerland for allowing us to show you their Long Term Supply Contract which appears in this chapter. The team consisted of Niklaus Eberle (Director of Operations), Rolf Senn (Supply Manager), Jürgen Roller (Commodity Manager), Martin Paulï (Commodity Manager) and Walter Hartmeier (Commodity Manager). They were assigned the task of adopting a standard contract so that it could be used for Direct Material suppliers. The idea behind the team was to create a document that would be developed by the people who use the contract.

The Supplier Cooperation Agreement was prepared by a team at ABB Semiconductors in Lenzburg, Switzerland. The team consisted of Andy Nilarp (President), Andreas Ruegg, Lise-Lotte Malmgren (Supply Manager) and Klaus Hoffman (Project Manager). With their dedicated support of Supply Management concepts and applications, they have been able to launch a successful program.

Our work with ABB has been a great success and proof that the Supply Management process works well with project procurement and production.

LEGAL NOTICE:
Included in this chapter are a Supplier Cooperation Agreement, a Master Subcontractor Agreement, a Confidentiality Agreement and a Long Term Supply Contract.
You should have your Legal Department or legal counsel review these documents before utilizing them. We have included them here for informational purposes only.

SUPPLIER COOPERATION AGREEMENT

1 PARTIES

A Supplier Cooperation Agreement, hereinafter referred to as the "Agreement" made this day of _____ 19__ between
<u>Your Company's Name</u>, hereinafter referred to as the "Company"
and <u>Supplier's Company Name</u>, hereinafter referred to as the "Supplier" together, hereinafter referred to as the "Parties."

1.1   Agreement Documents
All appendices to this Agreement shall form an integral part thereof as if they were set out in full in this Agreement.

1.2   Products Covered
The products covered under this agreement are _____
_____, hereinafter referred to as "Products."

1.3   Related Documents
The commercial relations between the Supplier and the Company are determined in a separate Supply Contract.

2 DECLARATION OF INTENT

Both the Company and the Supplier are committed to a philosophy of total customer satisfaction.

This Agreement is entered into with the intention of raising the level of quality and reducing cycle time throughout the whole supply chain, for the mutual benefit of the Parties. The Parties shall work towards achieving zero defects, on-time deliveries, minimal lead times and reduction of costs.

The means for reaching the goals set out above shall be the elimination of activities that do not increase the value for the customer, such as delivery control, build up of stores and incorrectly executed work that requires amending. Other means shall be the adjustment of specifications, so that the customer's requirements are met within the most appropriate way, the development of new products in cooperation between the Parties and the review of materials, methods of production and administrative routines. Both Parties shall, moreover, internally work towards quality management, reduction of lead time and product improvement.

Cooperation Agreement

3 COOPERATION TEAM

A joint cooperation team shall be formed between the Company and the Supplier. It will be led by a Supplier's Manager, and comprised by employees from Quality, Manufacturing, Engineering, and Customer Service. Their task is to identify improvements, resolve problems, and implement solutions. The Team would open a line of communications between the Company and the employees of the Supplier who design, manufacture, package and service products used by the Company to allow better understanding of where and how these products are used and, in turn, to initiate and drive continuous improvement activities.

The Supplier will make customer satisfaction a top priority both for the Company and for the Company's customers.

    A) Map Supplier Process
    B) Identify Process Gaps
    C) Eliminate Nonvalue-added Steps
    D) Reduce Product Cost

4 COOPERATION MUTUAL DISCLOSURE

The Parties shall in a spirit of trust and in the best way cooperate to achieve the goals set out in this Agreement. This entails cooperation at all levels. The Parties shall openly discuss the requirements of the end customer, procurement of materials, methods of production resources, design, delivery times and costs.

The Supplier shall give the Company access to any relevant information that may affect the Company's end product. The Supplier shall, for example, continually give the Supplier information about new experiences, positive as well as negative, in connection with the utilization and development of the products that are the subject matter of this Agreement. Such information may be used by the Company and its customers, within the framework of their normal activities, without payment to the Supplier. The Supplier and the Company shall give each other information about changes in their organizations that may affect this Agreement.

5 TERMINATION

This Agreement shall come into force immediately upon execution by the parties and shall remain in force for 1 year thereafter. Unless the Agreement is terminated, by notice given in writing by the Company or the Supplier at least three months before its expiry, it shall automatically be renewed for periods of twelve months at a time, but with the above provision for termination remaining in force.

6 PERFORMANCE MEASUREMENT

A critical aspect of this Cooperation Agreement are the continuous improvements the Supplier implements to satisfy the Company's delivery, quality, cost reduction and service requirements.

The Supplier will be rated on these parameters to measure how well the Supplier satisfies the Company's requirements. It will be used to track improvements in performance over time and allows the Parties to jointly identify problems and implement corrective actions when necessary. The results from this rating shall be taken into consideration by the Company when assessing future business.

7 SCOPE OF TECHNICAL COOPERATION

The Supplier is expected to continually develop the Products, so that they continue to be of high quality, compared to similar products available on the market.

The Parties shall work together to provide Products satisfying the customer's need by jointly learning how the end product functions and how it is utilized.

The Parties shall work together to develop new applications and provide cost improvements to have the most effective solution for new and current designs for the Company. The Company agrees to disclose appropriate costings for the surrounding design to the Supplier in order to optimize total costs.

The cost reductions that will result from this technical cooperation cannot be passed on to the Company's competitors for a period of two years.

The Parties shall furthermore endeavor to reduce the time for developing new products.

The Company shall be informed without delay of proposed technical or other changes to the Products that may affect the Company's or the end customer's utilization of them.

The Parties shall, at the beginning of each calendar year, agree to a plan for technical cooperation during the year to be executed by the Technical Cooperation Team.

The plan shall set out the Company's requirement of technical assistance from the Supplier. This may be, for example, participation in product development, product improvement or design.

The plan shall also set out the Supplier's requirement of technical cooperation with the

Company, such as participation in product development, product improvement, selection of materials, quality assurance and the implementation of simplified ordering and invoicing routines. The technical cooperation plan shall be set out in writing and shall be approved by both Parties.

Unless otherwise agreed, each party shall defray its own costs in connection with technical cooperation.

According to the present clause regarding technical cooperation, the Company does not overtake or accept any responsibility whatsoever for the Supplier's products.

The Supplier shall at any time be solely and fully responsible for all and any products manufactured or distributed by the Supplier or under the responsibility of the Supplier.

8 DELIVERY CYCLE TIME REDUCTION

The Supplier will work with the Company to develop progressively shorter delivery cycle times and manufacturing cycle times through accurate projections. The ultimate goal is direct shipment from the Supplier's manufacturing line to the Company's manufacturing line.

The Supplier will work with the Company to shorten order processing time and to improve the efficiency of order communication.

The ultimate target is a paper-free transaction with zero-defect order processing and the implementation of Electronic Data Interchange (EDI) by 1995.

9 PACKING, RETURN PACKAGING

The Products shall be paced so as to be protected from corrosion and all other damage until they reach their final destination. Packing shall carry handling instructions and shall be marked as required.

The Supplier will work with the Company to develop environmentally compatible, returnable packaging. The Supplier will have bar coding capability by 1995.

10 QUALITY SYSTEMS REQUIREMENTS

The Supplier will obtain world class quality and reliability through superior design, process controls and continuous process improvements. The Company's suggestions for improvement of the quality system shall be taken into consideration. The Supplier agrees to follow agreed quality routines. The Supplier shall be aware that eventually the product will be delivered directly to the Company's productions/installation and that the Company then will not inspect the product upon receipt. The Company shall not be obliged to inspect the product. The Company shall be entitled to visit the Supplier or the Supplier's supplier, in order to review quality systems. The Supplier shall assist, insofar as it can be reasonably demanded of it, during such reviews and shall make available the results of any test conducted.

11 SUPPLIER SURVEY RESULTS

The Supplier shall endeavor to improve the results of surveys conducted by the Company. The goal is to achieve a sustainable world class level of Six Sigma.

12 MEETINGS

The Cooperation Team shall meet regularly to follow up on the execution of the technical cooperation plan in Section 7 of this document.

The agenda for the meetings shall include the following items:

1. Review of activities and discussion of results.
2. Activities to reduce costs.
3. New possibilities of improvements.
4. Quantification and timing of new part goals.

Minutes shall be kept of the meetings and these shall be approved by the Parties. The designated scribe for the Supplier shall be _____; the designated scribe for the Company shall be _____.

The Supplier shall be responsible for calling meetings monthly for the first six months and every month thereafter. The meeting location shall change on a regular schedule as well.

13 PREFERRED SUPPLIER

The Supplier shall be a preferred supplier for products to the Company as stated in the Supply Contract.
The Company's intention is to expand cooperation with the Supplier according to this Agreement.

The Supplier shall be given the opportunity of offering and delivering new products of the same type as the Products already supplied.

14 TOOLS, ETC.

The Company shall own all tools, models, prototypes and similar items produced specifically on behalf of the Company by the Supplier. Such tools, etc. shall be delivered to the Company immediately upon demand.

Maintenance and repairs of such tools, etc. shall be the responsibility, and for the account, of the Supplier for as long as they remain in its possession.

15 PATENTS AND OTHER RIGHTS

The Supplier shall hold the Company harmless of all damage that may ensue from disagreement concerning alleged or actual infringements of patents, copyrights, trademarks, trade names or other rights, through the utilization of the Supplier's products, systems, programs or documentation.

In case of infringement, the Supplier shall, at its own account, safeguard the Company's right to continue utilizing the Products, or alter the Products so that there is no longer an infringement, or replace the Products with equivalent products the utilization of which does not infringe. Rights to ideas, inventions, know-how emanating from the Parties' cooperation shall vest in the originator. Where the Supplier is the originator/ author, the Company shall be licensed to make use of the ideas, invention, etc. at no additional cost.

16 EDUCATION AND TRAINING

Both the Supplier and the Company shall share in the cost of education and training designed for continuous improvement and the attainment of world class status.

17 CONFIDENTIALITY

Technical or commercial information obtained by the Company from the Supplier, and vice versa, in the course of their cooperation and commercial relations, shall be treated in confidence by the recipient party for five years thereafter.

The duty of confidentiality shall not apply to information:

a) already known to recipient, when he partook in the circumstances above defined;
b) properly provided by third party to the recipient; or,
c) which is or becomes generally available through other means than breach of this clause.

18 TERMINATION — BREACH OF CONTRACT

The Supplier and the Company may immediately terminate this Agreement by giving written notice to the other party, if the other party has:

a) committed a fundamental breach of this Agreement or repeated delay of deliveries or nonfulfillment of quality level and notwithstanding written demand to remedy the breach and taken suitable measures to do so within 30 days of receipt of such demand;

b) become unable to pay its debts or entered into compulsory or voluntary liquidation or has compounded a meeting of its creditors or has had a receiver or manager or an administrator appointed or has ceased for any reason to carry on business or has taken or suffered to be taken any similar action which in the opinion of the party giving notice means that the other may be unable to pay its debts.

19 VARIATION

Variation of the Agreement must be agreed in writing.

20 EXECUTION

This Agreement is executed in two originals, of which each party has taken one.

_____   _____
The Supplier   The Company

Master Agreement

SUPPLY MANAGEMENT

Master Subcontractor Agreement

PREAMBLE
This agreement is made on the _____ day of _____, 19__, by and between _____ hereby referred to as the "Company," and _____ hereby referred to as the "Subcontractor," under which the work, the subject of this agreement, shall be conducted.

1. **SCOPE**
   Both the Company and the Subcontractor will work toward ensuring that the Subcontractor will supply the Company with products and services which fully conform to specifications.

   Subcontractor will provide their manufacturing, process and procurement expertise to the Company. The mutually agreed responsibilities are defined in the body of this Agreement.

2. **TERM OF AGREEMENT**
   This Agreement will be valid for a period of one year from _____ and by the consent of both parties may be extended annually for one year periods.

3. **RESPONSIBILITIES**
   a) the Company will be responsible for providing the Subcontractor with the following:

        i) Engineering Documentation and related specifications which includes the Company's authorized deviations.

        ii) Approved Supplier List (A.S.L.)
   It is the intention of the Company to advise the Subcontractor of new designs at least six months before manufacturing is scheduled to commence.

   b) The Subcontractor will be responsible for the following:

        i) Manufacturing, testing and supplying to the Company products and services which must conform to specification including Company authorized deviations.

        ii) Maintaining and regularly calibrating all equipment involved in processing.

iii)   Utilizing only those components as specified in the Company provided A.S.L. or sources listing. Substitute of an alternative or replacement is prohibited without approval in writing by the Company Corporation.

Note: It is understood that the responsibilities defined in this section are of general nature and are more fully covered in various other sections.

4. ENGINEERING CHANGE ORDERS (ECOs)

All ECOs supplied by the Company will be implemented in a time scale and at a cost to the Company agreed by both parties.

5. QUALITY

The Subcontractor accepts zero-defects as a quality standard and does not subscribe to the philosophy of acceptable levels of defective materials (A.Q.L.).

a)   Products which do not conform to specification will upon documented verification be returned to the Subcontractor at its expense for repair/replacement and failure analysis.

b)   The Subcontractor will provide the Company with Process and Failure information monthly.

c)   The Subcontractor undertakes to develop and implement a process of continuous quality improvement to achieve and maintain a zero defect quality rating.

d)   The Subcontractor will permit the Company free access to its facility to carry out inspection of work being performed. Such access should be on a non-interference basis and at dates and times to be mutually agreed.

6. INSPECTION

The Subcontractor will be responsible for inspection of material required per the bill of material associated with each contracted product. The Subcontractor will enforce adherence to all specifications and inspect accordingly. The Subcontractor will be responsible for maintaining a complete set of documentation at all times as well as supplying the appropriate documentation to its vendors.

7. DELIVERY

The subcontractor shall be responsible for meeting its delivery commitments as specified on individual purchase orders incorporated under this master manufacturing agreement. In addition to its commitment for on time delivery the Subcontractor is responsible for delivering each order complete. It will be incumbent upon the Subcontractor to notify the Company of any component whose lead time exceeds the Subcontractor's prescribed lead time and which could potentially impact the Subcontractor's ability to deliver on schedule or complete.

Master Agreement

8. **WARRANTY**

a) The Subcontractor warrants that the products supplied to the Company shall conform to the relevant specifications and any authorized deviations.

b) The Subcontractor warrants that products supplied to the Company be free of component failure and workmanship defects for a period of 12 months from date of shipment from the Subcontractor's facility.

c) In the event of failures occurring within the warranty period, the Company may elect to return defective products to the Subcontractor or alternatively to repair in house or at customer sites. Such components as are necessary to effect repairs, will be supplied by the Subcontractor free of charge.

d) This warranty shall not apply to breakdown, malfunction, or other failure of products if it is:

i) Used, operated or maintained in a manner, or subjected to any condition, not consistent with the intended purpose of the product.

ii) Improperly repaired by the Company.

iii) Damaged or affected by the negligence of the Company or the end user, or by causes external to the equipment, such as but not limited to, air conditioning failure, or negligent acts or conduct of third persons.

9. **PRICING/PAYMENT CONDITIONS**

a) Product and service pricing is valid for the calendar year ____ on the basis that the total volume purchased by the Company is between __ and __ units over a twelve month period.

b) In the event that the purchase orders placed by the Company over a twelve month period exceed or fall short of the stated volume, both parties will meet to review the situation and agree to price revision if appropriate.

c) All invoices by the Subcontractor to the Company will be paid by the Company forty-five days after shipment from the Subcontractor facility.

10. **COMPETITIVENESS**

The Company and the Subcontractor will cooperate to reduce costs. Cost improvement plans will include the following:

a) The Subcontractor will manufacture the products using the most competitive component prices consistent with quality and commercial conditions obtainable.

Master Agreement

b) The Subcontractor will apply best industrial processes at its disposal or as committed to by the Subcontractor via its demonstrated capabilities and proposed methodologies to reduce the manufacturing costs consistent with meeting the Company's specifications.

c) The Subcontractor will provide cost details of major components on a confidential basis so that cost trends may be monitored.

d) The Company undertakes to give full consideration to the Subcontractor requests to add alternative suppliers to the Company A.S.L. The Company reserves the right to approve the replacement of any supplier on its A.S.L. by another (or additional or second source) at the request of the Subcontractor. Substituting of an approved supplier by one not approved is prohibited without written approval from the Company.

e) Benefits of any cost improvements implemented will be reflected by negotiation in product and service pricing.

11. FORECASTING AND ORDER PROCESS

1. On the third week of each calendar month, the Company will provide the Subcontractor with firm orders covering the following 90 days requirements, together with a non-commitment forecast of requirements through a further 180 days.

   a) Quantities of products ordered for delivery within 0-30 days are noncancellable and no reschedule is allowed.

   b) Quantities of products ordered for delivery within 31-60 days are noncancellable; however, orders may be increased or decreased by up to 25%. Reschedules as a result of decreases may not extend initial delivery dates by more than 90 days.

   c) Quantities of products ordered for delivery within 61-90 days are noncancellable; however, orders may be increased or decreased by up to 50%. Reschedules as a result of decreases may not extend initial delivery dates by more than 90 days.

   d) Activities carried out under paragraphs (a) to (c) are without charge to the Company.

   e) In the event of cancellation (or hold placed on this order by the Company), the Company's liability shall be limited to the applicable cost of

Master Agreement

those items scheduled for delivery on this order during the ninety days following the date of cancellation (or hold date) or the actual cost of material completed or in work. The Company's liability should be limited to the final costs that would be subject to the Company audit.

12. FIRST ARTICLE QUALIFICATION

a) Each product type will undergo a First Article Qualification Program.

b) Upon successful completion of the Qualification program for each product type, the Company will authorize the Subcontractor in writing to commence production.

c) The time scale prior to Production Authorization will be referred to as Pre-Production Phase.

13. LEAD TIME

Lead time for supply of products will be __ weeks from receipt of order together with relevant documentation. First production deliveries will commence a maximum 3 weeks after First Article Approval. Thereafter, the order process outlined in Section 11 will apply.

14. END OF LIFE

a) It is the intention of the Company to provide the Subcontractor with a minimum of __ days notice of the end of life to the products which are covered by this Agreement and any extension thereof.

b) The Company will supply the Subcontractor with a purchase order __ days prior to the end of life of specified products.

15. REVIEW MEETINGS

a) Monthly meetings will take place between the two parties at agreed upon locations to review performance and delivery or other issues.

b) The Company or the Subcontractor, with the other party's agreement, may at its option alter the frequency of these meetings if conditions so warrant.

16. COMMUNICATION

a) All communications will be coordinated through Managers appointed by both parties.

b) Production issues will be communicated by the Subcontractor through material control to purchasing.

17. CONFIDENTIALITY

This Agreement and all supplements and data (verbal and written) of both a technical or commercial nature, all pricing and associated information and any such information relating to the work subject to this Agreement, either generated by or provided by the Company to the Subcontractor and the Subcontractor to the Company, shall at all times and for a period of _____ years following the expiration of this Agreement, be treated in fully confidential manner and shall not be divulged to third parties whatsoever without written permission of the other party, including but not limited, to any parent company; associated, affiliated or subsidiary companies division and departments of all such companies and the like of the Subcontractor. The dissemination of all said documents, data and the like, shall be limited to the Subcontractor employees and then only on a need to know basis.

18. EXCLUSIVELY

The Subcontractor will supply the products covered by this Agreement only to the Company and to other designated companies specified by the Company in writing.

19. FORCE MAJEURE

Neither party shall be liable in any way whatsoever to the other party in the event that the performance of this Agreement, or any part thereof, is delayed through causes beyond the reasonable control of the delaying party, such as but not limited to, acts of God, acts of civil or military authorities, fires, industrial disputes, floods, wars, riots. In the event of such delay, the performance of this Agreement or any part affected by such cause (Subcontractor) shall be suspended for so long and to the extent that such cause (Subcontractor) prevents or delays its performance. The delaying party shall immediately and fully inform the other party of such delay. In the event the delay exceeds 30 days (or is anticipated to exceed 30 days), the parties shall meet to mutually decide what action should be taken in respect of the work and this Agreement. Both parties undertake to make "best efforts" to recover from such situations as timely as possible with minimal impact on the other party.

20. LIMITATION OF LIABILITY

a) Excepting as provided for in Sub Para (b) below, neither party shall be liable in any way whatsoever to the other party for any collateral, consequential, indirect or incidental damages of any nature arising out of or related to the transactions the subject hereof.

b) The Subcontractor shall be liable to the Company or any other party for any collateral, consequential, indirect or incidental damages of any nature arising out of or related to any activity deemed to be the Subcontractor responsibility, including but not limited to, processes, non-conformance to specification, the Subcontractor substituted components, even though such activities may have been approved by the Company.

Master Agreement

21. MOST FAVORED CUSTOMERS

The Subcontractor undertakes to give the Company highest priority if and when demands are made on the Subcontractor from whatever source which could result in shortages of materials (including components) and/or labor likely to adversely affect the timely performance of this Agreement and/or deliveries of products and services to the Company.

22. GOVERNING LAW

This Agreement shall be construed and interpreted in accordance with the law of the State of _____.

23. APPROVALS

In witness whereof the parties hereto have caused this Agreement to be duly and properly executed by the duly authorized representatives as of the day and year written below.

_____
On Behalf of the Company

_____
On Behalf of Supplier

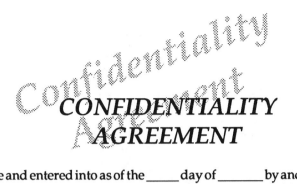

CONFIDENTIALITY AGREEMENT

This agreement was made and entered into as of the _____ day of _____ by and between _____ and _____. Since both parties to this agreement anticipate the possible need to disclose to and receive from the other party information which the furnishing party considers to be proprietary, they mutually agree as follows:

1. MARKING OF INFORMATION

    Any information exchanged by the parties and entitled to protection shall be identified as such by an appropriate stamp or marking on each document. The stamp or marking should designate that the information is "Proprietary."

2. PROTECTION AND USE

    The receiving party shall hold each item of proprietary information so received in confidence until ___ years after the expiration of this Agreement. During this period of time, the receiving party shall use the information only in connection with the purposes of the Supply Management Program and shall make the information available only to its employees having a "need to know." It is the responsibility of both parties to advise these employees of obligations under the Agreement of Confidentiality.

    The receiving party shall not use or disclose proprietary information during the aforesaid period, except when authorized in writing by the disclosing party. The only exception is when the receiving party must disclose the information to the cognizant U.S. Government agency in connection with proposals related to the Program; provided, however, that any such disclosure bears the restrictive legend as applicable of FAR 15.509, Use and Disclosure of Data, or FAR 52.215-12, Restrictions on Disclosure and Use of Data in effect on the effective date of this Agreement, or a successor provision substantially the same. No data provided under this agreement shall be delivered under a contract or otherwise made subject to a contract "rights of data" clause.

    Neither party can, without the prior written consent of the other, use proprietary information to manufacture or enable the manufacturing by third parties of the disclosing party's products, products similar thereto, or products derived therefrom.

    The disclosed information and all copies shall, upon the expiration or termination of this Agreement, be returned or destroyed and a written certificate of destruction provided to the disclosing party.

© 1995 PT Publications, Inc.

Agreement of Confidentiality

3. EXCLUSIONS FROM PROTECTION

Information is not protected by this Agreement if, on the effective date of this Agreement, the information:

(a) was already developed by the receiving party independently of the disclosing party; or

(b) rightfully obtained without restriction by the receiving party from a third party; or

(c) publicly available other than through the fault or negligence of the receiving party; or

(d) released without restriction by the disclosing party to anyone including the United States Government; or

(e) known to the receiving party at the time of its disclosure.

4. LEGAL ACTIONS AND GOVERNMENT REGULATIONS

If the receiving party is faced with legal action or required under U.S. Government regulations to disclose received proprietary information, the receiving party must notify the disclosing party, and upon the request of the latter, the receiving party shall cooperate in contesting such disclosure. Neither party shall be liable in any way for any disclosures made pursuant to judicial action or U.S. Government regulations, unless they failed to discharge the responsibilities set forth in the preceding sentence.

5. NO RIGHTS GRANTED

Nothing in this agreement shall be construed as granting or conferring any rights on the part of either party by license or otherwise, expressly or implied, to any invention or discovery or to any patent covering such invention or discovery.

6. INDEPENDENT CONTRACTOR

Each party in undertaking its responsibilities hereunder shall be deemed an independent contractor and nothing in this Agreement shall constitute, create, or in any way be interpreted as a joint venture, partnership, or formal business organization of any kind.

IN WITNESS WHEREOF, the parties hereto have caused this agreement to be duly executed and in effect on the day and year first above written.

By: _____   By: _____
Title: _____   Title: _____

Long Term Supply Contract

Long Term Supply Contract

WITNESSETH

WHEREAS, our Company wishes to develop with and purchase from the Supplier certain kinds of _____ which are based on our specifications.

WHEREAS, the Supplier _____ is willing to accept such requirements.

WHEREAS, both parties designed this contract according to a cooperation agreement that complements the Total Cycle Time and Total Quality objectives of elimination of nonvalue-added activities across the entire supply chain of mutual benefit. The scope of such partnering includes the following cooperation objectives: zero defects, on-time deliveries, lead time reduction, quality improvement, inventory reduction, unit cost reduction, standardization and optimizing administrative costs.

The duration of this agreement dated _____ is for _____ years; each year it automatically renews.

NOW THEREFORE, the parties hereto agree as follows:

1. <u>Cooperation</u>

    The parties will in full confidence and at their best ability endeavor to achieve the intentions of this contract. This will include cooperation between our Company and the Supplier at all levels.

    In good faith for this agreement, our Company is willing to provide the following to the Supplier:

    - forecast (released as needed)
    - share savings
    - communicate requirements
    - give long term purchase orders
    - establish inventory levels
    - establish quarterly meetings
    - define the requirements

    Therefore the Supplier agrees to work with our Company in the areas of:

    - process mapping
    - sharing material, labor and overhead cost
    - reduction of lead time
    - reduction of cycle time
    - reduction of inventory
    - attendance at meetings
    - share savings

    Based on this agreement with our Company, the Supplier agrees not to share any benefits derived with competitors of our Company for a period of 12 months.

Long Term Contract

2. <u>Disclosure</u>

Our Company encourages the Supplier to be involved early in new product development. For that purpose, the Supplier is ready to provide design and technical assistance to our Company. The Supplier will keep our Company informed about all technological breakthroughs at our regular meetings.

3. <u>Non-Disclosure</u>

All information, data, drawings and/or other subject matter regarding products communicated between the Supplier and our Company hereunder or in connection with this agreement, including under any and all orders placed by our Company to the Supplier (hereinafter termed "Confidential Information") shall remain the legal property of the disclosing party. No license is granted by this agreement. For a period of five (5) years from the date of receipt of the Confidential Information disclosed by the disclosing party hereunder, the parties shall not disclose, communicate, cede, grant, dispose of or give, use for itself or for benefit of any third party including but not limited to subsidiary and/or affiliate companies, and shall take all necessary precautions to prevent the disclosing, communicating, ceding, granting, disposing or giving to any third party in any way whatsoever, or impermissible use of any such Confidential Information without the prior written consent of the disclosing party. Both parties shall consult with the other when and if requested, as to procedures established to maintain the secret and confidential nature of such Confidential Information and shall, from time to time upon request, advise the requesting party as to the procedures currently in effect.

Both parties undertake and agree upon the termination or suspension of this agreement for any reason, to cease to use any such Confidential Information and promptly return to the disclosing party (without retaining copies thereof in whole or in part) all documents, artwork and other media containing Confidential Information unless instructed otherwise by specific written communication from the disclosing party. Both parties agree to promptly obtain and to maintain agreements with its employees to maintain the confidential nature of such Confidential Information. No information shall be within the protection of this agreement if such information:

    a)   is a matter of public knowledge;

    b)   is or becomes publicly available or in the public domain other than through the fault of our Company or the Supplier, or their agents;

    c)   is obtained from a source other than our Company or the Supplier when the source has the unrestricted right to disclose the information without a breach of any agreement;

    d)   independently of any information supplied by our Company or developed by the Supplier, or vice-versa; or

    e)   is subsequently designated non-confidential and is treated non-confidential by the disclosing party.

"CONFIDENTIAL" must be clearly marked on all documents considered confidential or proprietary. This includes documents provided to date. This agreement supersedes any previous agreement between the parties and shall survive. Each party will not file any patent applications if such filing requires divulging Confidential Information of the other party.

4.   Technical Cooperation

Our Company intends to develop a technical agreement that combines both production and engineering development into a single agreement. The purpose of such an agreement is to improve the process through problem solving and technical assistance. Our Company's expectation is that the Supplier, through technology, can transfer the method in process to the production environment. Our Company encourages the Supplier to present opportunities for joint ventures, joint development projects and in investments that will lower our total cost.

5.   Pricing

Our Company's product price should be the same or lower than the equivalent to market and must be maintained to ensure our Company's competitive pricing. In all cases, the Supplier must meet competitive prices.

The prices agreed to in Appendix 1 will be reviewed and adjusted through value analyses, learning curves, technology changes and our Company's demand for the product. Based on this agreement, it is our Company's intent for the Supplier to maintain his standard profit margin of _____.

The Supplier agrees to _____% as a yearly production increase over this contract.

    5.1   Currency

    A)   Currency of the supplying country, or

    B)   Currency fluctuations up to ____% will not influence the price;

           Currency fluctuations of more than ____% up to ____% will be shared equally between Seller and Buyer;

           Currency fluctuations of more than ____% will be reason for renegotiation of the prices.

    5.2   Terms of Payment

           Terms of payment other than the development fee will be net ____ days after receipt of invoice. Shipments must be complete with corresponding documentation.

    5.3   Cancellation

           Our Company may cancel undelivered products or components in whole or part of the purchase agreement without a cancellation charge according to the flexibility window:

		Responsibility		
Days	Flexibility cancel/change	R	W	FG
0 - 30	XX% (20 - 25)			
31 - 60	XX% (50)			
61 - 90	XX% (100)			
91 ->	XX% (100)			
R = Raw Material, W = Work, FG = Finished Goods				

           Prior to delivery dates, our Company agrees to change purchase orders in accordance to the formula set. Our Company may also cancel any purchase orders which are past due without any cancellation charge, via written notice to the Supplier.

6. <u>Packaging</u>

The goods shall be marked according to our Company's purchase order. Articles belonging to different orders shall be packed separately. Each package shall be clearly marked with our Company's article number as stated in our Company's purchase order.

All of our Company's packing material must be environmentally safe. Our Company prefers reusable standard containers and palettes where applicable. The Supplier must follow our Company's instructions as per Appendix 2.

Upon agreement, the Supplier will provide our Company with a return authorization policy and instruction. The Supplier shall have bar coding capability.

7. <u>Delivery</u>

7.1 <u>Cycle Time and Inventories</u>

Both parties will cooperate to reduce the total cycle time on a continuous basis from issue of purchase orders to supplier.

7.2 <u>Delivery Performance</u>

The Supplier will provide 100% on-time delivery of product to our Company. On-time is defined as meeting a delivery window of 7 calendar days early, zero days late to our receiving dock on the required date as specified on our Company's purchase orders and acknowledged by the Supplier.

Our Company will not specify delivery requirements within an agreed to lead time which is specified to be ___ weeks for the first delivery and ___ weeks for delivery after that. The Supplier will provide a plan including specific benchmarks for the reduction of this lead time.

7.3 <u>Late Charges</u>

On orders which are late due to the Supplier's responsibility, the Supplier will pay freight and any extra costs to ship the order to our Company, using any mode of transportation deemed necessary by our Company.

7.4 <u>Delivery Incentive</u>

Delivery performance shall be monitored semiannually by the parties. The seller shall pay penalties amounting to 0.5% of the total sales during the monitored period for each percent the delivery performance falls short of what is agreed. Penalties shall not be paid for the first late delivery during the period of measurement.

Our Company expects freight and duty to be calculated as separate line items.

The forwarding agent and/or transporter for this commodity will be _____ and they understand the delivery terms and conditions set forth in this agreement.

All material is insured by our Company. Therefore, the Supplier shall not charge any insurance fees.

The Supplier must have the capability within ____ months to deliver product directly to the factory floor or to designated areas without receiving inspection or testing. The Supplier keeps our Company informed on demand with the ability to track and trace scheduled deliveries.

The parties intend to develop Electronic Data Interchange (EDI) to become the media of communication and data transfer between our Company and the Supplier.

7.5 Classification

Our Company expects the Supplier to classify all of our products and services at the lowest possible duty code. The Supplier is responsible for notifying our Company of changes in duty codes.

8. Quality Requirements

8.1 Objectives

The Supplier will maintain process controls to detect deviations from agreed to specifications prior to completion of product manufacturing and delivery to our Company. The goal is to achieve conformance to requirements so that incoming inspection by our Company will not be necessary.

8.2 Certification

Our Company shall perform annual supplier quality surveys or audits at the Supplier's plant. Audit scores will determine the certification level of the Supplier when combined with delivery and quality performance measurements.

The Supplier shall inform our Company about any plans to change its quality control or its production well in advance of the change.

8.3 Quality Assurance

Our Company has the right to visit the Supplier at any time for quality audits or for quality assurance of products to be delivered. The time shall be agreed upon in advance.

The Supplier will develop its quality system to comply with ISO 9002 by the end of the ____ quarter of 19___.

8.4 Non-Conforming Deliveries

In the event that the Supplier delivers non-conforming products, our Company shall, in writing, notify the Supplier about the nature of the non-conformance and when a replacement must be delivered. The Supplier shall take all necessary actions to deliver a replacement at the time deemed necessary by our Company. If the Supplier is not capable of supplying a replacement at a time acceptable to our Company, our Company can, at our own choice and at the Supplier's expense, either bring the product into conformance or cancel the purchase order.

Long Term Contract

8.5   Quality Level

The Supplier warrants that 100% of the delivered products shall be without quality defects and meet our Company's specifications. Within 3 years from the contract dates, our Company expects the Supplier to achieve six sigma performance.

8.6   Designing for Producibility

The Supplier agrees to assist our Company in establishing design standards of producibility. Our Company expects during the life of the contract that the Supplier will reduce its failure and appraisal costs and concentrate efforts on prevention.

Statistical process control must be implemented in the production environment within ___ months of signing the agreement. The Supplier will furnish our Company with any certificates or documentation required according to this contract for proof of implementation.

9.   Tooling and Equipment

The ownership of tools and/or equipment needed to produce parts covered by this contract remains our Company's. Upon request by our Company, the Supplier has to hand over all tools and/or equipment partly or fully paid by our Company or the Supplier must credit the amount paid by our Company without written permission of our Company. The Supplier is not allowed to produce any parts using this tooling or equipment for other customers.

Based on our Company's information on the estimated quantity of parts, the Supplier is responsible for the construction of tools/equipment in order that no other cost occurs but maintenance during the life of the product. Furthermore, the Supplier guarantees a quick die change and "state of the art" storage. Upon request, the Supplier must inform our Company of the quantity produced with this tool/equipment, using SPC charts for verification.

Without the written permission of our Company, the Supplier is not allowed to dispose of tools/equipment. The Supplier must guarantee correct disposal of all tools/equipment and hold our Company harmless. The cost for disposal will be shared.

10.   Patents and Proprietary Rights

The Supplier shall indemnify and hold harmless our Company from and against all claims, actions, costs, expenses, liabilities and proceedings whatsoever resulting from all alleged or actual infringement of any letters registered, designs, copyright, trademark or trade name or other proprietary rights arising by reason of the use by our Company of any systems, programs or documentation supplied to our Company by the Supplier in fulfillment of the Supplier's obligations under this contract.

Our Company shall have the non-terminable, unrestricted worldwide rights to use all systems, programs, documentation and other know-how supplier to our Company by the Supplier under this contract provided, however, that such use shall be limited to internal use by our Company's personnel only.

(Royalties to be defined)

If any invention is made by an employee of either Party in the course of or in connection with any work under or relating to the Contract, such inventions and any patent or patents issued thereon shall remain the sole property of the Party whose employee made such invention.

Any invention made jointly by employees of both Parties in the course of or in connection with any work under or relating to the Contract and any patent or patents issued thereon shall at equal shares be owned jointly by both Parties who shall also be entitled to sue such invention and patent or patents free of charge. Noted to any third party, provided, however, that the execution of the Contract shall be deemed to constitute the Contractor's prior written consent to any such license which may be granted by the purchaser to any of his affiliated companies.

Any inventor's compensation shall be for the account of the Party whose employee made the invention.

The Contractor shall at no cost grant to the Purchaser the nonexclusive and irrevocable right to use free of charge and without any restrictions whatsoever any inventions made by the Contractor in the course of or in connection with any work under or relating to the Contract, and any patent or patents issued thereon.

11. <u>Warranty</u>

The Supplier is responsible for all faults 12 months from the date upon which the goods are put into service, maximum of 24 months after the delivery date from the Supplier's plant. The guarantee also covers the test runs carried out before the final commissioning when performed within 24 months after delivery from the Supplier's plant.

Upon detecting a fault or defect, our Company shall make a written claim and within one week from receipt of the claim, the Supplier shall begin corrections or repairs.

All faults and defects, which are not caused by faulty or careless operation, shall be repaired or replaced by the Supplier or its service agent at their own expense during the guarantee period, including the repair, alteration and installation work caused by the defective goods and also the freight costs. In the case of the Supplier not fulfilling its repair obligation, our Company is entitled to do the necessary repairs at the Supplier's cost.

The Supplier agrees — insofar as the cause of product liability would be attributable to it — to indemnify and hold our Company harmless from third-party product liability claims raised against our Company and originating from faulty or defective products of the supplier.

The Supplier is responsible for providing the products with all necessary warning labels and safety instructions.

Both the parties shall inform the other party of any product liability matter that may have legal implications on the other party.

Prior to the execution of the contract, the Supplier shall submit to our Company a certificate issued by the Supplier's third liability insurer certifying that during the validity of the contract, the Supplier's liability for damage to property and personal injury is covered up to an amount of _____ per occurrence and that the Supplier has paid the corresponding premiums for such third party's liability insurance.

12. <u>Spare Parts</u>

Our Company requires the Supplier to make spare parts available for ____ years. The Supplier must maintain tooling, gages, fixtures for the same period of time. The Supplier can only make components available to our Company or our designee. Pricing for spares will be a maximum based on a cost index and not to exceed 3.5% per year.

Long Term Contract

13.   <u>Performance Measurements</u>

      13.1   <u>Rating</u>

Suppliers will be rated by our Company and the rating will be used when assessing the business. A high rating will earn the Supplier recognition as a premium when evaluating quotations and reflected in actual supplier selection.

      13.2   <u>Goals and Measurements</u>

Our Company shall initiate that goals and measurements be defined and followed for on-time deliveries, quality, yearly productivity improvement, cost and cycle time reduction. Initial goals and measurements are agreed upon and will be reviewed quarterly.

      13.3   <u>Certification Process</u>

The Supplier agrees to enter into the certification process according to the enclosure.

14.   <u>Meetings</u>

      14.1   <u>Meeting Frequency</u>

The parties shall endeavor to continuously strengthen their competitiveness by meeting four times a year to agree on ways and means to improve the total cost structure, quality, on-time deliveries, and product improvements. The seller shall each schedule two meetings per year.

      14.2   <u>Agenda for the Meetings</u>

    1.   Forecasts for the next year and market situation.

    2.   Delivery record, their consequences, and actions for improvements.

    3.   Quality records, their consequences, and actions for improvement.

    4.   Product improvements.

Members of the team will be comprised of people from both the Supplier and Customer plants. Team minutes will be recorded by a leader from both the Supplier and Customer.

15.   <u>Termination Convenience</u>

Both parties have the right to terminate this agreement upon ___ days written notice of intention to terminate. The terms of this agreement shall remain in full force during the 12-month period of termination.

Our Company may, by written notice of default to supplier, terminate the whole or any part of this contract or any purchase order issued hereunder in any one of the following circumstances:

a)   If the Supplier fails to meet the delivery dates acknowledged upon acceptance of the purchase order of our Company, or

b)   If the Supplier fails to perform any of the other provisions of this contract, or so fails to prosecute the work as to endanger performance of this contract in accordance with the terms, and in either of these two circumstances does not cure such failure within a period of 60 days (or such longer period as our Company may authorize in writing) after receipt of notice from our Company specifying such failure.

16.   <u>Termination Provided Default</u>

In the event our Company terminates this contract or purchase orders in whole or in part as provided in this contract, our Company may make or produce, upon such terms and in such manner as our Company may deem appropriate, commodities similar to the commodities so terminated and the Supplier shall be liable to our Company for any excess costs for such similar commodities and also for any other costs incurred by our Company as a result of our Company having to procure elsewhere. The Supplier further agrees to continue the performance of this contract to the extent not terminated under the provision of this Article.

Either party may terminate this contract effective upon written notice to the other party should any of the following events occur:

a)   The other party files a voluntary petition for bankruptcy;

b)   The other party is adjudicated bankrupt;

c)   The other party makes assignment for the benefit of its creditors;

d)   A court assumes jurisdiction of the assets of the party under bankruptcy; or

e)   The other party is unable to pay its debts as they become due.

Either party may terminate this contract if the other party fails in its performance of this contract and such breach continues for a period of sixty (60) days after receipt of written notice thereof.

Either party may terminate this contract if, in its sole judgment, official government policy directives or rulings are announced that substantially affect or change the economic liability of this contract and the parties are unable to renegotiate this contract in a mutually satisfactory manner within a reasonable period of time following such official action(s).

17.   <u>Export Control</u>

Each party here acknowledges its obligations to control access to and the export of technical data furnished by the other party hereunder and any direct products (including any products) of such technical data under the U.S., non-U.S. or Japanese export laws and regulations, and hereby agrees not to export or re-export, or cause to be exported or re-exported, any technical data received hereunder or the direct products (including any products) of such technical data until all necessary export licenses or approvals required under the U.S., non-U.S. or Japanese export laws and regulations have been obtained.

In all cases, the party providing the technical data and any direct product (including products) are obligated to obtain the required authorizations or licenses. In addition, both parties have the responsibility to inform the other party of the requirement for authorizations or licenses in advance and provide information required for obtaining such required authorizations or licenses by the other party in a timely fashion so that the time necessary for obtaining the government approvals does not impinge on delivery contracts between the parties.

Long Term Contract

18. Force Majeure

    Neither party may hold the other party in breach of its obligations hereunder if the performance of their obligations is hindered by circumstances beyond the other party's control provided they could not or should not have been anticipated by such party. Such circumstances shall include but not be limited to labor disputes, war mobilization, embargo, requisition, riots and similar events.

19. Assignment

    Neither party shall assign, transfer or otherwise dispose of this contract or any of its rights, interests or obligations hereunder without the prior written consent of the other party.

20. Disputes and Governing Law

    Any dispute arising in connection with the interpretation or execution of this contract not settled by amicable arrangements shall be finally settled under mediation and if not resolved, then settled under the Rules of Conciliation and Arbitration of the International Chamber of Commerce having its Head Office in Paris by one or more arbitrators appointed by such rules.

    This contract and any individual contract shall be governed by the laws of _____.

21. Precedence

    Unless otherwise expressly agreed by the parties hereto, this contract takes precedence over any terms and conditions or any implementation documents including, but not limited to, purchase orders or acknowledgments used during the effective period of this contract by either party in the performance of their obligation under this contract.

22. Entire Agreement

    This contract supersedes all prior discussion and writings between the parties with respect to the subject matter hereto, and may not be changed, altered or amended except in writing signed by duly authorized representatives or the parties.

Long Term Contract

23.   <u>Contact Persons</u>

Our Company   _____

                      _____

The Supplier   _____

                      _____

<u>Our Company</u>   <u>The Supplier</u>

_____   Name   _____

_____   Title   _____

_____   Address   _____

_____   _____

IN WITNESS WHEREOF, the parties have caused this contract to be signed by their duly authorized representatives in duplicates on the days specified below.

Chapter Fourteen

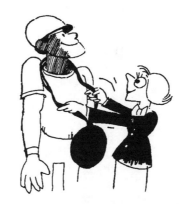

The Certification Process

Chapter Fourteen Contents

How to Use the Tools in this Chapter

Use the Supplier Certification Flow Chart which heads this chapter to give your supplier an overall picture of where you are in the process and an illustration of your involvement in the process. More detailed Flow Charts are included with each phase. These tools provide you with a visual outline of each step in that phase. The explanations of each step are taken from **Supplier Certification II:** *A Handbook for Achieving Success Through Continuous Improvement* (PT Publications, West Palm Beach, FL). We recommend that you consult our handbook for further explanation and clarification.

In Phase 1, we have included a form called Supplier Part Number Selection. You can use this tool to take a snapshot of each part number which you are planning to put through the certification process. The Component Certification Initiation Checklist can be used to show what you have done in the initial stages of certification and what needs to be completed.

In Phase 2, we have inserted a key form called Process Evaluation. This tool is used to determine whether a supplier has its process under control. Different sections of the form address Statistical Process Control, Second-Tier Supplier Requirements, Tooling and Gaging, etc. The "yes" and "no" questions should be presented to the supplier and the answers evaluated by the Supplier Certification Team.

In Phase 3, there is a Finalization form which is used to check off whether critical actions have been taken by the supplier. If these conditions have been met, the supplier then enters the certification phase.

In Phase 4, we have included a sample of a Letter of Approval for the supplier that successfully completes the certification phase. We have also drawn you an example of what a Certified Suppliers' plaque could look like. Recognition of achievement is an effective way of cementing bonds between customer and supplier.

In Phase 5, we have inserted two forms. The Decertification form is used in the event of a supplier failing to meet the requirements of the Supplier Certification Program. The Recertification form is used when a supplier once again meets the requirements.

Phase Flow Chart

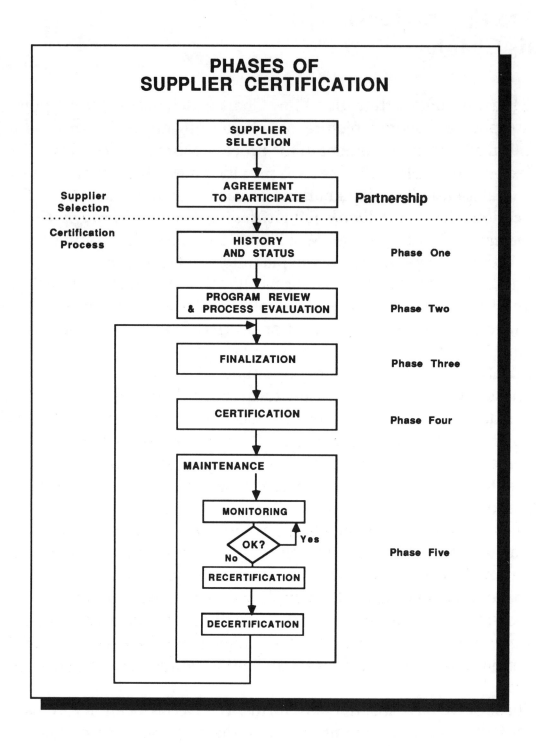

PHASES OF
SUPPLIER CERTIFICATION

SUPPLIER SELECTION	
AGREEMENT TO PARTICIPATE	**Partnership**
HISTORY AND STATUS	**Phase One**
PROGRAM REVIEW & PROCESS EVALUATION	**Phase Two**
FINALIZATION	**Phase Three**
CERTIFICATION	**Phase Four**

Supplier Selection

Certification Process

MAINTENANCE

MONITORING

OK? — Yes / No

RECERTIFICATION

DECERTIFICATION

Phase Five

PHASE ONE:
History and Status

The purpose of Phase One is to work with suppliers who are qualified as a result of their involvement in the process to work in a symbiotic relationship with our company. To determine this, we gather and assess the present state of product quality as well as supplier processes and controls. We then generate a History and Status Report to use in Phase Two. The areas to probe for each supplier and part number to be certified are listed below:

First Article Inspection Status
A first article inspection requires that a production component be checked for each attribute and then determine if all standards and specifications have been met. We want to be sure that a sample or culled-out component is *not* sent for review.

- Was a first article inspection performed on the part?
- If a first article inspection was performed, does its results measure up to our requirements?
- Does a part taken from the production line today match the original first article?

Incoming Quality Control History (IQC) and Line Fallout
Gather all available information so we can determine the major areas in which rejects occur. Equally important is determining whether parts are rejected for the same reason every time despite notices of previous corrective action notification to correct the problem. Quality problems must help us determine cause and effect on the production line. By reviewing the percentage of reject types, we can begin to isolate where the problems are located and what courses of action are required.

Part Documentation Review and Update
Ensure that all specifications, blueprints or drawings we send to the supplier are accurate and understood. There are few things more annoying and eventually detrimental than incorrect specifications from which the supplier must then build.

Packaging Specification/Method of Shipment
Identify the type of packaging required for each line item as well as the standard number of parts per unit. In addition to packaging, determine the best inbound routing and shipment method for each part.

Status of Production Tooling
Every tool has a production life expectancy and this data is required to ensure control over the process. Since this data is often hard to find, estimate the status of production tooling by asking the supplier for tool purchase orders. From this data, we can determine how many tools were bought and when and then we can estimate how many parts can be produced off of a tool.

The Certification Process

Status of Inspection Tooling and Gages

How often and when are inspection tools calibrated? Also determine whether the present inspection tools are tied into the process. In other words, do they test the part in process or do they inspect after the fact? Lastly, survey the existing inspection tools to see whether they are adequate for the job and whether the supplier may need duplicate tooling or more advanced fixtures.

Delivery Performance

If a delivery window has been established with a +/- tolerance, then a review of adherence to the exact date is required to see what the actual performance is. On-time delivery can only be measured against a committed delivery date with the supplier.

For more information and material on Phase One, refer to our book, **Supplier Certification II:** *A Handbook for Achieving Excellence Through Continuous Improvement.*

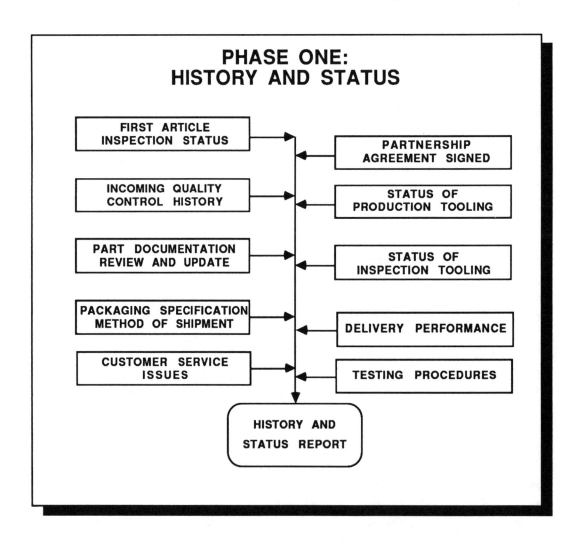

SELECTION OF PART NUMBERS
FOR CERTIFICATION PROCESS

Phase One

SUPPLIER PART NUMBER SELECTION

Qualified Supplier		Supplier Code		Part Family Matrix (Y or N?)	
Part Number		SIC Code			

Dollar Value (per unit)		Quality History Percent	
Current Requirements (units)		Forecast Quantity (units)	
Contract Number			

CERTIFICATION TEAM MEMBERS

Buyer:	
Administrator:	
Manufacturing Engineer:	
Quality Assurance:	

STEERING TEAM COMMITTEE APPROVALS

Manufacturing Engineering:	
Procurement Quality Assurance:	
Purchasing:	
Administration:	

KICK-OFF MEETING

Date:	
Time:	
Place:	

PART NUMBER CERTIFICATION INITIATION CHECKLIST

COMPONENT CERTIFICATION INITIATION CHECKLIST

Part # _____ Supplier _____ V/C _____

Date Initiated _____ Supplier Code _____

Buyer requesting Certification Initiation

_____
Yes   No

Has supplier been qualified? ☐   ☐
If yes, on what date _____

Date
Com-
pleted

Purchasing shall obtain the following:
   Delivery History ☐   ____
   Cycle time requirements ☐   ____
   Supplier History ☐   ____

Quality Assurance shall obtain the following:
   Quality History ☐   ____
   Specification Adherence ☐   ____
   Supplier Inspection Records ☐   ____
   Process Capability ☐   ____

Mfg. Engineering shall obtain the following:
   Supplier Process Planning and History ☐   ____
   Packaging Requirement ☐   ____

_____

Team agrees that component should
proceed to Phase 2. ☐   ☐

Review Meeting Date: _____

PHASE TWO:
Supplier Program Review and Process Validation

Submit Phase 1 Findings to Supplier

Documentation consists of process and quality data either required or existing on a part number. Review all the documentation and analyze all the data to establish performance benchmarks.

Supplier Process Review

Complete the checklist for Process Evaluation. Determine whether the supplier's process is under control and what areas need to be brought under control. If process is not under control, determine the steps required to achieve process control.

Quality Survey and Continuous Improvement Plan

Determine whether the supplier meets the minimum requirements established under the supplier selection criteria. If no, then look for ways to work with supplier to improve their position or look for a new source.

Evaluation Memo

Document any problems and weak areas which need strengthening in an Evaluation Memo. Summarize all corrective actions and construct a time frame for their completion. Assign the responsibility and authority for addressing each issue to one specific person who commits to a finish and start date.

Review of Supplier Responses

Review of all the documentation until it is mutually agreed that the specifications can be met. Determine whether or not the supplier is committed and capable of making the part to specification each time. If no, then either keep seeking improvement, change the specifications so that the supplier can meet them or find another supplier.

Reference: Supplier Certification II: *A Handbook for Achieving Excellence Through Continuous Improvement*, **Chapter Eight.**

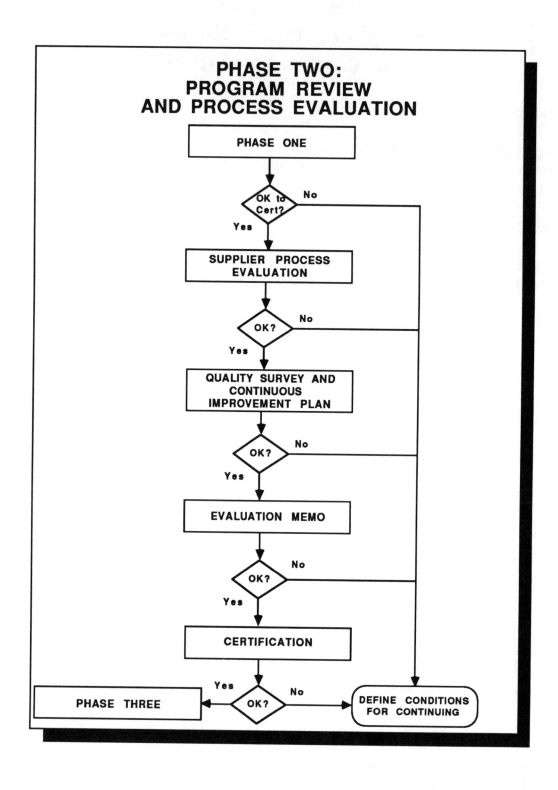

Phase Two

PROCESS
EVALUATION

Date:		**PROCESS VALIDATION**

Company Name:	
Supplier Code:	
Supplier Contact:	
Part Number:	
Description:	

SECTION ONE: Review of the Supplier's Commitment	YES	NO
1. Is the supplier's sequence of operations adequate to assure compliance to the design's requirements?		
2. Is the supplier utilizing the latest blueprints, specifications and other processing information as applicable?		
3. Does the supplier utilize separate work instructions for each part number?		
4. Is the part manufacturable as depicted on the Engineering specification?		
5. Would the manufacturability of the part be improved with a change to the Engineering Design?		
6. Has a Change Request been submitted or discussed with the Concurrent Engineering Coordinator, for the appropriate product line, to enhance the manufacturability? CHANGE REQUEST #: _____ DATE SUBMITTED: _____ COORDINATOR CONTACTED: _____		
7. Does the supplier maintain adequate testing points for detection of nonconformances?		
8. Are the machines and process depicted capable of producing conforming material?		

PROCESS EVALUATION

SECTION TWO: Identification of key operations, services, processes and characteristics	YES	NO
1. Has the supplier identified the key operations, within the manufacturing process, that present the greatest potential for opportunity?		
2. List the supplier identified operations that present the greatest potential for opportunity. (Attach a separate sheet if necessary.) _____ _____		

SECTION THREE: Process changes requiring notification	YES	NO
1. Has the supplier been advised that changes to the critical processes/operations identified in Section 2 require prior notification to the company?		
2. Has the supplier been advised that changes to the above stated processes without prior notification will result in decertification of this part number?		

SECTION FOUR: Statistical Process Control	YES	NO
1. Has the supplier identified the key characteristics for all critical operations for monitoring via control charts?		
2. Have the process control limits been calculated for all key characteristics?		
3. Has the supplier performed process capability studies?		
4. Does the supplier rely on control charting and capability data for acceptance?		

PROCESS EVALUATION

SECTION FOUR: Statistical Process Control	YES	NO
5. Is the Detailed Testing Plan to the latest Blueprint revision on file?		
6. Is there a First Article Inspection Report on file?		
7. Are the supplier's sampling levels and testing techniques adequate?		
8. Is there a better or more economical way to test the characteristics? If YES, state below and communicate them to supplier: _____ _____		
9. Does the supplier have clear specifications and instructions available and do they include clear accept/reject criteria?		
SECTION FIVE: Requirements to Second Tier Suppliers	YES	NO
1. Does the supplier provide to their second tier suppliers detailed work instructions to insure compliance to the specifications?		
2. Are the blueprints, specifications and other processing information flowed to the second tier supplier, at the correct revision level defined on the Purchase Order?		
SECTION SIX: Tooling and Gaging	YES	NO
1. Does the supplier have adequate tooling and gaging?		
2. Will additional tooling and/or gaging be required ? If YES, make a list with costs.		
3. Is the tooling in good condition and capable of producing conforming components?		
4. Is the gaging in good condition and within calibration limits?		

Phase Two

PROCESS
EVALUATION

	YES	NO
SECTION SEVEN: Packaging and Shipping Requirements	YES	NO
1. Does the supplier utilize adequate Material Handling devices before and during manufacturing to prevent damage to the material and components?		
2. Does the supplier package and ship in the prescribed methods as stated in the Purchase Order?		
SECTION EIGHT: Supplier/Company Agreed Upon Corrective Actions	YES	NO
1. Has the supplier been briefed on the actions necessary to complete Process Validation on this part? AGREED UPON DATE FOR REVIEW:		
2. Has the supplier agreed upon a date to verify that the corrective actions have been completed and implemented? VERIFICATION DATE:		
SECTION NINE: Verification of Completed Action	YES	NO
1. Is the supplier in compliance with the agreed upon specification and process? COMPLIANCE DATE:		

ADDITIONAL COMMENTS/OBSERVATIONS:

	Signature	Date
Supplier's Acknowledgment		
Team Verification		

PHASE THREE:
Finalization

Determine that all the courses of corrective action delineated in the Evaluation Memo have been completed. The team then works with the supplier on how to handle testing and methods of inspection for the supplier's product in order to reach full certification.

First determine the number of acceptable lots that will prove a supplier can consistently deliver zero-defect parts. Set a level of lots which must come in to our factory with no defects before the supplier can be certified. Next determine the type of inspection. The number of lots and the type of inspection will be determined by what it takes to satisfy our requirements.

Once the finalization process is finished, the team meets to evaluate whether a supplier should be moved to the certification phase.

FINALIZATION AND CERTIFICATION

Part # _____   Supplier _____

Date Initiated _____   Supplier Code _____

Certification

	Yes	No
Has Process Validation been completed?	☐	☐
Have all agreed upon actions for validation been completed? Date: _____	☐	☐
Have required # of lots been accepted? Date Complete _____	☐	☐
Has ongoing periodic audit plan been defined? Date Complete _____	☐	☐
Add part number to certified list? Date Added _____	☐	☐
Has the acceptance plan been revised? If yes, send copy to buyer/planner.	☐	☐

Manufacturing Engineer: _____

Quality Engineer: _____

Purchasing: _____

Phase Three

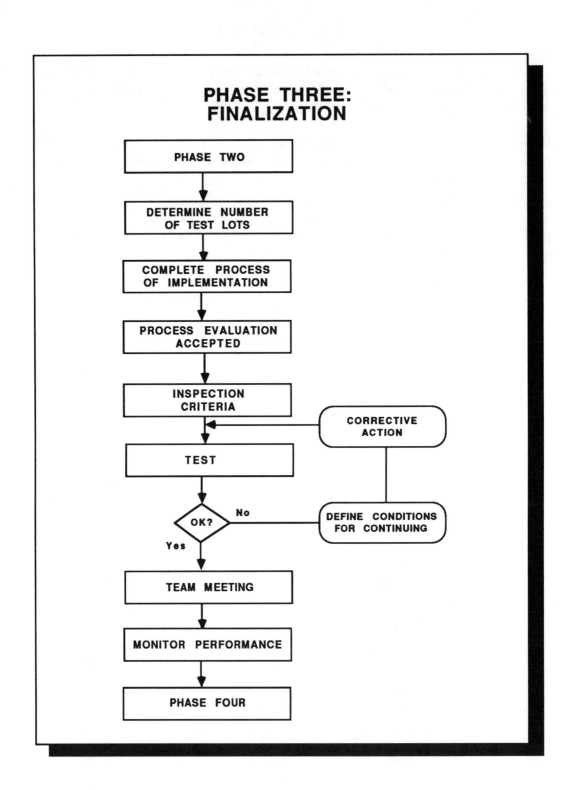

PHASE THREE: FINALIZATION

PHASE TWO

↓

DETERMINE NUMBER OF TEST LOTS

↓

COMPLETE PROCESS OF IMPLEMENTATION

↓

PROCESS EVALUATION ACCEPTED

↓

INSPECTION CRITERIA

CORRECTIVE ACTION

↓

TEST

↓

OK?

No → DEFINE CONDITIONS FOR CONTINUING

Yes

↓

TEAM MEETING

↓

MONITOR PERFORMANCE

↓

PHASE FOUR

Phase Four

PHASE FOUR:
Certification

The first three phases clarify specifications and establish testing procedures to receive parts that conform to established requirements. Once this has been done successfully, certify the supplier for each *specific part number*.

Once certified, send a Letter of Approval (like the one below) and acknowledge the achievement with a certificate, plaque or some type of ceremony.

Ms. Mary Aaron, President
Travel Access
2273 Palm Beach Lakes Blvd.
West Palm Beach, FL 33409

Dear Ms. Aaron:

I am pleased to announce that Travel Access has met all the requirements of Pro-Tech's Supplier Certification Program and is now a Certified Supplier.

As a Certified Supplier, Travel Access is Pro-Tech's supplier of choice. We expect our working relationship to foster the development of new technologies relating to travel that will benefit both of our companies.

In becoming a Certified Supplier, Travel Access has demonstrated its superiority in quality, delivery, service, and pricing in providing Pro-Tech with the lowest cost for travel. Being a Certified Supplier changes the way Pro-Tech will do business with Travel Access. Effective with this letter, we will no longer inspect 100% of Travel Access's tickets and itinerary.

We look forward to working with all of our Certified Suppliers. The consolidation of our supplier base allows us to reduce the occasion for special cause variation in our product. We believe that with Travel Access and our other Certified Suppliers we can concentrate on adding value — not adding cost with inspections.

Congratulations. We are pleased Travel Access has become a Certified Supplier. Travel Access is important to Pro-Tech and we value our relationship with you.

Sincerely,

Leslie Boyce
Assistant to President
Professionals for Technology Associates, Inc.

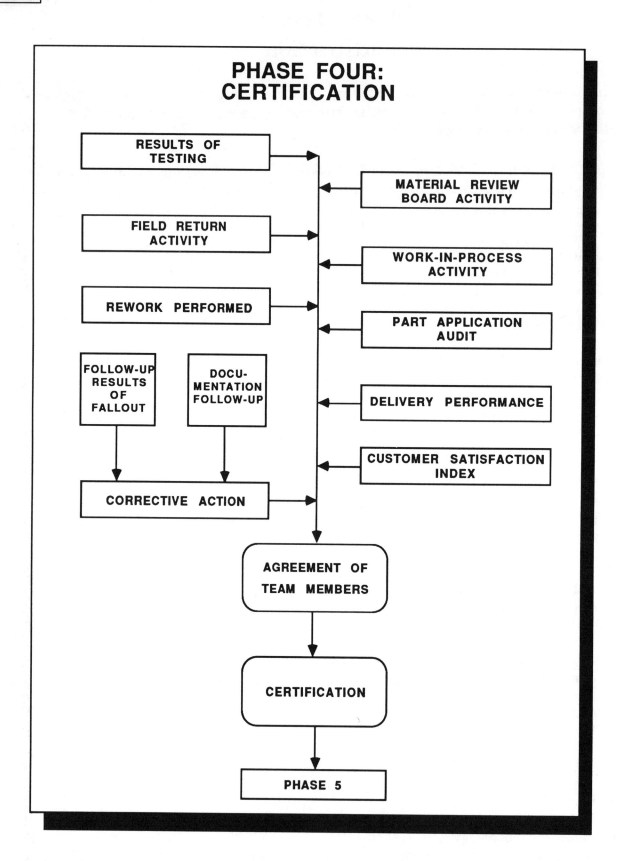

PHASE FOUR: CERTIFICATION

RESULTS OF TESTING

MATERIAL REVIEW BOARD ACTIVITY

FIELD RETURN ACTIVITY

WORK-IN-PROCESS ACTIVITY

REWORK PERFORMED

PART APPLICATION AUDIT

FOLLOW-UP RESULTS OF FALLOUT

DOCU-MENTATION FOLLOW-UP

DELIVERY PERFORMANCE

CUSTOMER SATISFACTION INDEX

CORRECTIVE ACTION

AGREEMENT OF TEAM MEMBERS

CERTIFICATION

PHASE 5

CERTIFIED SUPPLIERS

Certified Suppliers

The following suppliers have joined with us in the achievement of World Class status. These suppliers are our partners in a win/win relationship which seeks to eliminate waste in all activities throughout our respective organizations.

PHASE FIVE:
Maintenance

Audit and maintain the supplier certification program by conducting random audits of material and the supplier's process. While auditing, take samples from lots and inspect 1) to see that the product meets the print, 2) to see if capability ratios have changed or not, and 3) to see that the supplier's process is under control.

Disqualification
A supplier loses its certified status if it ships a lot with any discrepancies. Alert the supplier with a Memo of Disqualification which outlines the problem and suggestions for how it can be solved. Problems will, of course, occur from time to time, but how the supplier handles them makes all the difference.

Requalification
If disqualified, a supplier should be given *one* more opportunity to succeed. If disqualified again, then look for a new source. The two checklists on the next page show how decertification and recertification can be handled.

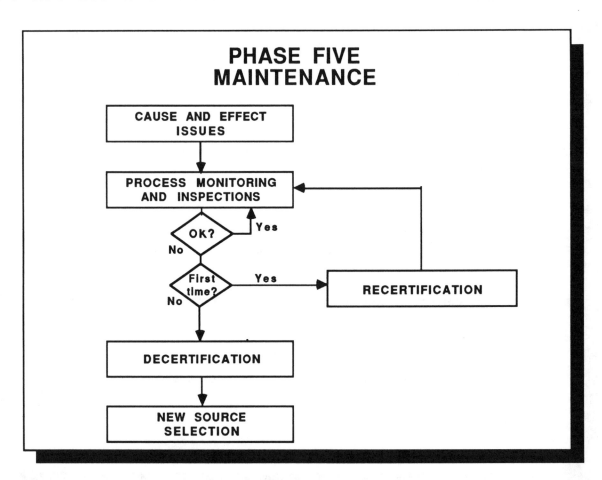

PART NUMBER DECERTIFICATION

Part # _____　　　Supplier _____

Date Initiated _____　　Supplier Code _____

DELIVERY 100% ☐　　　　QUANTITY ☐
　(For Certified Parts Only)

PROCESS ☐　　　　　　　CORRECTIVE ☐
　　　　　　　　　　　　ACTION PLAN

QUALITY ☐　　　　　　　TECHNOLOGY ☐
　　　　　　　　　　　　CHANGE

When all information is completed, forward to Procurement, Quality Assurance.

PART NUMBER RECERTIFICATION

Part # _____　　　Supplier _____

Date Initiated _____　　Supplier Code _____

PROCESS REVALIDATION ☐

CLEARING INTERVAL ☐　　　　PHASE I ☐
(Mfg. lot acceptance)

　　　　　　　　　　　　　　PHASE II ☐

DELIVERY ☐　　　　　　　　　PHASE III ☐
(3 consecutive months above 98%)

Quality Assurance: _____
Manufacturing Engineering: _____
Purchasing: _____

When all information is completed, forward to Procurement, Quality Assurance.

Chapter Fifteen

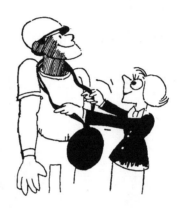

Supplier Ratings

Chapter Fifteen Contents

How to Use the Tools
in this Chapter

In this chapter, all of our tools rate suppliers using the same criteria - Certification, Product Quality, Delivery Performance, Cost Performance, Cooperation, and Quantity. Whether you choose to use our criteria or select others, the tools will be used in the same manner.

The first tool, the Commodity Rating Worksheet, is used to compare the ratings of two or more suppliers. Many of our clients refer to it as a "Supplier Report Card." It gives your Supplier Certification Team a quick means of seeing the relative strengths and weaknesses of different suppliers.

The second tool, the Supplier Yearly Performance Summary, is used to evaluate the performance of one supplier over a year. Put the scores for each criteria in the appropriate month and look for trends. A period of declining scores is cause for concern and the Supplier Certification Team should determine why it is occurring.

The Supplier Performance Rating Form is the meat of the chapter. It contains detailed descriptions of how to assign points to the criteria used in our rating tools and the means for quantifying performance. For further explanation of supplier rating, read Chapter 9 of **Supplier Certification II:** *A Handbook for Achieving Excellence Through Continuous Improvement*.

The last tool in this chapter is a list of features which should be contained in a software application which rates suppliers. Test all applications at your site before purchasing software and ask for the names of current users. Interview these people to see whether the software does what it claims.

Introduction to Rating

INTRODUCTION TO SUPPLIER RATING

Supplier rating is a method used to compare suppliers and is often conducted, or updated, on a quarterly basis. Every supplier earns points in different areas according to the proven level of performance with 100 points being the maximum. The areas which are most often rated include:

1) Quality of received material.

2) Delivery.

3) Cost.

4) Cooperation.

5) Certification.

Most companies believe, and we would agree, that it is essential to include total quality costs when rating a supplier. This would include extra costs such as proven field failures and production stoppages.

A team consisting of people from purchasing, engineering, production and QA is often used to assign points in each of the categories being rated.

Keep in mind that once you certify a supplier, it may not be necessary to rate them. There are many schools of thought on the subject of rating. We believe that a certified supplier's performance speaks for itself.

Commodity Rating Worksheet

Elements		Supplier Ratings		
	Max Pts.	A	B	C
Certification	10			
Product Quality	25			
Delievery Performance	30			
Cost Performance	15			
Cooperation	10			
Quantity	10			
Totals	100			
% of Business				
Ranking				

Notes: _____

_____

_____

_____

_____

_____

_____

Yearly Summary

Supplier Yearly Performance Summary

Elements	Max Pts.	Months											
		1	2	3	4	5	6	7	8	9	10	11	12
Certification	10												
Product Quality	25												
Delievery Performance	30												
Cost Performance	15												
Cooperation	10												
Quantity	10												
Totals	100												
% of Business													
Ranking													

Notes: _____

_____

_____

_____

_____

_____

SUPPLIER PERFORMANCE RATING FORM

Supplier Rating Form

SUPPLIER | |
Address | |
Phone/Fax | |
RATING PERIOD | |

TOTAL VALUATION
Rating Table

Function	Max. Pts.
Certification	20
Product quality	25
Delivery performance	20
Cost performance	15
Cooperation	10
Quantity	10
Total	100

Field failures	-10
Production stoppages	-10

Status in Supplier Certification Program (select one)	Subtotal	Balance Factor	Total
Approved Supplier		1.5	
Qualified Supplier		1.3	
Certified Supplier		1.0	
		Total Score	

Scoring

1	Excellent
2	Good
3	Satisfactory
4	Not satisfactory
5	Not acceptable

CERTIFICATION

Certification

A supplier nets points for the level of Supplier Certification which it has obtained. The chart below shows the number of points to award a supplier for completion of various phases of the program.

PHASE	MAX. PTS.
Phase One: History and Status	5
Phase Two: Program Review and Process Validation	8
Phase Three: Finalization	13
Phase Four: Certification	20

Field Failures

A supplier with field failures receives negative points, if the failures can be proved to be caused by the supplier's components when used within specifications.

If the failures are considered non-significant, deduct 10 points from the rating. If the failures are considered severe (causing loss of sales), you may want to consider a more drastic point reduction.

Production Downtime

A supplier can also earn negative points in this category, if the downtime can be proved to be caused by the supplier's components when used within specifications. We suggest a deduction of 10 points in this area, again depending on the severity and length of lost production.

PRODUCT QUALITY

Goal

A zero-defect objective to the customer (free from electrical and mechanical failures or defects) and meeting customer requirements.

Valuation Criteria	Score	Balance Factor	Total
Material Reject Rate (MRR)		0.40	
Production Downtimes		0.30	
Field Failures		0.30	
		Subsystem Score	

$$\text{MRR} = \frac{\text{Total number of rejected incoming and line}}{\text{Total units received}} \times 100\%$$

Legend for MRR:

1	Excellent	99.8%	>
2	Good	99.5%	< 99.8%
3	Satisfactory	99.0%	< 99.5%
4	Not satisfactory	98.0%	< 99.0%
5	Not acceptable		< 98.0%

Legend for Production Downtimes:

1	< 24 equivalent man hours (machine hours)
2	24 < 70 equivalent man hours (machine hours)
3	70 < 300 equivalent man hours (machine hours)
4	300 < 600 equivalent man hours (machine hours)
5	< 600 equivalent man hours (machine hours)

Legend for Field Failures:

1	No field failures/not applicable
2	No significant field failures
3	Severe field failures

The points are based on the relative number of returns during the rating period according to the chart shown here. Note that returns can also be made for components which have been received before the rating period.

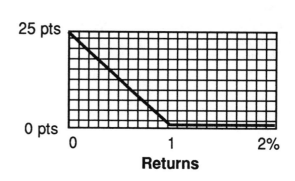

Supplier Rating Form

DELIVERY PERFORMANCE

Goal — reduction in cycle time
— keep agreed delivery dates
— short lead times
— quick deliveries for urgent needs
— supply fulfillment in case of market shortages

Valuation Criteria	Score	Balance Factor	Total
Material Reject Rate (MRR)		0.80	
Lead Times (in relation to competitors) including behavior for urgent needs		0.20	
		Subsystem Score	

Legend for On-Time Deliveries:

1	Excellent	99%	>
2	Good	97%	< 99%
3	Satisfactory	94%	< 97%
4	Not satisfactory	90%	< 94%
5	Not acceptable		< 90%

Legend for Lead Times:

1	Excellent	shorter than customer's cycle time
2	Good	best of the suppliers of this product
3	Satisfactory	equal to market
4	Not satisfactory	1 day longer than best
5	Not acceptable	2 days longer than best

The points are based on correct time of deliveries according to the chart shown here. Times are calculated as averages during the rating period (one quarter). The score is calculated from the chart.

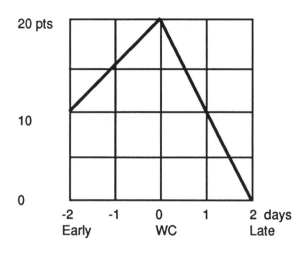

On-Time Delivery

COST PERFORMANCE

Goal

— best cost/performance relation

Valuation Criteria	Score	Balance Factor	Total
In comparison to other manufacturers and other sources (same product)		0.50	
Price Tendency (frequent increases/reductions		0.50	
		Subsystem Score	

Cost includes two factors: relative direct cost in comparison to other manufacturers for a maximum of 15 points, and
relative cost trend in comparison to an industry index for a maximum of 5 points.

Scoring:

	Comparison to Competitors	Price Tendency
1 Excellent	> 5% lower	> 5% below industry index
2 Good	0 < 5% lower	2 - 5% below industry index
3 Satisfactory	meets competition	±1% industry standard
4 Not satisfactory	0 < 5% higher	2 -5% above industry index
5 Not acceptable	> 5% higher	> 5% above industry index

Relative Cost

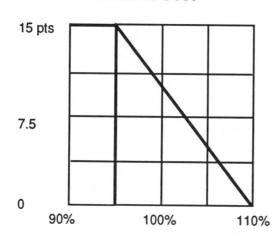

Relative Cost Trend

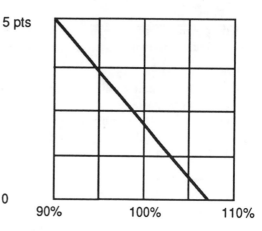

Supplier Rating Form

COOPERATION

Goal
— partnership relations

Valuation Criteria	Score	Balance Factor	Total
1. Commercial		0.25	
2. Technical		0.25	
3. Forwarding		0.25	
4. Service (after sales)		0.25	
		Subsystem Score	

Scoring:

1 Excellent
2 Good
3 Satisfactory
4 Not satisfactory
5 Not acceptable

Cooperation results in a score of 10 points if the following items are fulfilled:
— fast response to customer contacts
— application support
— problem solving
— mutual information sharing (quality and test data, etc.)
— development and research support

Moderate cooperation results in 5 points if the following items are fulfilled:
— fast response to customer contacts
— problem solving

If none of the above are fulfilled, a score of 0 points is given.

Criteria for Cooperation

1. Commercial
— Competence of the internal/external sales organization
— Initiative in case of problems
— Reaction on inquiries
— Information about trends, market fluctuations, technical changes, etc.
— Contract/Order processing
— Openness toward cost reduction programs

2. Technical
— Competence of advisory and support services
— Documentation (quality, completeness, transitions)

3. Forwarding
— Completeness and quality of shipping documentation (export)
— Reliability of packing
— Completeness and quality of shipping advice notes (import)
— Reliability in meeting shipment deadlines
— Labeling/identification of material

4. Service (after sales)
— Type, extent and quality of service network
— Quality of services
— Response in case of technical problems
— Fairness

QUANTITY

Goal
— 100% quantity delivered to order
— small lot sizes
— ship to stock

Valuation Criteria	Score	Balance Factor	Total
Correct quantity		0.80	
Window adjustment		0.20	
		Subsystem Score	

<u>Legend for Quantities:</u>

1	Excellent	99%	>
2	Good	97%	< 99%
3	Satisfactory	94%	< 97%
4	Not satisfactory	90%	< 94%
5	Not acceptable		< 90%

The points are based on correct quantity delivered according to schedule or release. Calculations are based on a quarter rating period. The score is calculated from the chart.

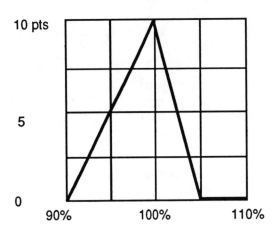

Correct Quantity

Computer Rating System

Computer Rating System Specifications

A number of software companies are developing products for use in Supply Management Programs. Before you buy a Supplier Rating System, we suggest that you find out if the program has the following features:

- **Flexibility** — has the capability of allowing the user to change the parameters for measuring supplier criteria, setting criteria weights, and assigning nonconformance costs while building a system suited to your particular requirements.

- **User-Friendly** — simple, intuitive menus and graphic interface which allows users to quickly learn the program.

- **Industry Standards** — program should be based on industry standards and provide supplier performance measurements, such as delivery, quality, supplier price, company profile, quality audits and defects per million.

- **Traceability** — tracks reject actions and lists reason codes and dates for evaluations.

- **On-line Inquiry** — gives user the ability to search supplier performance statistics by any category.

- **Report Generation** — ability to print supplier performance package, including summary supplier performance, per rating reports, supplier detailed delivery and quality reports.

- **Supplier History** — capability of storing as much historical data as your hardware allows and ability to access this information with ease.

- **Ease of Implementation** — easily configurable with present equipment.

- **Benchmarking** — ability to measure activity versus other suppliers against a World Class standard for each commodity.

- **Graphics** — capable of visually plotting and graphing trends in either a pie or bar graph.

- **Measurements** — able to predict trends based on data, history and benchmarking; this should be a preventive method.

- **Quality** — ability to track trends for continuous improvement.

Chapter Sixteen

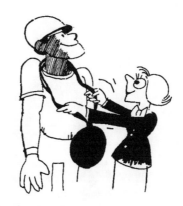

Implementation

Chapter Sixteen Contents

How to Use the Tools in this Chapter

Pages four through seven of this chapter contain a tool called the Mission Statement. It serves as a basis for introducing suppliers to a Supply Management program. We suggest that you look over our example and use what is appropriate to your company's requirements. Adapt or add to our generic statement as you need. This is really a tool to get you thinking about how you are going to implement a Supply Management Program. Before you can go out and ask suppliers to join, you must know what you want. We recommend that you read Chapter 10 in **Supplier Certification II:** *A Handbook for Achieving Success Through Continuous Improvement* and **People Empowerment:** *Achieving Success from Involvement*. Both books are available from PT Publications, West Palm Beach, FL.

The next tool is a sample Minutes of a meeting. Note how all important actions are noted. Minutes should also give an indication on what should be done before the next meeting. Don't forget to add when and where the next meeting will be.

The Meeting Schedule is included to show you how to arrange meetings with different departments and people while visiting a supplier. Make this schedule available to your people and to your supplier well in advance of your arrival.

We have also supplied you with a Target Cost Reduction Worksheet. This form is filled out by both the supplier and customer and delineates the size of the expected cost reduction for a number of areas. This tool should be used as a means of getting agreement by the two parties.

Tom Peters recently indicated that companies who can't use tools like Fishbone Diagrams will not survive into the next century. We have provided a filled-out diagram to show you how to use a Fishbone and a blank diagram for your own use. Fishbones are filled out by placing a problem on each branch and then brainstorming about possible causes. As each cause is investigated and eliminated, the diagram shows your progress toward final resolution.

The final tool is an Action Plan which simply puts into writing who performs what action and when the action will be completed. It is a scheduling and documentation tool.

MISSION STATEMENT
Quality Policy

"The hallmark of our company is quality." That means that we recognize every one of our commitments, actions and products as an expression of quality. The foremost criteria of quality is the satisfaction of our customers. We aim to attain their full confidence in our company as a supplier. We shall succeed by meeting customer demands and stipulations and by conforming to agreed terms. Every delivery we make of our product or service should create a recommendation for further business.

The achievement of World Class status will be determined by our attitude to quality.

Company Mission

Our mission is to be the leader in delivering quality products and services in our industry. Our products and services will meet the needs and requirements of all our customers and contribute to their success.

To ensure customer satisfaction, products and services are provided by employees who are committed to leadership standards in applying our unique combination of experience and resources to meeting our customer's goal of remaining competitive in the global marketplace.

Mission Statement

Company Goals

Our company pledges to take the following actions to ensure continuous improvement in quality:

Customers — To become an organization that is measured by the contributions we make to our customers' success and satisfaction.

Shareholders — To achieve leadership results and competitive advantage in the areas of return on capital and orderly rate growth through the appropriate focus on management of risk and cash flow.

Employees — To create an environment of openness and trust in which employees take pride in the organization and feel responsible for its success.

Community — To assure good corporate citizenship by actively contributing to the welfare of the local communities where our employees live and work.

COMMITMENTS AND EXPECTATIONS
Statement of Commitment

We are proud of our history of providing customers with quality products and services. Furthermore, we are committed to 100% customer satisfaction throughout the '90s and beyond in order to remain globally competitive.

We aim to serve our customers by focusing on continuous improvement in exceeding their expectations and achieving excellence in all that we do. The Supply Management Program is an integral and necessary component of this effort.

We will also seek input from our Suppliers on how we may become a better customer since we believe Supply Management is a two-way street in which suppliers and customers discuss requirements. Our intention is to reduce the supply base over time and to work with a lesser number of highly qualified suppliers. We will also continue to identify new suppliers who are able and willing to work with us in the Supply Management Program to build an environment of mutual trust and confidence.

We have set developing strategic partnerships with key suppliers as our ultimate goal. In these partnerships, we will strive to continuously improve quality, technology, delivery performance and to reduce total costs.

MINUTES OF THE
SUPPLY MANAGEMENT
TEAM MEETING
April 16, 19___

1.0   **The Supply Management team** met Thursday morning, April 16.

2.0   **Next Meeting**   Friday, May 15
                               8:00 a.m.
                               R&D Conference Room

3.0   **Meeting Minutes**
We spent the meeting brainstorming on the kind of Symposium we might have and the agenda for it.

3.1   **Schedule**
We decided that we will try and have a combined Supplier and Customer Symposium on the same day. Maybe 8 a.m. to 4 p.m., including lunch.

And have an open bar from 4 p.m. to 6 p.m. with hot hors d'oeuvres. Dinner will follow the "attitude adjustment time."

We developed and signed up for Supplier Symposium tasks:

> Develop a Supplier Certification Program presentation.
> Prepare briefing for symposium speakers.
> Develop a color brochure on our company.
> Invite Keynote speaker.
> Prepare a Quality Statement form.
> Develop guest list, suppliers and customers, for the symposium.
> Invite guests and monitor responses.
> Develop follow-up literature.
> Do follow-up mailings.
> Prepare Certification Implementation form.

4.0   **Action Items**

Next week, as a team, we will develop an agenda for the Symposium. During this week, think about: how to arrange the day, should we do this over two days, what time should we start, exactly what do we want to cover.

MINUTES (continued)

5.0   **Attachments — Sample Symposium Agendas**

Agenda Sample #1

1.   Who we are
2.   Philosophy of Quality
      Partners in Quality
3.   Certification Program
      Definition
      Goals
      What it will do for us
      What it will do for the supplier
      What we have done so far
      What we will be doing in the near future
4.   Review of Symposium literature
      Quality Statement
      Certification Implementation Worksheet
      Review PT Publications' book: Supplier Certification II
5.   The Next Steps
6.   Wrap-Up Statement by President
7.   Keynote Speaker
8.   Plant Tour

Agenda Sample #2

1.   Introduction to the Company
2.   Introduction to the Local Plant
3.   Philosophy of Quality
4.   Certification Program
5.   What This Does for You — Supplier or Customer
6.   Keynote Speaker
7.   Review of Symposium literature
8.   What's Next
9.   Wrap-Up
10.   Plant Tour

When utilizing outside assistance for implementation, it is extremely important to plan an agenda. The sample agendas we have provided are for your information.

MEETING SCHEDULE

TO: World Class Teams
SUBJECT: Pro-Tech Visit/Team Meetings

For the upcoming Pro-Tech visit on November 19, 20, and 21, the following schedule has been established. If there are any conflicts, please try to resolve them with your team leader. Note: all meetings will be held in the Purchasing Conference Room.

November 19

8:00 a.m.	Commodity C Team Meeting
10:00 a.m.	Team Building Session
2:00 p.m.	Software Team Meeting
4:00 p.m.	Team Leader Meeting

November 20

9:00 a.m.	Inventory Team Meeting
10:00 a.m.	Commodity B Team Meeting
2:00 p.m.	Specification Team Meeting
3:30 p.m.	Supplier Certification Steering Committee Meeting

November 21

10:00 a.m.	Survey Team Meeting
11:00 a.m.	Design for Producibility Team Meeting
1:30 p.m.	Information Systems Team Meeting
3:00 p.m.	Management Wrap-Up Meeting

In addition to the above, Wayne Douchkoff will be available to meet with team members individually as necessary to help resolve any questions or problems.

TARGET COST REDUCTION WORKSHEET — CUSTOMER/SUPPLIER

Cost Worksheet

Cost Factor	Customer	Supplier	Agreement	Action Item
Logistics				
Lead time				
Lot size				
Freight				
Packing				
Recycling cost				
Inventory carrying cost				
Safety stock				
Penalty				
Inventory reduction				
Pricing				
Price				
Volume pricing				
Market price				
Future pricing				
Currency conversion				
Payment terms				
Quality				
Cost of supplier testing				
Cost of customer testing				
Failure cost in Engineering				
Failure cost in Production				
Failure cost in Order Entry				
Failure cost in Specifications				
Audit cost				
Guarantee cost				
Goodwill cost				
Planning cost				
Delivery delay for quality				
Returns				
Performance Stability				
Life cycle				
Substitution cost				
Replacement cost				

Cost Worksheet

TARGET COST REDUCTION WORKSHEET — CUSTOMER/SUPPLIER

Cost Factor	Customer	Supplier	Agreement	Action Item
Supply Base				
Second source cost				
Change of supplier				
Cost Reduction Program				
Continuous improvement process				
Cost coordination				
Order Processing				
Order entry				
Engineering				
Qualification cost				
Selection range				
Cost of prototype				
Evaluation of prototype				
Consulting cost				
New development				
Design options				
Special component cost				
Design modification				
Production				
Process capability				
Learning curve				
Supplier capacity				
Capacity utilization				
Set-up cost				
Special order cost				
Cost of quality				
Plan capacity				

Fishbone Diagram

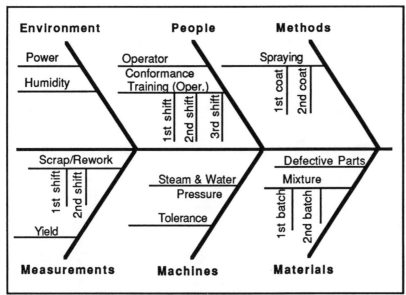

Cause Enumeration Fishbone

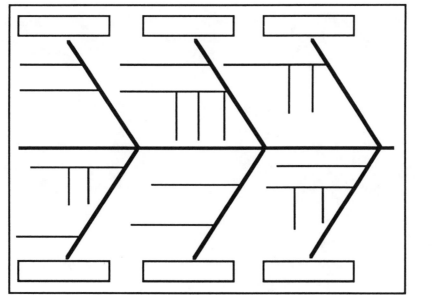

Cause Enumeration Fishbone

SUPPLY MANAGEMENT TEAM

ACTION PLAN

ACTION	WHO	WHEN

Chapter Seventeen

Cost
Reduction

Chapter Seventeen Contents

How to Use the Tools in this Chapter

The tools in this chapter are designed to assist you in cost reduction and negotiation. We suggest that you read two of our publications, **Activity Based Costing:** *The Key to World Class Performance* and **The World of Negotiations:** *Never Being a Loser,* for more detailed information about these areas. Both books are available from PT Publications, West Palm Beach, FL.

The first tool in this chapter asks you to list your Cost Reduction Goals by Commodity. There are columns for you to track the savings in dollars and by percentages. This tool works in conjunction with the tool on Page Six which you can use to expand upon the goals and objectives for one particular commodity. Every commodity you are tracking for cost reduction should have its own sheet.

What these tools ask you to do is benchmark your progress. We have found no better way to keep the Continuous Improvement Process moving forward. Our new book, Cycle Time Management, includes an entire chapter on benchmarking's importance and how to implement it.

The purpose of the Cost Reduction Road Map is to show what actions have taken place for each commodity. By using this tool, you can see where your effort to improve needs more attention and where it is meeting expectations. Both the Supply Management Projected Savings and Material Budget tools are used in similar ways.

The next two tools, the Sourcing Team Action Plan and the Team Brainstorming Worksheet, are used to keep track of what teams are doing in their cost reduction efforts. The intent is to focus teams on finding opportunities and to indicate specific steps they are going to take.

(continued on next page)

An extremely important tool comprises the bulk of this chapter. The Negotiation Worksheet encapsulates the entire negotiation process in one chart. The "Min" and "Max" columns allow you to stay within your own terms while the other columns represent how your negotiation partner has responded. The worksheet also covers all the pertinent factors affecting negotiation and allows you to add others important to your company.

The next tool is a useful example of a chart which can show how well your company's investment in cost reduction has fared.

In the area of Total Cost, we have included a Total Cost Equation that you can use to determine how much money is spent on all the cost elements in the price of a product or service. The next tool provides you with a snapshot view of what percentage of the total cost is spent on each cost element. The last tool is useful in determining how a supplier stacks up against its competitors and to industry averages.

COST REDUCTION GOALS
by COMMODITY   Date:

Cost Reduction Goals

COMMODITY LIST	Dollars Purchased	SAVINGS PER PRODUCT		PROJECT		
		Dollars	Percent	A	B	C
Sheet metal						
Winding wires						
Insulating material						
Injection molding						
Welding construction						
Sheets						
Fastening parts						
Bearings						
Castings						
Cooler						
Fans						
Instrumentation						
Copper						
Plastic						
Electricity						
Telecommunications						
Printed circuit boards						
TOTAL SAVINGS						

Supply Management Goals

SUPPLY MANAGEMENT GOALS AND OBJECTIVES

Commodity	
Volume Purchased	Year
Date	
Schedule	

Year

Sourcing Team

Leader _____
Scribe _____
Date _____

GOALS:

Products	1	2	3	4	Total
Cost					
Quality					
Quantity					

COST HISTORY

GOALS:

Date												
Period	Jan	Feb	Mar	Apr	May	Jun	Jul	Aug	Sep	Oct	Nov	Dec
1995												
1996												
1997												

RESULTS/ACTION PLAN:

COST REDUCTION ROAD MAP

Date _____

Action	Commodity	Jan	Feb	Mar	Apr	May	Jun	Jul	Aug	Sep	Oct	Nov	Dec	Remarks
Knowledge Gathering	1													
	2													
	3													
	4													
	5													
Feasibility Development Phase	1													
	2													
	3													
	4													
	5													
Design to Cost: supplier involvement, teamwork, contract proposal, cost goals	1													
	2													
	3													
	4													
	5													
Preproduction: supplier, customer	1													
	2													
	3													
	4													
	5													
Design Release	1													
	2													
	3													
	4													
	5													
Procurement: final contract	1													
	2													
	3													
	4													
	5													
Production: supplier, customer	1													
	2													
	3													
	4													
	5													

Cost Reduction Road Map

Projected Savings

Date _____

SUPPLY MANAGEMENT PROJECTED SAVINGS

Commodity Teams	No. of Suppliers	No. of Parts	'94 Cost	'95 Cost	'94 Savings	'95 Savings
Sheet metal						
Fasteners						
Insulation material						
Copper products						
Welded construction						
Printed circuit boards						
Fans						
Injection molding						
Castings						
Bearings						
Service						
Telecommunications						
Office supplies						
Total						

1994 MATERIAL BUDGET: Cost Reduction by Percent

Commodity Teams	$ Volume	Content	Reduction Total	Reduction Net	ACTION/RESPONSIBILITY
Sheet metal		15%	20%	3%	
Shafts		3%	50%	1.5%	
Glass bottles		2%	50%	1%	
Welding		10%	40%	4%	
Copper and insulation		20%	20%	4%	
Copper products		10%	10%	1%	
Bearings		5%	10%	0.5%	
Injection moldings		10%	20%	2%	
Casting		10%	40%	4%	
Other		15%	5%	0.75%	
Total	$	100%		21.75%	

Date _____

Material Budget Plan

Material Budget Plan

Date _____

199__ MATERIAL BUDGET: Cost Reduction by Percent

Commodity Teams	$ Volume	Content	Reduction Total	Reduction Net	ACTION/RESPONSIBILITY
	$				

SOURCING TEAM ACTION PLAN

COMMODITY _____

LEADER _____

ACTION	WHO	WHEN

Action Plan Worksheet

17-12

Team Brainstorming

TEAM BRAINSTORMING WORKSHEET
Presentation of Results

COMPANY _____

PRODUCTS _____

Opportunities for Cost Reduction	Impact on				
	Price	Quality	Lead Time	Other	

SUPPLY MANAGEMENT NEGOTIATION WORKSHEET (MIL)

SUPPLIER:

COMMODITY:

SUBJECT:

NAME: **DATE:**

TEAM MEMBERS:

Negotiation Worksheet

Ref	Points of Contract	Min	Max	Concession	Offer	Agreement	Offer	Agreement	Offer	Agreement
1	**Cost**									
	material									
	labor									
	overhead									
	cost of quality									
	cost of inventory									
	benefit cost									
	price range									
	Total									

Negotiation Worksheet

Ref	Points of Contract	Min	Max	Concession	Offer	Agreement	Offer	Agreement	Offer	Agreement
2	**Extra Costs**									
	freight									
	tariffs									
	packing									
	duty									
	customs									
	Total Extra Costs									
3	**Conditions**									
	payment terms									
	delivery									
	discounts									
	step function pricing									
4	**Currency**									
	currency base									
	cost index									
	currency clause									
	a) all price factors									
	b) components									
	fixed currency									
	soft country currency									
	options									
5	**Quantity**									
	total quantity									
	lot size									
	quantity tolerances									
	% of business									
	just-in-time									

© 1995 PT Publications, Inc.

Negotiation Worksheet

Ref	Points of Contract	Min	Max	Concession	Offer	Agreement	Offer	Agreement	Offer	Agreement
6	**Quality**									
	First Pass yields									
	quality requirement									
	First Pass yield									
	penalties									
	ISO 900X/other									
	corrective actions									
7	**Inventory**									
	warehouse									
	ship-to-stock									
	turns									
	raw									
	wip									
8	**Delivery Time**									
	lead time									
	move time									
	duty									
	customs									
	carrier									
	freight terms									
	method of transportation									
	commodity code									
9	**Duration of Contract**									
	start									
	end									

Negotiation Worksheet

Ref	Points of Contract	Min	Max	Concession	Offer	Agreement	Offer	Agreement	Offer	Agreement
10	**Tests**									
	internal testing									
	external testing									
	receiving									
	RMA (Return Material Authorization)									
	warranty									
11	**Certification Program**									
	criteria									
	a) chosen suppliers									
	b) survey points									
	c) actual results									
	agreement to certification									
	agreement to CIP									
	a) on-time delivery									
	b) quality									
	c) costs									
	d) cooperation									
	quantity									
12	**Improvement of Results**									
	yearly improv. of production									
	team members									
	meeting dates									
	CIP milestones									

Negotiation Worksheet

Ref	Points of Contract	Min	Max	Concession	Offer	Agreement	Offer	Agreement	Offer	Agreement
13	**General Points**									
	force majeure									
	general conditions									
	partnership agreement									
	terms and conditions									
14	**Commission Process**									
15	**Other Points**									

Negotiation Worksheet

DEFINITIONS AND REMARKS

Ref	Descriptions
1	Possible formula: **Company CFO Input**
2	Consult freight group team.
3	Look at extra costs for packing, release, return, etc.
3	Payment in 45 days, 2% or 90 days net.
4	In general, only orders in supplier's currency. NO SPECULATIONS.
	Protection against currency instabilities with following formula:
	Price x (Currency old – Range width 3%)/(Currency new – Range width 3%)
5	Quantity tolerance is ±0%.
6	Define FPY per time period. Define penalties.
	Possible penalties: For a FPY delay of x% during the measuring period, there will be a discount of x% for the following period.
7	Quick deliveries must be guaranteed.
8	Durations for deliveries must be defined.
9	Contract period should be at least 3 to 5 years.
10	Document results. Supplier should keep test documents and certificates. Define process for corrective action.
11	Compare with industry.
12	Improvement of productivity should match our rate to compensate for increasing price factors.
13	Our conditions for orders must be accepted before talking about sales conditions.
14	Define order process.
15	Define case by case.

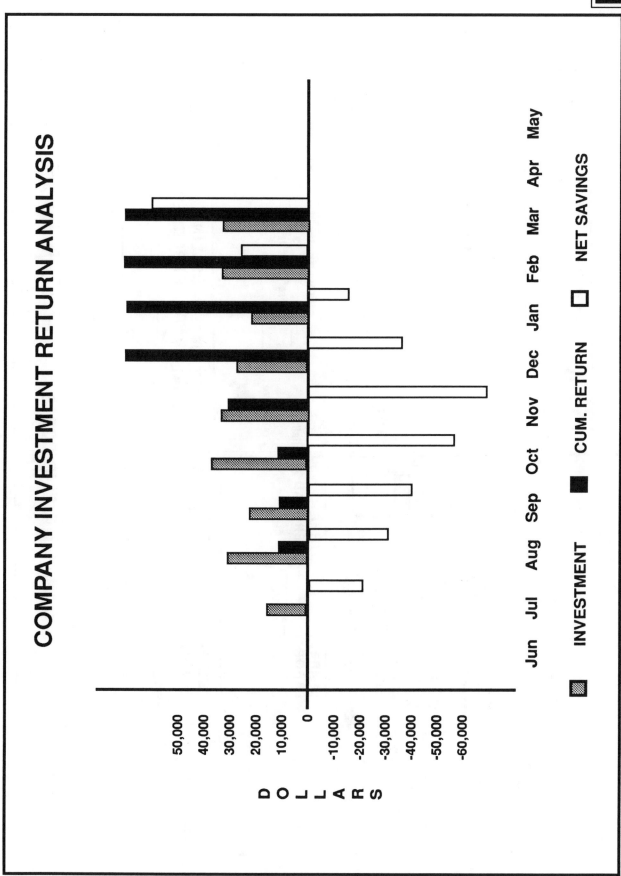

COMPANY INVESTMENT RETURN ANALYSIS

Return on Investment

INVESTMENT   CUM. RETURN   NET SAVINGS

TOTAL COST EQUATION

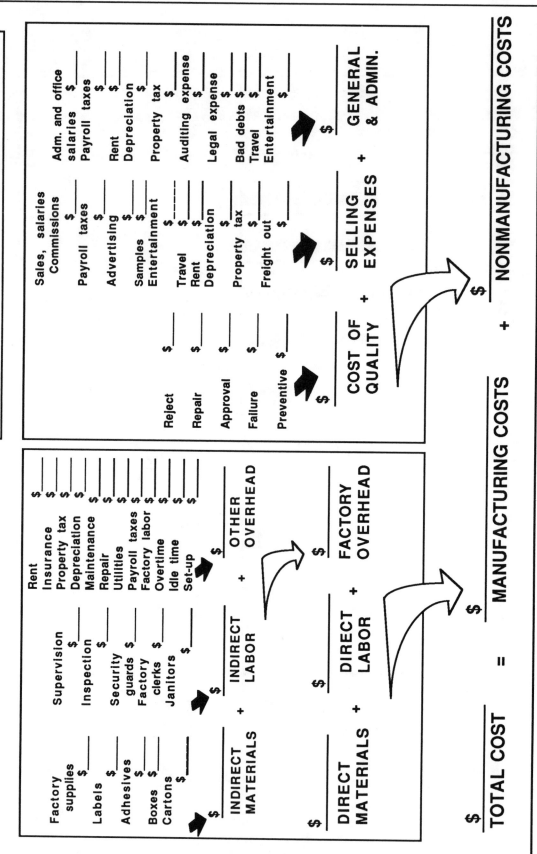

General & Admin.
Adm. and office salaries $___
Payroll taxes $___
Rent ___
Depreciation ___
Property tax ___
Auditing expense $___
Legal expense $___
Bad debts $___
Travel ___
Entertainment $___
= GENERAL & ADMIN. $___

Selling Expenses
Sales, salaries Commissions $___
Payroll taxes $___
Advertising $___
Samples $___
Entertainment $___
Travel $___
Rent ___
Depreciation ___
Property tax $___
Freight out $___
= SELLING EXPENSES $___

Cost of Quality
Reject $___
Repair $___
Approval $___
Failure $___
Preventive $___
= COST OF QUALITY $___

SELLING EXPENSES + GENERAL & ADMIN. + COST OF QUALITY = NONMANUFACTURING COSTS $___

Other Overhead
Rent $___
Insurance $___
Property tax $___
Depreciation $___
Maintenance $___
Repair $___
Utilities $___
Payroll taxes $___
Factory labor $___
Overtime $___
Idle time $___
Set-up $___
= OTHER OVERHEAD $___

Indirect Labor
Supervision $___
Inspection $___
Security guards $___
Factory clerks $___
Janitors $___
= INDIRECT LABOR $___

INDIRECT LABOR + OTHER OVERHEAD = FACTORY OVERHEAD $___

Indirect Materials
Factory supplies $___
Labels $___
Adhesives $___
Boxes $___
Cartons ___
= INDIRECT MATERIALS $___

Direct Labor $___

Direct Materials $___

INDIRECT MATERIALS + DIRECT LABOR + DIRECT MATERIALS + FACTORY OVERHEAD = MANUFACTURING COSTS $___

TOTAL COST $___ = MANUFACTURING COSTS + NONMANUFACTURING COSTS

COST ELEMENTS

Take the figures from the Total Cost Equation and calculate the percentages for each cost element. Make a chart to show the relationship of cost elements to Total Cost.

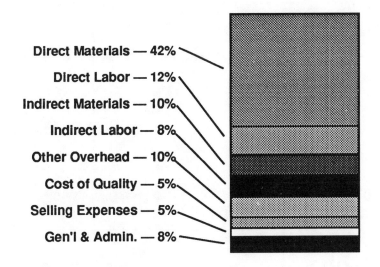

Direct Materials — 42%
Direct Labor — 12%
Indirect Materials — 10%
Indirect Labor — 8%
Other Overhead — 10%
Cost of Quality — 5%
Selling Expenses — 5%
Gen'l & Admin. — 8%

Direct Materials —   %

Direct Labor —   %

Indirect Materials —   %

Indirect Labor —   %

Other Overhead —   %

Cost of Quality —   %

Selling Expenses —   %

Gen'l & Admin. —   %

Variance Range

SUPPLIER'S VARIANCE RANGE

SUPPLIER: _____

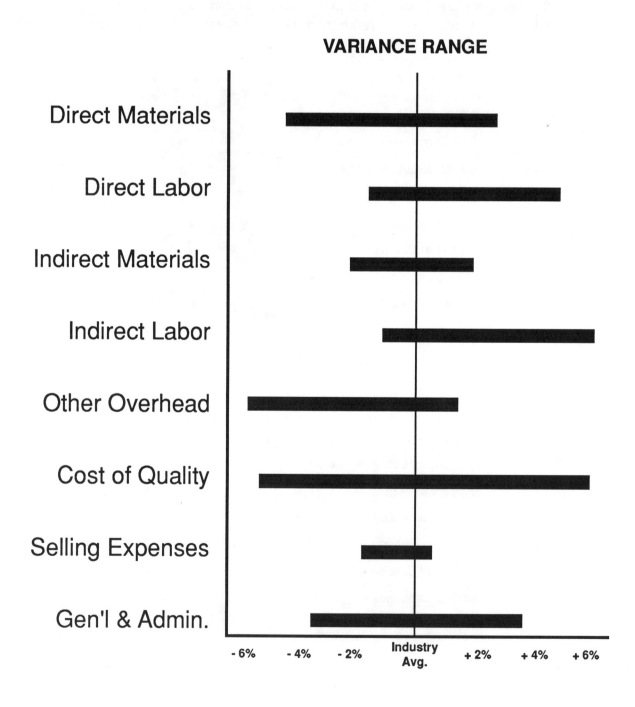

VARIANCE RANGE

Direct Materials

Direct Labor

Indirect Materials

Indirect Labor

Other Overhead

Cost of Quality

Selling Expenses

Gen'l & Admin.

- 6%   - 4%   - 2%   **Industry Avg.**   + 2%   + 4%   + 6%

SUPPLIER'S VARIANCE RANGE

SUPPLIER: _____

Variance Range

VARIANCE RANGE

Direct Materials

Direct Labor

Indirect Materials

Indirect Labor

Other Overhead

Cost of Quality

Selling Expenses

Gen'l & Admin.

- 6%   - 4%   - 2%   Industry Avg.   + 2%   + 4%   + 6%

Chapter Eighteen

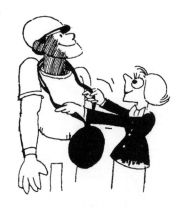

Supplier
Quality
Agreement

Chapter Eighteen Contents

How to Use the Tools in this Chapter

The first three tools in this chapter are used to determine the frequency of occurrence for each item and to calculate the costs each month and cumulatively for each of three categories of the cost of quality. Each category is further divided into activities which can be tracked. The intent is to get the user to identify which components are causing quality problems so they can be reduced or eliminated.

The Process Flow Chart is a very powerful tool for reducing costs and eliminating waste. The tool is used to help a team observe and define the different activities which comprise a company method or operation. This tool can be used on the factory floor or in administrative settings. The lower portion provides you with a means of breaking an activity down and assigning values to each part. These parts can then be summarized in the middle section. The point is to reduce or eliminate nonvalue-added activities.

Both the Measurement Record Sheet and Spread and Target Worksheet are used in the application of Statistical Process Control (SPC) in order to achieve Six Sigma performance. Although these tools may initially look difficult, you will find by reading Chapter Six of **Supplier Certification II:** *A Handbook for Achieving Excellence Through Continuous Improvement* that the tools are easily mastered. The use of SPC tools is one of the most important business techniques for an organization to learn. It is essential to the attainment of World Class status.

Other important SPC tools are included next. Again refer to Chapter Six of **Supplier Certification II**. There, you will see how to take measurements for SPC charts and how to interpret your results.

Eventually, the results you obtain will indicate courses of actions for teams in your company to take. The Activity Worksheet is a tool designed to help you keep track of the people working on a particular problem and the activities for which they are responsible. Our Activity Worksheet also provides a column for putting the activities into the order which they should be completed.

How to Use the
Tools in this Chapter (continued)

Standardization of your Supply Management Process requires that teams keep minutes of their meetings. Our Problem Solving Minutes provides you with a form to be utilized in achieving this standardization. Filling out the form is as simple as answering the questions.

Another problem solving tool we have found useful summarizes the Process of Problem Solving. This form is filled in by writing in what has been completed or needs to be completed in each category.

The last tool in this chapter is indispensable. By now, almost everybody in the business world has seen a Fishbone or Cause and Effect Diagram. They are used by filling in the boxes with suggested causes and then breaking down these broad categories into more detailed categories below. When a cause has been investigated and eliminated, then it is denoted on the diagram by some sign. Some companies put parentheses around work they have finished. Fishbones not only give you a snapshot view of the underlying causes, but a report on your progress as well.

FAILURE COSTS

Failure Costs	Base Line Formula	Freq. of Occurrence	Month Actual Dollars	YTD Actual Dollars	Benchmark Company
Scrap					
Rework					
Warranty					
Product liability					
Corrective action					
Service					
Purch. change orders					
Eng. change orders					
Redesign					
Customer relations					
Total					

Failure Costs Form

Appraisal Costs Form

APPRAISAL COSTS

Appraisal Costs	Base Line Formula	Freq. of Occurrence	Month Actual Dollars	YTD Actual Dollars	Benchmark Company
Prototype inspection					
Acceptance testing					
Supplier qualification					
Product inspection					
Mkt. service survey					
Incoming inspection					
Inventory audit					
Mat'l review board					
Process control tests					
Production spec.					
Conformance testing					
Total					

PREVENTION COSTS

Prevention Costs	Base Line Formula	Freq. of Occurrence	Month Actual Dollars	YTD Actual Dollars	Benchmark Company
Design reviews					
Qualification testing					
Parts qualification					
Supplier qualification					
Quality seminars					
Specification reviews					
Proc. control studies					
Tool control					
Eng. quality training					
Operational training					
Quality orientation					
Acceptance planning					
Zero-defect pgms.					
Statistical training					
Quality audits					
Drawings reviews					
Preventive maint.					
Automation					
Total					

Process Flow Chart

QUESTION EACH DETAIL

Analysis Why?

Where | When | What | How

SUMMARY	Present # Time	Proposed # Time	Diff # Time
◯ Operation			
⇨ Transport			
▢ Inspection			
D Delay			
▽ Storage			
	Ft.	Ft.	Ft.

Job _____
Person Or Material _____
Chart begins _____
Chart ends _____
Charted by _____
Date _____

Details of Present or Proposed Method	Operation	Transport	Inspection	Delay	Storage	Distance	Quantity	Time	Eliminate	Combine	Sequence	Place	Person	Improve	Notes
	◯	⇨	▢	D	▽										
	◯	⇨	▢	D	▽										
	◯	⇨	▢	D	▽										
	◯	⇨	▢	D	▽										
	◯	⇨	▢	D	▽										
	◯	⇨	▢	D	▽										
	◯	⇨	▢	D	▽										
	◯	⇨	▢	D	▽										
	◯	⇨	▢	D	▽										
	◯	⇨	▢	D	▽										
	◯	⇨	▢	D	▽										
	◯	⇨	▢	D	▽										

Supplier Quality Management

Process Flow Chart

Details of Present or Proposed Method	Operation	Transport	Inspection	Delay	Storage	Distance	Quantity	Time	Eliminate	Combine	Sequence	Place	Person	Improve	Notes
	○	⇨	□	D	▽										
	○	⇨	□	D	▽										
	○	⇨	□	D	▽										
	○	⇨	□	D	▽										
	○	⇨	□	D	▽										
	○	⇨	□	D	▽										
	○	⇨	□	D	▽										
	○	⇨	□	D	▽										
	○	⇨	□	D	▽										
	○	⇨	□	D	▽										
	○	⇨	□	D	▽										
	○	⇨	□	D	▽										

Notes: _____

_____

_____

_____

_____

_____

_____

_____

_____

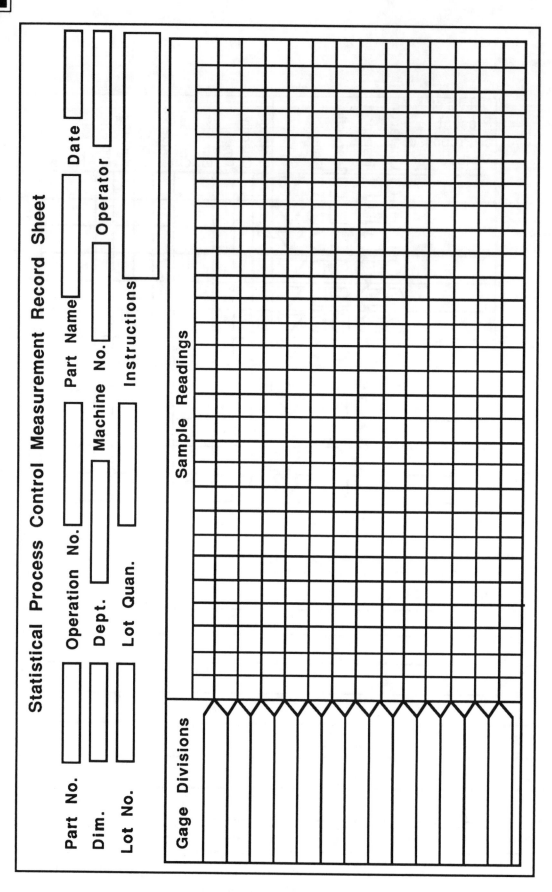

Measurement Record Sheet

Statistical Process Control Measurement Record Sheet

Part No. [   ]   Operation No. [   ]   Part Name [   ]   Date [   ]

Dim. [   ]   Dept. [   ]   Machine No. [   ]   Operator [   ]

Lot No. [   ]   Lot Quan. [   ]   Instructions [   ]

Sample Readings

Gage Divisions

Spread and Target Worksheet

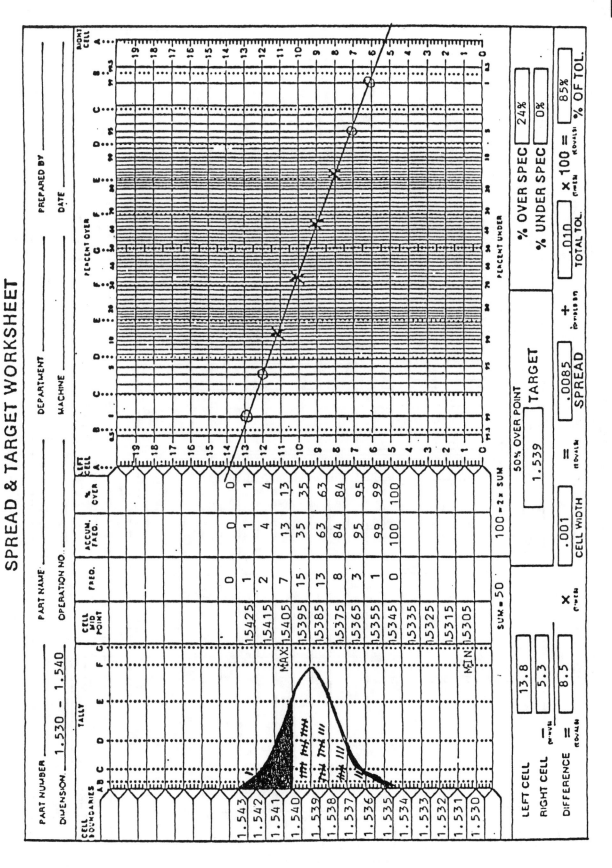

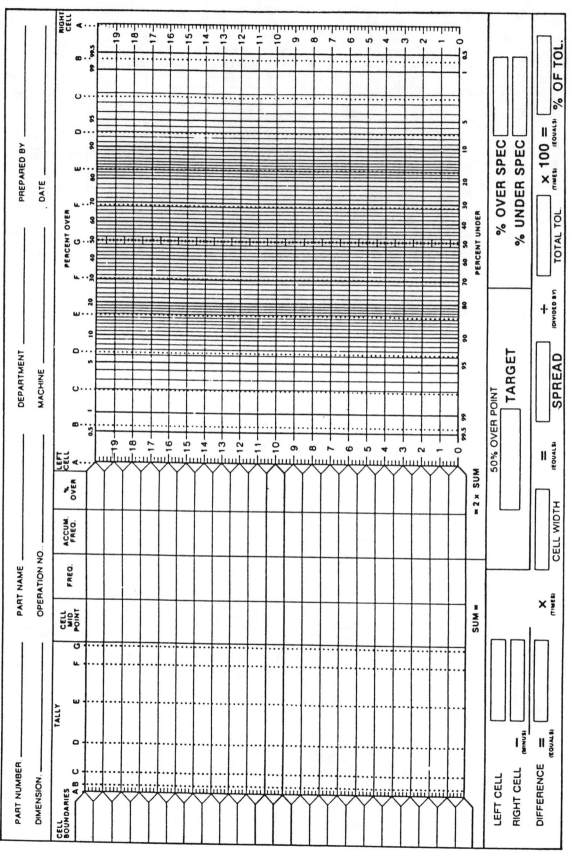

SPC CHARTS

Control Chart for Attribute Data

Part No. and Name	□ P	□ NP	□ C	□ U	Dept./Section
What are you charting?		Average sample size		Frequency	

AVG. =   UCL =   LCL =

.11

UCL
.10

.09

p
.08

.07

LCL

.06

.05

.04

.03

D i s c r e p a n c y

Fraction (pu)																										
Number (npc)																										

Sample (n)																										
Date																										

REMARKS

SPC CHARTS

SPC Charts

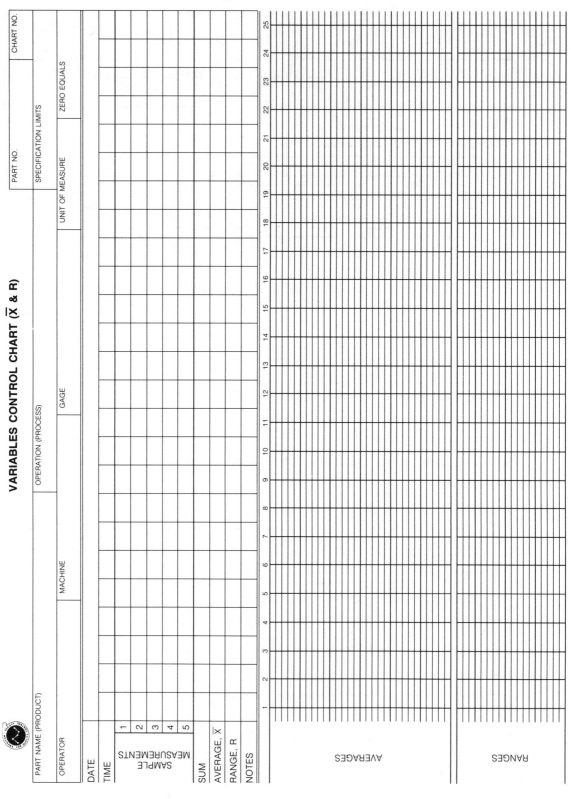

ACTIVITY WORKSHEET

Team/Project _____   Date _____

1. List activities needed to accomplish project.
2. Put in names of people who will be responsible for the project's completion.
3. Record completion date of each activity.
4. Number the activities in order.
5. Put "Responsibility Code" in square for each person and activity.

Responsibility Codes:

PR — person has primary responsibility
AP — person who must give approval for activity
SP — person whose support or help is needed
IP — person who should be kept informed of progress
NR — no responsibility for this activity

Responsible People

Order	Activity							Date

Problem Solving Worksheets

PROBLEM SOLVING MINUTES

Team/Project: _____

Date: _____

Next Meeting: _____ (time)   (day)
                      _____ (location)

Scribe: _____

Participants: _____
_____

What did you discuss during this meeting?

1 _____
2 _____
3 _____
4 _____
5 _____
6 _____
7 _____
8 _____
9 _____
10 _____
   _____
   _____
   _____

What actions were decided? And who is responsible for seeing them completed.

Actions: _____   Person: _____
_____   _____
_____   _____
_____   _____
_____   _____
_____   _____

What do you plan to discuss at the next meeting?

_____
_____
_____
_____
_____
_____

THE PROCESS OF PROBLEM SOLVING

IDENTIFY PROBLEM	
CLARIFY PROBLEM	
EVALUATE CAUSES	
DEVELOP ALTERNATIVES	
SELECT SOLUTION	
IMPLEMENT SOLUTION	

Fishbone Diagram

SUGGESTED CAUSES
policies, methods, material machinery, services, manpower, environment, procedures, equipment, measurements

FISHBONE CAUSE & EFFECT DIAGRAM

PROBLEM

RESULTS

FISHBONE CAUSE & EFFECT DIAGRAM

© 1995 PT Publications, Inc.

Chapter Nineteen

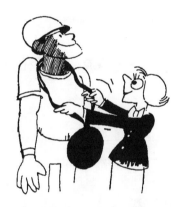

Measurements

Chapter Nineteen Contents

How to Use the Tools in this Chapter

Most of the tools in this chapter show an example of the tool in use and a blank form for you to fill out. Use the samples as a guide. Adapt to the conditions in your company.

The first three tools in this chapter (Parts on Shortage List, Purchase Order Changes, and Lead Time Requested) all work in the same manner. They can be used to identify those areas within each sector which need the most attention and which will have the greatest effect on keeping the Continuous Improvement Process moving forward. Using these tools begins with the collection of the data shown in each pie graph or any data which is more appropriate to your organization. Much of this information is already available in most companies. Take the data and compute the percentages and then display the percentages as a pie chart in the blank form we have provided. The visual display of data helps educate both senior management and the work force about what needs to be done. Teams can then direct their focus on the area with the most payback.

The second set of tools (Past Due Percentage — Purchase Orders, Past Due Percentage — Purchase Requisitions, and Change Orders) are used to identify trends in the area being measured. Like the tools described above, you begin by collecting information. If the information is not readily available, this is your opportunity to begin its collection. The data is then represented as a bar graph which displays the progress made by the organization in each area. We have found tools such as these to be effective ways of instilling team spirit as everybody tries to improve upon this month's "score."

Quality Yields is a very important tool because it can help you pinpoint the precise areas where the operation is failing to produce 100% quality. With this tool, you record quality yields and defect percentages by discrepancy type on a regular basis. The sample chart readily shows where the major problems are and, when the tool is used over a period of time, it shows the rates of improvement for each discrepancy. Again, this tool shows where you are and where you are headed.

How to Use the Tools

How to Use the Tools in this Chapter (continued)

The next three tools (On-Time Delivery Performance, Count Accuracy Performance, and Supplier Quality Rating) are used to measure individual suppliers. Performance measurements are collected for each month and charted as either a line or bar graph. The Supplier Quality Rating tool is a good overall indicator of a supplier's performance.

The next tool (Reject Rate) is used to measure both how well an individual supplier meets a target and how one supplier measures up against others. In our sample, we have shown how three suppliers have fared over three quarters. The chart provides you with a snapshot view of which company is improving by the greatest amount and which company has come closest to meeting or beating the target. For example, Supplier B in our example has improved the most, but Supplier C still has the best scores. This tool is used by the Supply Management team to evaluate which supplier deserves to become a partner.

The last tool (Material Cost Goals) is an internal measurement of your company's progress toward generating savings. It also demonstrates whether or not you were able to beat the projected budget for each commodity. This tool shows how well all the efforts at cost reduction and waste elimination have progressed.

Major Reasons For Parts On Shortage List

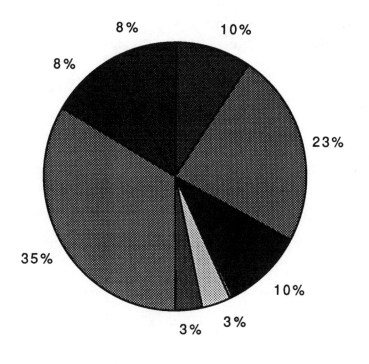

8%   10%

8%

23%

35%

3%   3%   10%

■	In House Builds Qty 14
▨	Spares, Unplanned Sales Orders Qty 34
■	Supplier Delinquent Qty 15
▫	Insufficient Lead Time Qty 5
▨	Unplanned Usage Qty 5
▨	Other Qty 49
■	Lost Stock Qty 3
■	Pulled Ahead Of Schedule Qty 12

19-6

Major Reasons For Parts On Shortage List

Complete this pie chart with the percentages of the following items:

_____%　　　In house builds
_____%　　　Pulled ahead of schedule
_____%　　　Lost Stock
_____%　　　Other
_____%　　　Spares, Unplanned Sales Orders
_____%　　　Supplier Delinquent
_____%　　　Insuffcient Lead Time
_____%　　　Unplanned Usage

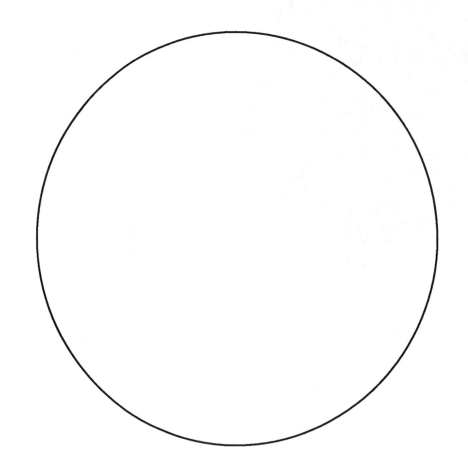

Major Reasons For
Purchase Order Changes

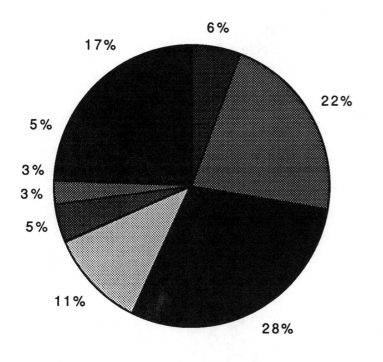

■	Revise Changes Qty 49
▨	Cancel Qty Qty 177
■	Add Qty Qty 238
░	Change Header Data Qty 92
■	Price Increase Qty 36
▨	Price Decrease Qty 22
■	Wrong P/N Received Qty 22
■	Revise Due Dates Qty 42
■	Reject Replacement Qty 135

Major Reasons For
Purchase Order Changes

Complete this pie chart with the percentages of the following items:

_____%   Reject Replacements
_____%   Revise Changes
_____%   Cancel
_____%   Add Qty
_____%   Change Header Data
_____%   Price Increase
_____%   Price Decrease
_____%   Wrong P/N Recieved
_____%   Revise Due Date

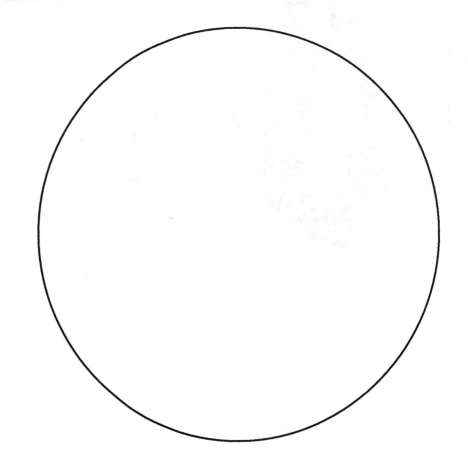

Lead-Time Requested
On Purchase Requisitions

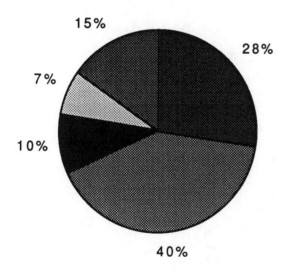

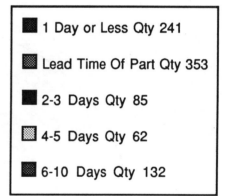

■ 1 Day or Less Qty 241

▦ Lead Time Of Part Qty 353

■ 2-3 Days Qty 85

□ 4-5 Days Qty 62

■ 6-10 Days Qty 132

Lead Time Requested

Lead-Time Requested
On Purchase Requisitions

Complete this pie chart with the percentages of the following items:

_____%	1 Day or Less
_____%	Lead-Time of Part
_____%	2-3 Days
_____%	4-5 Days
_____%	6-10 Days

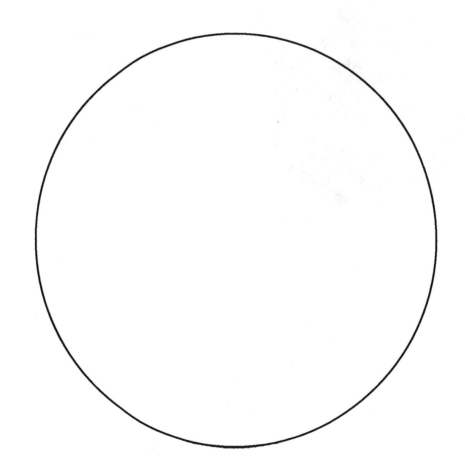

Past Due % Of
Open Purchase Orders

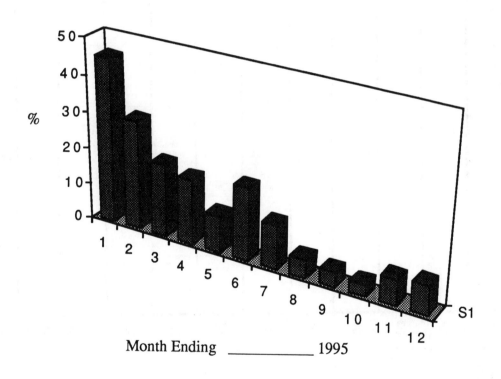

19-12

Past Due — Purchase Orders

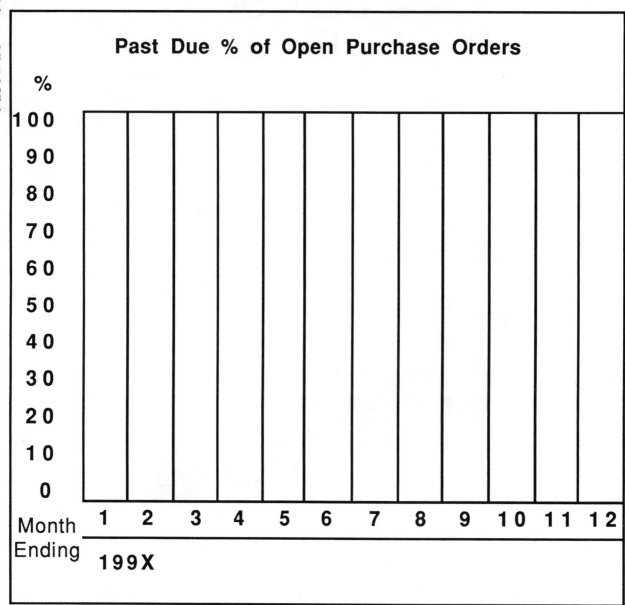

Past Due % of Open Purchase Orders

%

100
90
80
70
60
50
40
30
20
10
0

Month Ending

1 2 3 4 5 6 7 8 9 10 11 12

199X

Past Due % Of Open Purchase Requisitions

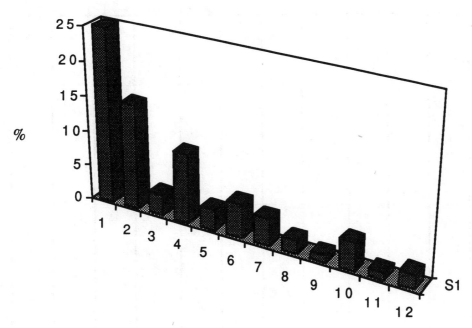

Month Ending _____ 1995

Past Due — Purchase Requisitions

Past Due % of Open Purchase Requisitions

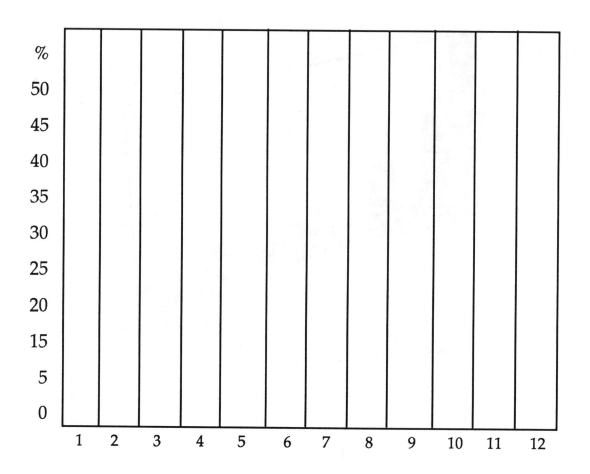

Month Ending 199X

Purchase Change Orders Written

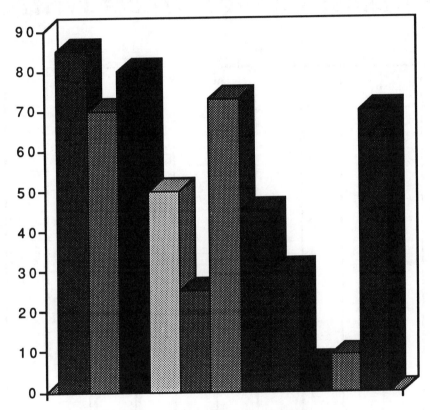

Month Ending 1995

Purchase Change Orders

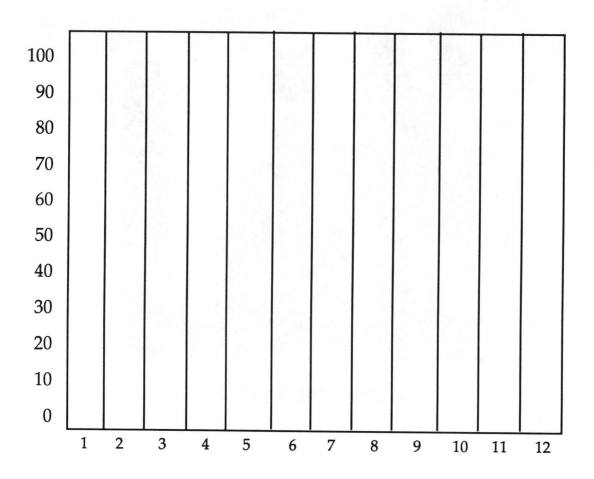

Purchase Change Orders Written

100
90
80
70
60
50
40
30
20
10
0

1 2 3 4 5 6 7 8 9 10 11 12

Month Ending 199X

QUALITY YIELDS AND PERCENT DEFECTIVES BY DISCREPANCY TYPE

Part #	Supplier			Machine						Dept.			
Week	1	2	3	4	5	6	7	8	9	10	11	12	13
Total Quantity	197	391	627	569	325	490	360	675	381	0	0	0	0
Quantity Rejected	30	45	43	62	52	36	31	37	27	0	0	0	0
Total Percent Accepted	84.8	88.5	93.1	89.1	84.0	92.7	91.4	94.5	92.9	NA	NA	NA	NA
Construction	23.3	19.6	15.9	34.8	28.3	22.2	6.5	21.6	11.1	0.0	0.0	0.0	0.0
Workmanship	30.0	17.4	54.5	42.4	54.7	33.3	19.4	32.4	55.6	0.0	0.0	0.0	0.0
Operate	3.3	32.6	0.0	1.5	3.8	11.1	19.4	5.4	0.0	0.0	0.0	0.0	0.0
Comp Fail 1	13.3	4.3	13.6	4.5	7.5	14.8	19.4	8.1	0.0	0.0	0.0	0.0	0.0
Comp Fail 2	10.0	13.0	9.1	0.0	3.8	3.7	3.2	10.8	14.8	0.0	0.0	0.0	0.0
Comp Fail 3	0.0	2.2	0.0	3.0	1.9	3.7	9.7	8.1	14.8	0.0	0.0	0.0	0.0
Comp Fail 4	6.7	10.9	4.5	12.1	0.0	11.1	19.4	10.8	3.7	0.0	0.0	0.0	0.0
Comp Fail 5	13.3	0.0	2.3	1.5	0.0	0.0	3.2	2.7	0.0	0.0	0.0	0.0	0.0

Quality Yields

QUALITY YIELDS AND PERCENT DEFECTIVES BY DISCREPANCY TYPE

Part #	Supplier					Machine				Dept.			
Week	1	2	3	4	5	6	7	8	9	10	11	12	13
Total Quantity													
Quantity Rejected													
Total Percent Accepted													
Construction													
Workmanship													
Operate													
Comp Fail 1													
Comp Fail 2													
Comp Fail 3													
Comp Fail 4													
Comp Fail 5													

On-Time Delivery Performance

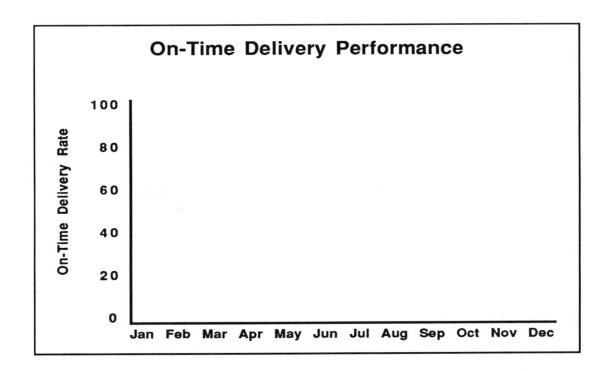

On-Time Delivery Performance

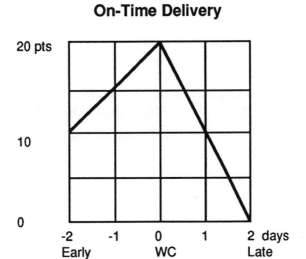

On-Time Delivery

Count Accuracy Performance

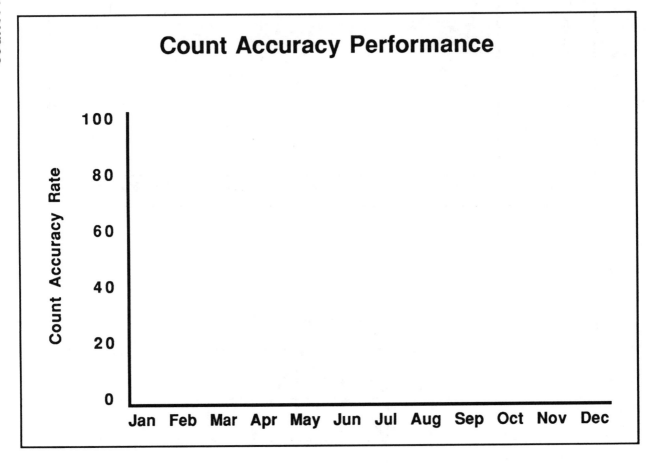

Count Accuracy Performance

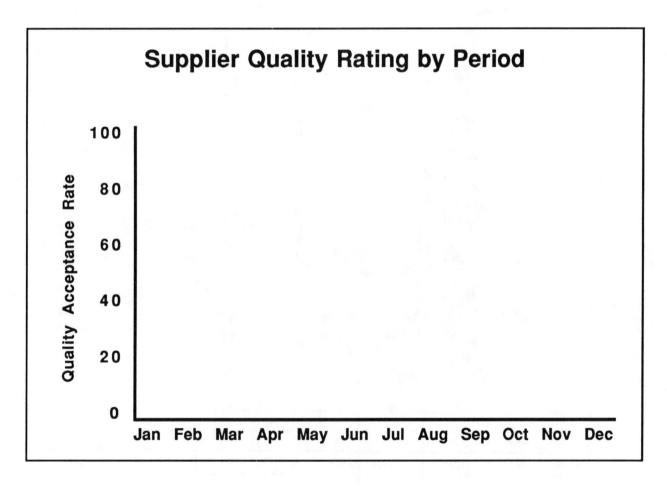

Reject Rate

Reject Rate By Quarter

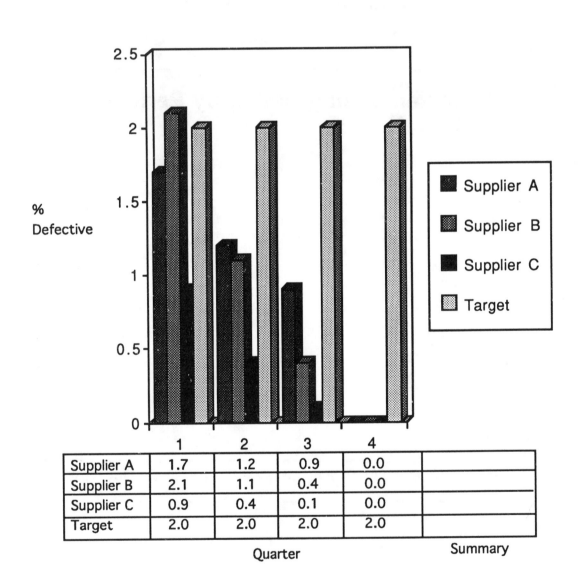

% Defective

	1	2	3	4	
Supplier A	1.7	1.2	0.9	0.0	
Supplier B	2.1	1.1	0.4	0.0	
Supplier C	0.9	0.4	0.1	0.0	
Target	2.0	2.0	2.0	2.0	

Quarter   Summary

Legend:
- Supplier A
- Supplier B
- Supplier C
- Target

Reject Rate By Quarter

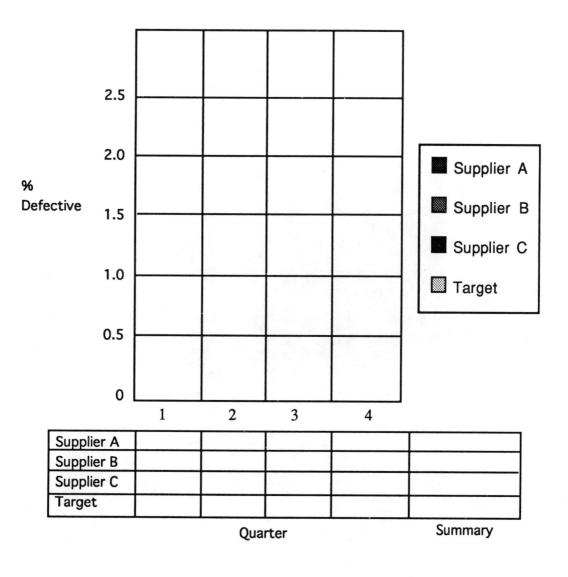

	1	2	3	4	Summary
Supplier A					
Supplier B					
Supplier C					
Target					

Quarter

Supply Management

Group: _____   Commodity: _____

Material Cost Goals (Savings)

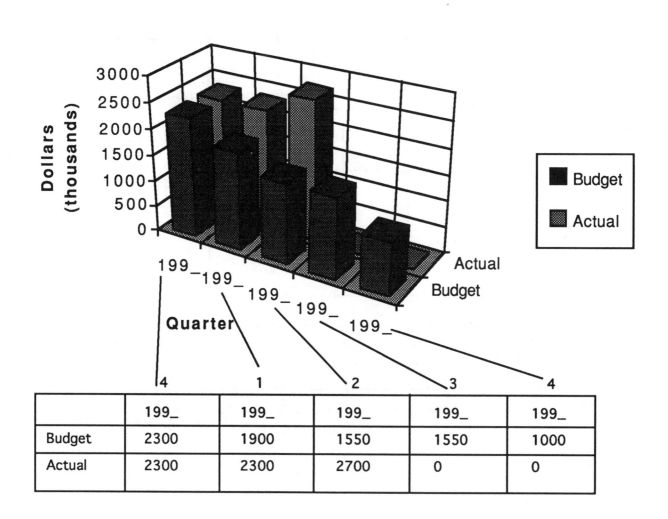

	199_	199_	199_	199_	199_
Budget	2300	1900	1550	1550	1000
Actual	2300	2300	2700	0	0

Supply Management
Group: _____ *Commodity:* _____

Material Cost Goals (Savings)

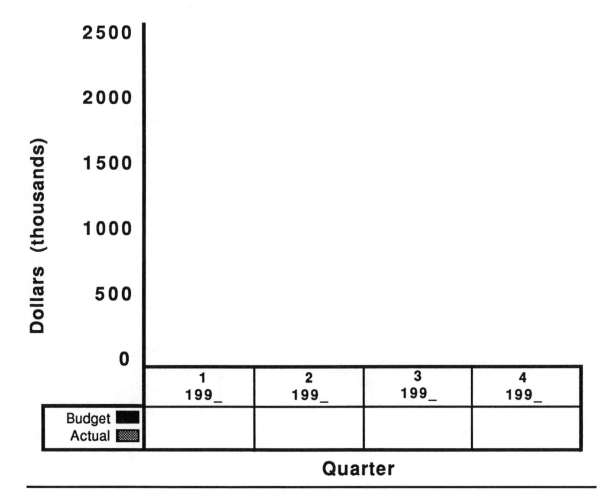

Chapter Twenty

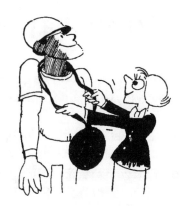

Generic
Company
Newsletter

How to Use the Tool in this Chapter

The generic newsletter that we have included on Pages 3–5 in this chapter should be used as a guideline. We have found, however, that the following combination works well:

- News items about what is happening in your organization, at one of your suppliers, or in the world at large as it directly applies to your company and your people. See the first page of our sample.

- A detailed report on one facet of your program which shows how the task was completed and the results. See the second page of our sample.

- Examples of tools which can be used by other members of your organization to help them do their job better. See the third page of our example.

- "Cheerleading" material which is designed to show your people that they are valued members of the team. See the third page of our sample.

SUPPLY MANAGEMENT *ToolBox*

n e w s l e t t e r

Volume 1 No. 1   "A Tool for Continuous Improvement"   ABC Company, Inc.

Generic Newsletter

ABC Names First Certified Supplier

All of the work of our Supplier Certification program paid off last week when XYZ Supply Company was designated a Certified Supplier. The XYZ Supply Company is the first firm to receive this award, but not the last.

Mary Nelson, the president of XYZ, was on hand to receive a plaque and certificate.

"We are delighted that ABC sees us as a partner and not an adversary," said Nelson in her acceptance speech. "I truly believe that we can profit more together than apart."

Our own president, Mark Warner, said that he was impressed with the speed with which the teams from both companies finished the certification process.

Pro-Tech Brings New Ideas

Peter Grieco and his international management consulting firm have been highly visible throughout the ABC Company during the past few months. They are not the type of consultants who spend all day in boardrooms.

You can see them down on the factory floor and in our offices, discussing problems with supervisors, secretaries, set-up people, and anybody else who has an idea for continuous improvement.

"There are no problems," Pete says, "only opportunities to improve."

"If this is an indication of the future, we are in good shape," he said.

Kevin Fremont who heads the Supplier Certification team said that his team will be making a number of awards in the coming months. There are five more companies on the verge of becoming Certified Suppliers.

"I'm busy," Fremont said, "but I'm happy that we are ensuring the survival of our company."

One of Pro-Tech's first actions was to begin educating all of us here at ABC in the theories and applications of Supply Management. That meant classes for executives, middle management, supervisors and for all of the people who build and sell our products and services.

"If you want to be World Class," Pete says, "everybody in the company must be knowledgeable about reducing waste. This isn't just a management program. This is a company-wide commitment to excellence. Everybody must be a part of the effort."

Index

• **Material Flow**
• **Process Flow Tool**
• **What is CERTain?**

ABC *Goes Into The Zone*

Kevin Fremont says that going into this zone feels better than scoring the winning touchdown in our annual touch football Super Bowl.

"This touchdown is for everybody," Fremont explains. "Everybody in the company will benefit from this new manufacturing layout."

Pete Grieco of Pro-Tech was instrumental in helping ABC Company understand and then implement the Zone Manufacturing concept.

Like all of Pro-Tech's endeavors, this one began with Pete helping Kevin form a Zone team.

A Zone team is an independent, self-managed team comprised of representatives from various departments whose activities affect or are affected by the manufacturing processes in the Zone.

The primary purpose of the team is to achieve conformance to requirements for all customer/supplier relationships. As you can see from the diagram above, that was a difficult task when the relationships were so convoluted.

Look at how much simpler the new flow is. Material never goes backward or even sideways. Each successive operation is only responsible to the one immediately behind or in front of it.

The next step is to take the lessons learned from implementing this prototype and

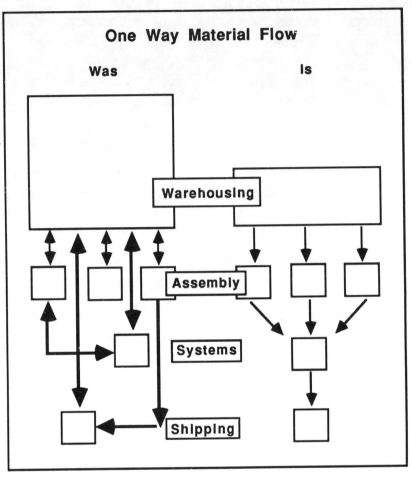

One Way Material Flow

Was   Is

Warehousing

Assembly

Systems

Shipping

What a difference an idea can make!

apply it to other areas.

"We will use the lessons we learned here to address the issues, dynamics and concerns of the next area," says Kevin Fremont.

Overall, the mission is to create Zones throughout the company. These Zones would operate as internal suppliers and customers. Pete Grieco explains that autonomous Zones are better able to manage the activities within their own segment of the company's operations.

What is most important is the fact that they are able to identify the real problems which have halted continuous improvement in the past.

Problems now truly become opportunities as the personnel in a Zone concentrate all their efforts on assessing and eliminating the wasteful activity.

"We are now in a better position to attain the continuous improvement we are all striving for," Kevin says in conclusion.

Generic Newsletter

A *Tool From The Tool Box*

QUESTION EACH DETAIL	Analysis Why? Where When What How

SUMMARY	Present # Time	Proposed # Time	Diff # Time
◯ Operation			
⇨ Transport			
☐ Inspection			
D Delay			
▽ Storage			
	Ft.	Ft.	Ft.

Job _____

Person Or Material _____
Chart begins _____
Chart ends _____
Charted by _____
Date _____

Details of Present or Proposed Method	Operation	Transport	Inspection	Delay	Storage	Distance	Quantity	Time	Eliminate	Combine	Sequence	Place	Person	Improve	Notes

The CERTain TEAM

What is CERTain?

- A responsibility to continuously reduce waste.
- A team approach to solving problems.
- An opportunity to improve.
- A forum for sharing your ideas and concerns.
- A time for all of us to take the initiative in the process to become World Class.

CERTIFICATION

action
is
now

FIRST

The

Glossary Of Purchasing Terms

KEY PURCHASING TERMS

KEY PURCHASING TERMS

ABC CLASSIFICATION — Stratification of Inventory items in decreasing order of annual dollar volume. This array is then split into three classes, called A, B, and C. Class A contains the items with the highest annual dollar volume and receives the most attention. The medium class B receives less attention, and class C, which contains the low dollar volume items, is controlled routinely.

ACKNOWLEDGMENT — A communication by a supplier to advise a purchaser that a purchase order has been received. It usually implies acceptance of the order by the supplier.

ACTION MESSAGE — An output of an MRP system that identifies the need for and the type of action to be taken to correct a current or potential material coverage problem.

ACTIVE INVENTORY — Covers raw material, work-in-process, and finished products which will be used or sold within the budgeted period without extra cost or loss.

ACTIVITY BASED COSTING (ABC) — A system for searching out cost drivers and assigning them directly to products and services. Frequently used to drive improvement efforts by monitoring and controlling activities in order to bring true costs into the open.

ACTUAL COSTS — Those labor and material costs which are charged to a job as it moves through the production process.

AGGREGATE FORECAST — An estimate of sales for some grouping of products; perhaps for all products produced by some manufacturing facility.

AGGREGATE INVENTORY — The sum of the inventory levels for individual items. For example, the aggregate finished goods inventory would be made up of one half the sum of all the lot sizes plus the sum of all of the safety stocks plus anticipated inventory plus transportation inventory.

ANNUALIZED CONTRACTS — A method of acquiring materials which helps ensure continuous supply of material, minimizes forward commitments, and provides the supplier with estimated future requirements.

APPRAISAL COSTS — Costs associated with ensuring that products conform to requirements. Activities in this area are typical of traditional quality methods and include testing, inspection and material review boards.

ARRIVAL DATE — The date purchased material is due to arrive at the receiving site. Arrival date can be input; can be equal to the current due date; or can be calculated from ship date plus transit time. Syn: expected receipt date.

ASSEMBLY — A group of subassemblies and/or parts which are put together: the total unit constitutes a major consolidation of the final product. An assembly may be an end item or a component of a higher level assembly. SEE: component, subassembly

AUDIT — A process to determine whether a supplier's quality and manufacturing processes are under control. Audits are also used as a method to improve a supplier's performance by pointing out weaknesses.

AVAILABLE MATERIAL — A term usually interpreted to mean "material available for planning" and thus including not only the on hand inventory, but also inventory on order. Material "available to promise" would, of course, be only the material on hand which has not been assigned.

AVAILABLE INVENTORY — In a simple inventory system, this is the sum of one-half the lot sizes plus the reserve stock in formula calculations.

BACKLOG — All of the customer orders booked, i.e., received but not yet shipped. Sometimes referred to as "open orders."

BACK ORDER — An unfilled customer order or commitment. It is an immediate (or past due) demand against an item whose inventory is insufficient to satisfy the demand.

BENCHMARKING — A strategic and managerial tool for identifying and emulating those companies who excel in a particular business area. Benchmarking is a continuous process whereby a company adopts the best-in-class practices of World Class companies.

BID — A price, whether for payment or acceptance. A quotation specifically given to a prospective purchaser upon their request, usually in competition with other suppliers.

BID ANALYSIS — Analysis of the provisions of a bid, usually for the purpose of comparing the strengths and weaknesses of the various bids received.

BILL OF LADING (UNIFORM) — A carrier's contract and receipt for goods which it agrees to transport from one place to another and to deliver to a designated person or assigns for compensation and upon such conditions as are stated therein.

BILL OF MATERIAL — A listing of all the subassemblies, parts and raw materials that go into a parent assembly showing the quantity of each required to make an assembly. There are a variety of formats for bills of material, including Single Level bill of material, Indented bill of material. Modular (Planning), Costed bill of material, etc.

BLANKET ORDER — A term commitment (usually one year or more) to a supplier for certain goods or services over a predetermined period of time at predetermined prices, most-favored customer prices, or prices to be revised due to market or other conditions. This practice is aimed at reducing the number of small orders, utilizing short-term releases to satisfy demand requirements.

BOOK INVENTORY — An accounting definition of inventory units or value obtained from perpetual inventory records rather than by actual count.

BREAK EVEN POINT — Point at which cost of goods sold equals sales.

BUDGET — The financial expression of objectives. The budget includes total cash flow income and outflow.

BUYER — An individual whose functions include supplier selection and development, negotiation, order placement, supplier follow-up, measurement and control of supplier performance, value analysis, evaluation of new materials and processes, etc.

BUYER CODE — A code used to identify the purchasing person responsible for a given item and/or purchase order.

BUYER'S MARKET — A "buyer's market" is considered to exist when goods are readily available and when the economic forces of business tend to cause goods to be priced at the purchaser's estimate of value.

BUYER/PLANNER — A functional title given to an individual whose duties combine the production planning and procurement function into a single position, called the buyer/ planner, who is in charge of a specific line of inventory. The concept is based on the idea that the same person should have the authority and responsibility for both the production planning and the purchasing decisions for specified items.

CANCELLATION CHARGES — A fee charged by a seller to cover the costs associated with a customer's cancellation of an order. If the seller has started any engineering work, purchased raw materials, or started any manufacturing operations, these changes would be included in the cancellation charge.

CAPACITY—It is a separate concept from priority. The highest sustainable output rate which can be achieved with the current product specifications, product mix, work force, plant and equipment.

CARRYING COST — The cost of carrying inventory is usually expressed as a percent. It represents the cost of capital invested, and costs of maintaining the inventory such as, taxes, and insurance, obsolescence, spoilage, and space occupied. Such costs vary from 35% or more annually, depending on type of industry.

CHANGE ORDER — A formal notification that a purchase order or shop order has changed.

COMMODITY BIDDING—Grouping like parts or materials under one grouping. It may be used to control buyer's items.

COMPETITIVE BIDDING — A common method of source selection; the offer of prices and specified elements of performance by firms competing for a contract. In industrial purchasing, preliminary bids are sometimes solicited with the stated intention of selecting those firms with whom negotiations will be conducted subsequently to arrive at a final sourcing decision.

COMPONENT — An inclusive term used to identify a raw material, ingredient, part or subassembly that goes into a higher level assembly, compound, or other item.

CONCURRENT ENGINEERING — An environment in which all functional disciplines contribute to the design, development, production, distribution and sale of a product or service. The company performs these activities concurrently and cooperatively instead of sequentially.

CONFIDENTIALITY AGREEMENT — An agreement between a company and a supplier which establishes the rights and obligations of both parties with respect to proprietary interests and data.

CONFIRMING ORDER — A purchase order issued to a supplier, listing the goods or services and terms of an order placed verbally, or otherwise, in advance of the issuance of the formal purchase document.

CONSIGNED STOCKS — Inventories which are in the possession of customers, dealers, agents, etc., but remain the property of the manufacturer by agreement.

CONTINUOUS IMPROVEMENT PROCESS — A process whereby a company uses and problem solving techniques to create a feedback cycle which eliminates waste.

CONTRACT—An agreement between two or more competent persons to perform a specific act or acts. A contract may be verbal or written. A purchase order, when accepted by a supplier, becomes a contract. Acceptance may be in writing or by performance.

CONTRACT DATE — The date when a contract is accepted by all parties.

CORRELATION — The relationship between two sets of numbers, such as between two quantities such that when one changes, the other is likely to make a corresponding change. If the changes are in the same direction, there is a positive correlation. When changes tend to go in opposite directions, there is negative correlation.

COST ANALYSIS — A review and an evaluation of actual or anticipated cost data (material, labor, overhead, G&A). This analysis involves applying experience, knowledge, and judgment to date in an attempt to project reasonable estimated contract costs. Estimated costs serve as the basis for buyer-seller negotiation which will arrive at mutually agreeable contract prices.

COST CENTER—The smallest segment of an organization for which costs are collected, such as the lathe department. The criteria in defining cost centers are that the cost be significant

Purchasing Terms

and the area of responsibility be clearly defined.

COST FACTORS — The units of input which represent costs to the manufacturing system, for example: labor hours, purchased material.

COST-PLUS — A pricing method whereby the purchaser agrees to pay the supplier an amount determined by the costs incurred by the supplier to produce the goods and/or services purchased plus a stated percentage or fixed sum.

COST REDUCTION — The act of lowering the cost of goods or services by identifying and eliminating non-value added cost/price or waste.

CURRENT PRICE — The price currently being paid.

CYCLE TIME MANAGEMENT (CTM) — The integration of all the activities of an organization from customer need to customer satisfaction under one operating philosophy which seeks to build better products or provide better services faster than its competitors.

DEBIT MEMO — Document used to authorize the shipment of rejected material back to the supplier and create a debit entry in accounts payable.

DELINQUENT ORDER — A line item on the customer open order which has an original schedule ship date prior to the current date.

DELIVERY CYCLE — The actual time from the receipt of the customer order to time of the shipment of the product.

DELIVERY SCHEDULE — The required or agreed time or rate of delivery of goods or services purchased for future period.

DEMAND — A need for a particular product or component. The demand could come from any number of sources, i.e., customer order, forecast, interplant, branch warehouse, service part, or to manufacturing the next higher level.

DEPENDENT DEMAND — Demand is considered dependent when it is directly related to or derived from the demand for other items or end products.

DEPRECIATION — An allocation of the original value of an asset against current income represent the declining value of the asset as a cost of that time period.

DESIGN FOR PRODUCIBILITY (DFP) — A process whereby quality is designed into the product and the process at the same time, thus guaranteeing that the product is producible and conforms to customer requirements.

DETAILED SCHEDULING — The actual assignment of target starting and/or completion dates to operations or groups of operations to show when these must be done if the manufacturing order is to be completed on time. These dates are used in the dispatching operation.

DIRECT COSTS — Variable costs which can be directly attributed to a particular job or operation.

DIRECT SHIPMENT — The consignment of goods directly from the supplier to the buyer. Frequently used where a third party (distributor) acts as intermediary agent between supplier and buyer.

DISCOUNT — An allowance or deduction granted by the seller to the buyer, usually when certain stipulated conditions are met by the buyer, which reduces the cost of the goods purchased.

DISTRIBUTOR — A business that does not manufacture its own products but purchases and resells these products usually maintaining an inventory of miscellaneous products.

DOCK-TO-STOCK — That part of purchased goods and material that skips incoming inspection and goes directly into inventory after delivery.

DROP SHIPMENT — A distribution arrangement in which the seller serves as a selling agent by collecting orders but does not maintain inventory. The orders are sent to the manufacturer which ships directly to the customer.

DUE DATE — The date at which purchased material or production on order is due to be available for use.

DUTY — A tax levied by a government on the importation, exportation, or use and consumption of goods.

EARLY SUPPLIER INVOLVEMENT (ESI) — A practice that involves one or more selected suppliers with a buyer's product design team early in the specification development process. The objective is to use the supplier's expertise and experience in developing a product specification designed for effective and efficient manufacturability.

ECONOMIC ORDER QUANTITY (EOQ) — Determines amount of product to be purchased or manufactured at one time in order to minimize total cost involved, including ordering costs (set-up of machines, writing orders, checking receipts, etc.) and carrying costs (costs of capital invested, insurance, taxes, space, obsolescence, and spoilage).

ELECTRONIC DATA INTERCHANGE (EDI) — The direct computer-to-computer exchange of business information in a standard format. Transaction documents, such as purchase orders, invoices, and shipping notices, are transmitted electronically and entered directly into a supplier's (or buyer's) computer or into a third-party network for processing.

ENGINEERING CHANGE — A revision to a parts list, bill of materials or drawings. Changes are usually identified by a control number and are made for "Safety," "Cost Reduction," or "Functionality" reasons. In order to effectively implement engineering changes, all affected functions such as Materials, Quality, Assurance, Assembly Engineering, etc., should review and agree to the changes.

ENGINEERING DRAWINGS — A blueprint that visually presents the dimensional characteristics of a part or assembly at some stage of manufacture.

ESCALATION — An amount or percent by which a contract price may be adjusted if specified contingencies occur, such as changes in supplier's raw material or labor costs.

EXPEDITING — The "Prioritization" or "Tracing" of production or purchase orders which are needed in less than the normal lead time.

EXPEDITOR — A person whose primary duties are expediting.

EXPLOSION — An extension of a bill of material into the total of each of the components required to manufacture a given quantity of upper-level assembly or subassembly.

FABRICATION — A term used to distinguish manufacturing from assembly operations.

FAILURE COSTS — Costs associated with ensuring that products conform to requirements. Activities in this area are typical of traditional quality methods and include scrap, rework, change orders, service and corrective action.

FAIR MARKET VALUE — The value of an item as determined by negotiation between purchasers and suppliers, which would be acceptable as a basis for a purchase and sale.

FAR (FEDERAL ACQUISITION REGULATION) — The acquisition uniform policy and procedure used by executive agencies of the federal government. FAR regulations are issued and maintained by the Department of Defense. FAR supersedes DAR (Defense Acquisition Regulation).

FINISHED GOODS INVENTORIES — Inventories on which all manufacturing operations, including final test, have been completed. These may be either finished parts, like replacement parts, or finished products which have been authorized for transfer to the finished stock account. These products are now available for shipment to the customer either as end items or replacement parts.

FISHBONE DIAGRAM — A brainstorming tool which shows causes and effects. The intent of this tool is to identify a problem and its possible causes and then to note the progress being made to eliminate those causes.

FOB (FREE ON BOARD) — The term means the seller is required to place goods aboard equipment of the transporting carrier without cost to buyer. The term "F.O.B." must be qualified by a name of location, such as shipping point, destination, name of a city, mill, warehouse, etc. The stated f.o.b. point is usually the location where title to the goods passes from the seller to the buyer. The seller is liable for transportation charges and the risks of loss to the goods up to the point where title passes to the buyer.

FORECAST — A forecast is the extrapolation of the past into the future. It is an objective computation involving data as opposed to a prediction or subjective estimate incorporating management's anticipation of changes.

FUTURES — Contracts for sale and delivery of commodities at a future time, made with the intention that no commodity be delivered or received immediately.

GROSS REQUIREMENTS — The total of independent and dependent demand for a component or an assembly prior to the netting of inventory and scheduled receipts.

HANDLING COST — The cost involved in handling materials.

INACTIVE INVENTORY — Designates the stocks that are in excess of contemplated consumption within planning period (typically 12-18 months).

INDIRECT COSTS — Costs which are not directly incurred by a particular job or operation.

INDIRECT LABOR — Workers required to support production without being related to a specific product or assembly line.

INDIRECT MATERIALS — Materials which become part of the final product but are used in such small quantities that their cost is not applied directly to the product. Instead the cost becomes part of manufacturing supplies or overhead costs.

INTEGRATED SUPPLY — A special type of partnering arrangement usually developed between a purchaser and a distributor on an intermediate to long-term basis. The objective of an integrated supply relationship is to minimize, for both buyer and supplier, the labor and expense involved in acquisition and possession of MRO products — items that are repetitive, generic, high-transaction, and have a low unit cost.

INVENTORY — Items which are in a stocking location or work-in-process location. Inventories usually consist of finished goods, work-in-process, purchased materials.

INVENTORY CONTROL — The activities and techniques of maintaining the stock of items at desired levels, whether they be raw materials, work-in-process, or finished goods.

INVENTORY INVESTMENT — The total cost of all inventory.

INVENTORY POLICY — A statement of philosophy which directs the management of inventory upon which procedures will be established.

INVENTORY SHRINKAGE — Losses resulting from scrap, deterioration, pilferage, etc.

INVENTORY TURNOVER — The number of times that the inventory dollar value is consumed by cost of goods sold during the year. The way to compute inventory turnover is to divide the cost of goods sold by the average inventory value.

INVENTORY USAGE — The amount of inventory used or consumed over a period of time.

INVENTORY VALUATION — The value of the inventory which can be calculated at either its cost or its market value. Because inventory value can change with time, some recognition must be taken of the age distribution of inventory. Therefore, the cost value of inventory, under accounting practice, is usually computed on a first-in-first-out (FIFO), last-in-first-out (LIFO) basis.

INVENTORY WRITE-OFF — A deduction of inventory dollars from the financial statement because the inventory is no longer saleable or because of shrinkage.

ISO 9000 — A comprehensive set of process and procedure quality management standards developed by the International Standards Organization. Suppliers selling to firms that have adopted the ISO 9000 standard must produce products using processes and methodologies that use quality management standards specified by ISO 9000.

ISSUE CYCLE — The time required to complete the cycle of material issues. It includes generating a requisition, pulling the material from an inventory location and moving it to its destination.

ITEM — Any unique manufactured or purchased part or assembly, such as, finished product, assembly, subassembly, component, or raw material.

ITEM MASTER FILE — A computer file that contains identifying and descriptive data, control values and data on inventory status, requirements and planned orders. There is normally one record in this file for each stock keeping unit.

JUST-IN-TIME (JIT) SYSTEM — The basic JIT concept is an operation management philosophy whose dual objectives are to reduce waste and to increase production. Operationally, JIT minimizes inventory at all levels; materials are purchased, transported, and processed "just in time" for their use in a subsequent stage of the manufacturing process.

KANBAN SYSTEM — A system of production flow control that utilizes Kanban cards to "pull" in-process inventories through a manufacturing process, where items are called for only as they are needed in the next step of the production process.

KIT — The components of an assembly which have been pulled from stock and readied for movement to the assembly area.

KITTING — The process of removing components of an assembly from the stockroom and sending them to the assembly floor as a kit of parts.

LABOR PRODUCTIVITY — The rate of output of a worker or group of workers, per unit of time, compared to an established standard or rate of output.

LEAD TIME — A period of time required to perform an activity such as the procurement of materials and/or the production of products from manufacturing facility.

LOAD — This is the amount of scheduled work ahead of a manufacturing facility, usually expressed in terms of hours of work units or production.

LOGISTICS — The process of planning, implementing, and controlling the efficient, cost-effective flow and storage of raw materials, in-process inventory, finished goods, and related information from point of origin to point of consumption for the purpose of conforming to customer requirements. (This definition was adopted in 1985 by the Council of Logistics Management.)

LOT NUMBER — A unique identification assigned to a quantity of material to be procured or manufactured.

LONG-TERM CONTRACTING — A decision to contract with a particular supplier over an extended period of time.

LOT SIZE — The quantity of goods purchased or produced in anticipation of demand.

Purchasing Terms

MAKE-OR-BUY— A determination of what products or services a firm should manufacture or provide in-house, as opposed to purchasing from outside sources.

MAKE-TO-ORDER PRODUCT—The end item is finished after receipt of a customer order. Frequently long lead time components are forecast prior to the order arriving in order to reduce the delivery time to the customer. Where options or other subassemblies are stocked prior to customer orders arriving, the term "assemble-to-order" is frequently used.

MAKE-TO-STOCK PRODUCT — The end item is manufactured to and shipped from finished goods, "off the shelf."

MANUFACTURING LEAD TIME — The total time required to manufacture an item. Included here are order preparation time, queue time, set-up time, run time, move time, inspection, etc.

MANUFACTURING ORDER—A document or group of documents conveying authority for the manufacture of specified parts or products in specified quantities.

MANUFACTURING PROCESS — The series of activities performed upon material to convert it from the raw or semifinished state to a state of further completion and of increased value.

MANUFACTURING RESOURCE PLANNING — A method for the effective planning of all resources of a manufacturing company. Ideally, it addresses operational planning in units, financial planning in dollars, and has a simulation capability to answer "what if" questions. It is made up of a variety of functions, each linked together: Business Planning, Production Planning, Master Production Scheduling, Material Requirements Planning, Capacity Requirements Planning and the execution systems for capacity and priority. Outputs from these systems are integrated with financial reports such as the business plan, purchase commitment report, shipping budget, inventory projections in dollars, etc. Manufacturing resource planning is a direct outgrowth and extension of MRP (Material Requirements Planning). Often referred to as MRP II (2).

MARKET SHARE — The actual portion of available customer demand that a company achieves.

MASTER FILE—A main reference file of information such as bills of material or routing files.

MASTER PRODUCTION SCHEDULE (MPS) — It represents what the company plans to produce expressed in specific configurations, quantities, and dates.

MATERIAL — Any commodity used directly or indirectly in producing a product, raw materials, component parts, subassemblies, supplies, etc.

MATERIALS MANAGEMENT—A term to describe the grouping of management functions related to the complete cycle of material flow, from the purchase and internal control of production materials to the planning and control of work-in-process to warehousing, shipping and distribution of the finished product.

MOVE TIME — See *TRANSIT TIME.*

MRO — Material, repairs and ordinary supplies.

NEGOTIATION—In the purchasing context, negotiation is an exploratory and a bargaining process (planning, reviewing, analyzing, compromising) involving a buyer and seller, each with their own viewpoints and objectives, seeking to reach a mutually satisfactory agreement on all phases of a procurement transaction — including price, service, specifications, technical and quality requirements, payment terms, etc.

NET CHANGE MRP — An approach in which the material requirements plan requires a change in requirements, open order or inventory status, or engineering usage. A partial explosion is made only for those parts affected by the change.

NET REQUIREMENTS — Requirements for a part or an assembly are derived as a result of netting gross requirements against inventory on hand and the scheduled receipts.

ON HAND — The balance shown in perpetual inventory records as being physically present at a stocking location.

ON ORDER — The stock on order is the quantity represented by the total of all outstanding replenishment orders. The on order balance increases when a new order is released, and it decreases when material is received to fill an order, or when an order is canceled.

ON-TIME DELIVERY — Delivery of material or product on time, 100% of the time. On-time is defined as a window in which both early and late deliveries are unacceptable.

ONE TOUCH CHANGEOVER (OTC) — A set-up reduction method which aims to reduce a changeover to one action with no setting, testing, resetting and retesting before a good part is made.

OPEN ORDER — The quantity of a purchase order, sales order or factory order yet to be satisfied.

OPTION — A choice or feature offered to customers for customizing the end product. The customer must select from one of the available choices.

ORDER POINT — When the inventory level of an item where stock on hand plus on order falls to or below the order point, action is taken to replenish the stock.

OUTSOURCING — A version of the make-or-buy decision in which a firm elects to purchase an item that previously was made in-house; commonly used for services.

OVERHEAD — Costs incurred in the operation of a business which cannot be directly related to the individual products or services produced.

OVERHEAD PERCENTAGE — The percentage applied to a labor cost to calculate the overhead cost of performing work in that work center.

OVER-RUN — The quantity received from manufacturing or a supplier that is in excess of the quantity ordered.

OVERTIME — Work beyond normal established working hours which usually requires that a premium be paid to the workers.

PACKING SLIP — A document which itemizes in detail the contents of a particular package or shipment.

PARETO'S LAW — A concept developed by Pareto, an Italian economist, that simply says that a small percentage of a group account for the largest fraction of the cost.

PART — Refers to an item which is used as a component, an assembly or subassembly.

PART NUMBER — A number which serves to uniquely identify a component, product, or raw material.

PARTIAL ORDER — Any shipment received or shipped which is less than the amount ordered.

PAST DUE — An order that has not been completed on time.

PIECE PARTS — Consists of individual items in inventory at the entry level in manufacturing. For example, bolts and washers.

PLANNED ORDER — A suggested order quantity and due date created by MRP processing, when it encounters net requirements. Planned orders are created by the computer; exist only within the computer; and may be changed or deleted by the computer during subsequent MRP processing if conditions change.

Purchasing Terms

PRE-EXPEDITING — The function of following up on open orders prior to the scheduled delivery date to ensure they will be delivered on time.

PREPAID — A term denoting that charges have been or are to be paid by the shipper.

PRESURVEY — A survey of a supplier which is used to determine whether they will continue in the Supplier Certification process.

PREVENTION COSTS — Costs associated with ensuring that products conform to requirements. Activities in this area are typical of Total Quality Management methods and include supplier qualification, process control, zero-defects and preventive maintenance.

PREVENTIVE MAINTENANCE — A program of maintenance which seeks through statistical methods to make routine repairs or maintenance before a breakdown occurs.

PRICE ANALYSIS — Price analysis is the examination of a supplier's price proposal (bid) by comparison with reasonable benchmarks, without examination and evaluation of the separate elements of cost and profit making up the price.

PRICE PREVAILING AT THE DATE OF SHIPMENT — An agreement between the purchaser and the supplier that the price of the goods ordered will be based on the price on the day of shipment.

PRICE PROTECTION — An agreement by a supplier with a customer to grant the purchaser a price which the supplier established should the price increase prior to shipment.

PRICE SCHEDULE — The list of prices applying to varying quantities or types of goods.

PRIME COSTS — Direct costs of material and labor; does not include general sales and administrative costs.

PRIORITY — In a general sense, refers to the relative importance of jobs, i.e., which jobs should be worked on and when.

PROCEDURE MANUAL — A formal organization and indexing of a firm's policies and practices.

PROCEDURES — Definitions of approved methods of operation.

PROCESS SHEET — Detailed manufacturing instructions issued to the shop. The instructions may include speeds, feeds, tools, fixtures, machines, and sketches of set-ups and semi-finished dimensions. (i.e. routing)

PROCESS TIME — The time during which the material is being changed, whether it is a machining operation or a hand assembly.

PROCUREMENT — This term has a broad and a narrow definition. The broad definition typically includes such duties as specifications development, value analysis, supplier market research, negotiation, buying activities, contract administration, and perhaps inventory control, traffic, receiving, and stores.

PROCUREMENT LEAD TIME — The time required by buyer to select a supplier, and to place and obtain a commitment for specific quantities of material at specified times.

PRODUCT — Any commodity produced for sale.

PRODUCT MIX — The combination of individual product types and the volume produced that make up the total production volume. Changes in the product mix can mean drastic changes in the manufacturing requirements for labor and material.

PRODUCT STRUCTURE — The way components go into a product during its manufacture. A typical product structure would show, for example, raw material being converted into fabricated components, components being put together to makes subassemblies, subassemblies going into assemblies, etc.

PRODUCTION CONTROL — The function of directing or regulating the movement of goods through the entire manufacturing cycle from the requisitioning of raw materials to the delivery of finished product.

PRODUCTION CYCLE — The lead time to produce product.

PRODUCTION MATERIAL — Any material used in the manufacturing process.

PRODUCTION RATES — The quantity of production usually expressed in units, hours. Expressed by a unit of time.

PRODUCTION REPORT — A formal, written statement giving information on the output of an organization for a specified period.

PRODUCTION SCHEDULE — A plan which authorizes the plant to manufacture a certain quantity of a specific item.

PROGRESS PAYMENTS — Payments arranged in connection with purchase transactions requiring period payments in advance of delivery.

PURCHASE ORDER — The purchaser's document used to formalize a purchase transaction with a supplier.

PURCHASE PART — A part purchased from a supplier.

PURCHASE PART VARIANCE (PPV) — The difference in price between what was paid to the supplier and the standard cost of that item.

PURCHASE REQUISITION — A document conveying authority to the procurement department to purchase specified materials in specified quantities within a specified time.

PURCHASING AGENT — The person authorized by the company to purchase goods and services for the company.

PURCHASING CAPACITY — The act of buying capacity or machine time from a supplier.

PURCHASING — One of the major business functions of an organization. The function typically is responsible for acquisition of required materials, services, and equipment used in the organization.

PURCHASING LEAD TIME — The total lead time required to obtain a purchased item. Included are procurement lead time, supplier lead time, transportation time, receiving, inspection and put away time.

QUANTITY DISCOUNT — An allowance determined by the quantity or dollar value of a purchase.

QUANTITY PER — The quantity of a component to be used in the production of its parent. Quantity per is used when calculating the gross requirements for production.

QUEUE TIME — The amount of time a job waits at a work center before set-up or work is performed on the job. Queue time is one element of total manufacturing lead time.

QUOTATION — A statement of price, terms of sale, and description of goods or services offered by a supplier to a prospective purchaser; a bid. When given in response to an inquiry, it is usually considered an offer to sell.

QUOTATION TO EXPIRE DATE — The date at which time quotation price is no longer valid.

RECEIVING — This function includes the physical receipt of material; the inspection of the shipment for conformance with the purchase order (quantity and damage); identification and delivery to destination; and preparing receiving reports.

RECEIVING POINT — Location to which material is being shipped.

RECEIVING REPORT — A form used by the receiving function of a company to inform all departments of the receipt of goods purchased.

REJECTED INVENTORY — Inventory which does not meet quality requirements but has not yet been sent to rework, scrapped, or returned to a vendor.

Purchasing Terms

REJECTION — The act of rejecting an item by the buyer's receiving inspection as not meeting the quality specification.

RELEASE — The authorization to produce or ship material which has already been ordered. (i.e. blanket order).

REPROMISE DATE — Revised delivery date obtained from the supplier which differs from the original contracts delivery date.

REQUEST FOR PROPOSAL (RFP) — A solicitation document used to obtain offers to be used either in a firm-bid purchasing process or in a negotiated purchasing process, as stipulated in the request.

REQUEST FOR QUOTATION (RFQ) — In the private sector, The RFQ usually is considered to be the same as the RFP. In some organizations, however, an RFQ is used to obtain approximate information for planning purposes. In such cases, this fact should be clearly stated in the request. In federal government purchasing, the RFQ is used only for the purpose of obtaining planning information.

RESCHEDULING — The process of changing order or operation due dates, usually as a result of their being out of phase process or customer requirements.

RETURN TO SUPPLIER — Material that has been dispositioned, rejected by the buyer's inspection department and is awaiting shipment back to the supplier for repair or replacement.

ROUTING — A document showing the sequence of operations to be followed in a company environment.

RUN TIME — The actual time a job is on a machine or process in manufacturing

SAFETY STOCK — A quantity of stock planned to be in inventory to protect against fluctuations in demand and/or supply.

SEMI-FINISHED GOODS — Products which have been stored uncompleted awaiting final operations.

SERVICE PARTS — Parts used for the repair and/or maintenance of an assembled product.

SET-UP COST — The costs incurred with changing over a machine.

SET-UP TIME — The time measured from the last good part to the first good part produced off the next manufacturing run.

SHIP-TO-WIP — Product shipped directly to work-in-process.

SHIPPING — Includes packaging, marking, weighing, routing, and loading materials for transportation from one location to another.

SHIPPING LEAD TIME — The number of working days normally required for goods in transit between a shipping and receiving point, plus acceptance time in days at the receiving point.

SHIPPING POINT — The location from which material is shipped.

SINGLE MINUTE EXCHANGE OF DIE (SMED) — A method of set-up reduction in which the amount of time is reduced to a single digit, that is, nine minutes or less.

SINGLE SOURCING — The practice of using one source, among others in a competitive marketplace which, for justifiable reasons, is found to be the most advantageous for the purpose of fulfilling a given purchasing need.

SIX SIGMA — A statistical term which designates the achievement of only 3.4 defective components for every 1,000,000 components produced.

SOLE SOURCING — The use of one source when that source is the only available firm possessing the ability to fulfill the purchasing firm's needs.

SPECIFICATION — A detailed description of a material, an item, or a service.

SPLIT DELIVERY — A method by which a larger quantity is ordered but delivery is spread out over several dates.

SPLIT LOT — A manufacturing order quantity that has been divided into smaller quantities.

SPREAD AND TARGET WORKSHEET — A statistical tool which provides a precise and quick overall picture of how a process is performing and analytical paths to pursue when problems do exist.

STANDARD COSTS — The normal expected cost of an operation, process, or product including labor, material, and overhead charges, computed on the basis of past performance costs, estimates, or work measurement.

STATISTICAL PROCESS CONTROL (SPC) — The collection of statistical data which is used to determine whether a process is in control, that is, performing within acceptable limits.

STOCK — Stored products or service parts ready for use.

STOCK STATUS — A report showing the inventory quantity on hand.

STOCKLESS PURCHASING — A general practice whereby the buyer negotiates a purchasing arrangement, including price, for a group of items for a predetermined time period, and the supplier holds the inventory until the buyer places orders for specific items. Blanket orders, open-end orders, and systems contracts can be used as stockless-purchasing techniques.

SUBASSEMBLY — A component or assembly which is used at a higher level to make up another assembly.

SUBCONTRACTING — The practice in which a prime contractor contracts with another party for performance of all or part of the prime contractor's work.

SUPPLIER — An organization that supplies goods and/or services to a purchasing organization.

SUPPLIER ALTERNATE — Other than the primary supplier. The alternate supplier may or may not supply a percentage of the items purchased, but is usually approved to supply the items.

SUPPLIER CERTIFICATION — A long-term commitment by a supplier to produce and deliver goods and services which conform to the customer's requirements 100% of the time. Supplier agrees to work with the customer to continuously improve its performance levels.

SUPPLIER DEVELOPMENT — A systematic organizational effort to create and maintain a network of competent suppliers, and to improve various supplier capabilities that are necessary for the purchasing organization to meet its increasing competitive challenges.

SUPPLIER EVALUATION — Objective analysis of either existing suppliers by evaluating past performance, or as a preliminary assessment of potential new suppliers. Suppliers typically are evaluated on the basis of their technical quality, delivery, service, cost, and managerial capabilities.

SUPPLIER LEAD TIME — The time that normally elapses between the time an order is placed with the supplier and shipment of the material.

SUPPLIER MEASUREMENT — The act of measuring the supplier's performance to the contract. Measurements usually cover delivery, quality, and total cost.

SUPPLIER NUMBER — Numerical code used to identify one supplier from another.

SUPPLIER PARTNERSHIP — A supplier partnership between a purchasing and a supplying firm involves a mutual commitment over an extended time horizon to work together

Purchasing Terms

to the mutual benefit of both parties in the relationship. These relationships require a clear understanding of expectations, open communication and information exchange, mutual trust, and a common direction for the future. Such relationships are a collaborative business activity that does not involve the formation of a legal partnership. The term, strategic alliance, is used by many firms to mean the same thing as a supplier partnership. In some firms, however, the term strategic alliance is used to describe a more inclusive relationship involving the planned and mutually advantageous joint utilization of additional operating resources of both firms.

SUPPLIER PERFORMANCE REPORT — A record of supplier quality, delivery, and service performance.

SUPPLIER RATING SYSTEM — A system used to evaluate and rate suppliers' performances, which generally involves quality, service, delivery, and price. Rating formulas vary depending upon the nature of the item being purchased, the quality required, and competition within the supplying industry.

SUPPLIER SELECTION — A process by which suppliers are evaluated according to a set of criteria to determine whether they are capable of entering a Supplier Certification process.

SUPPLIER STRATEGY — The tactics and strategy used by a company to identify and work with suppliers who will be able to attain World Class standards.

SUPPLIER SURVEY — A rigorous appraisal of a supplier's operations which includes site visits. The intent is to determine whether the supplier has its operations under control and if the supplier can enter into a partnership.

SUPPLY MANAGEMENT (SM) — A systems management concept employed by some organizations, designed to optimize the factors of material costs, quality, and service. This is accomplished by consolidating the following operating activities: purchasing, transportation, warehousing, quality assurance for incoming materials, inventory management, and internal distribution of materials. These activities normally are combined in a single department, similar to the arrangement under a material management form of organization.

TERMS AND CONDITIONS — A general term used to describe all of the provisions and agreements of a contract.

TOTAL COST — Sometimes called "all-in costs." In purchasing, total cost generally includes the price of the purchase and transportation cost, plus indirect handling, inspection, quality, rework, maintenance, incremental operations, and all other "follow-on" costs associated with the purchase.

TOTAL QUALITY CONTROL (TQC) — A process whereby a company commits itself to doing it right the first time, that is, it builds products or provides services in conformance to requirements.

TRANSIT TIME –– An allowance given on any order for the physical movement of items from one place to the next.

UNIT OF MEASURE (PURCHASING) — The unit used to purchase an item. This may or may not be the same unit of measure used in the internal systems.

UNIT PRICE — A price associated with each individual unit of an inventory item.

USE AS IS — Material that has been dispositioned as unacceptable per the specifications, however, the material can be used within acceptable tolerance levels.

VALUE ANALYSIS — A systematic and objective evaluation of the value of a good or service, focusing on an analysis of function relative to the cost of manufacturing or providing the item or service. Value analysis provides insight into the inherent worth of the final good or service, possible altering specification and quality requirements that could reduce costs without impairing functional suitability.

VALUE MANAGED RELATIONSHIP (VMR) — A term used for a long-term agreement with a specific supplier. Emphasis is on quality and on-time delivery and a supplier partner who lends value to the business process. VARIABLE COSTS — An operating cost that varies directly with production volume.

VARIANCE — 1. The difference between the expected and the actual. 2. In statistics, the variance is a measure of dispersion of data.

VENDORS AS PARTNERS (VAP) — A program in which a company enrolls its suppliers in a program where each party enters a mutually beneficial partnership.

VISUAL INSPECTION — A term generally used to indicate inspection performed without the aid of test instruments.

VOUCHER — A written instrument that bears witness to an act. Generally a voucher is an instrument showing services have been performed, or goods purchased, and authorizes payment to be made to the vendor.

WAIT TIME — The time that material would sit after being produced at an operation while it waits to be moved.

WARRANTY — An undertaking, either expressed or implied, that a certain fact regarding the subject matter of a contract is presently true or will be true. The word should be distinguished from "guarantee" which means a contract or promise by one person to answer for the performance of another.

WASTE — Anything other than the absolute minimum resources of material, machines and manpower required to add value to the product.

WORLD CLASS — Being the best at what you do. Product, Process, or Service.

WORK-IN-PROCESS (WIP) — Product in various stages of completion throughout plant including raw material released for initial processing and completely processed material awaiting final inspection and acceptance as finished product or shipment to a customer.

YIELD — Ratio of usable material from a process compared to the manufacturing capacity plan.

ZERO DEFECTS — Free of defects; 100% quality. A program in which quality levels and performance meet requirements 100% of the time.

ZERO INVENTORY — Condition in which there is no excess inventory in warehouses or on the floor and production is fed by JIT delivery of products or material with no defects.

Purchasing Terms